BUREAUCRACY AND DEMOCRACY
ACCOUNTABILITY AND PERFORMANCE

William T. Gormley Jr.
Georgetown University

Steven J. Balla
George Washington University

CQ PRESS

A Division of Congressional Quarterly Inc.
Washington, D.C.

CQ Press
1255 22nd Street, N.W., Suite 400
Washington, D.C. 20037

202-729-1900; toll-free, 1-866-4CQ-PRESS (1-866-427-7737)

www.cqpress.com

∞ The paper used in this publication exceeds the requirements of the
American National Standard for Information Sciences—Permanence of
Paper for Printed Library Materials, ANSI Z39.48-1992.

Printed and bound in the United States of America   *2447478*

07   06   05   04   03   5   4   3   2   1   *24132373*

Library of Congress Cataloging-in-Publication Data

Gormley, William T., Jr. 1950–
    Bureaucracy and democracy : accountability and performance / William
T. Gormley Jr., Steven J. Balla.
        p. cm.
    Includes bibliographical references and index.
    ISBN 1-56802-760-5 (alk. paper)
    1. Bureaucracy--United States. 2. Administrative agencies--United
States. I. Balla, Steven J. II. Title.
JK421.G6447 2003
352.6'3'0973--dc22

                                        2003015903

To Rosie
 —B.G.

To Mom and Dad
 —S.B.

Contents

Tables and Figures

Preface

It is not easy to describe what government bureaucracy does and why it is important. It is also tough to explain to family and friends why you are writing a book that attempts to do just that. Why not choose a more glamorous topic? Why force yourself to master dozens of acronyms, to decipher bureaucratese, and to grapple with such concepts as satisficing, delegation, diffuse costs and benefits, and networks? Despite these difficulties and occasional taunts from skeptics, we have persisted in seeking to bring to life a subject matter often viewed as tedious and impenetrable.

There is no doubt that myths about public bureaucracy abound. Many people believe the bureaucracy simply carries out public policies made by politicians. In reality a large number of our most important policies are formulated and implemented in the bureaucracy. Many people also believe the bureaucracy is a huge, inanimate, insensitive, rule-driven machine that produces enough red tape to choke progress on any front. In reality the bureaucracy can be remarkably responsive to outside pressure—partly because agency officials enjoy considerable discretion and partly because they often use this discretion to solve problems and improve conditions for individuals and organizations throughout society.

We hope students reading this book will develop an appreciation of these myths and realities and will come to view the bureaucracy as important, problematic, redeemable, and intriguing (all at the same time!). Bureaucracy is important because agency officials determine whether public policies succeed or fail. It is problematic because bureaucrats are unelected public officials and because many factors conspire against superior performance in executive branch organizations. It is redeemable because bureaucrats and agencies are capable of significant reform. And it is intriguing because the bureaucracy is far less predictable than simple myths, metaphors, or theories imply.

Bureaucratic accountability and performance are our specific focus in the book. We aim to lay out just how the bureaucracy is accountable, as well as to whom, under what circumstances, and with what results. In thinking about these issues, we draw on insights from several different academic disciplines, including political science and public management. Political science offers a plethora of empirical research and an appreciation of the importance of the bureaucracy's external environment. Public management provides a wide array of useful concepts and a rich understanding of the interior life of agencies.

Analytically, the book is organized around four prominent social scientific theories—bounded rationality, principal-agent theory, interest group mobilization, and network theory. These frameworks have a lot to say about normative issues regarding bureaucratic accountability in a democratic political system. In selecting these four theories for special emphasis, we tried to ensure close attention to a range of factors affecting the variations that inevitably emerge in agencies' performance. Bounded rationality helps us capture the pragmatic side of bureaucratic problem solving and the bureaucracy's remarkable capacity to make reasonably good decisions with limited time and information. Principal-agent theory highlights the challenges of delegation from politicians to bureaucrats and the difficulties of bureaucratic surveillance. Interest group mobilization draws our attention to the important role interest groups play and the circumstances under which they are most active and effective. Network theory and the tools of government approach stress relationships inside and outside government that cannot be reduced to hierarchical form. Together with a series of short vignettes and four in-depth case studies in chapter 6, the theories go a long way toward helping us see the bureaucracy as an understandable and fascinating set of public institutions.

In selecting public policy examples to illustrate our points, we were deliberately eclectic. Readers will find many examples from health care, environmental protection, education, homeland security, and other areas that receive prominent attention in the mass media. Readers will also find examples from child care, emergency management, public utility regulation, transportation, and other activities that usually receive less public exposure. Despite the fact that we both teach in Washington, D.C., we cite numerous examples from state and local government agencies. We take federalism seriously, and we recognize that state agencies are important not only because they implement federal laws but also because they make policy in their own right.

A number of pedagogical tools help bring all of this into focus. We include at the beginning of each chapter a series of core questions to foster students' critical thinking about a particular aspect of the bureaucracy or a chapter's approach. At the end of each chapter we include a list of key terms for students to review. An appendix of annotated Web resources follows the last chapter so students can more easily pursue further study of the topics we raise. Most important, we feature throughout the book excerpts from interviews we conducted with four former cabinet secretaries. Insights from these interviews, featured conveniently as "Inside Bureaucracy" boxes within the text, bring bureaucratic decisions and disputes to life and illustrate how prominent practitioners view theoretical appraisals of themselves and their agencies. We would like to thank each of these distinguished public servants—James Baker III, Dan Glickman, Donna Shalala, and Richard Thornburgh—for taking the time to share their insights with us.

We would also like to thank many others for their help at various stages during the preparation of the book. Brint Milward, David Rosenbloom, Patrick Wolf, and Carolyn Hill provided sage advice on particular chapters or themes. Belinda Creel Davis, Michigan State University; Euel W. Elliott, University of Texas at Dallas; Sean Gailmard, University of Chicago; and Gregory Huber, Yale University, reviewed a draft of the entire book and offered thorough and insightful commentaries. Michael McGuire, University of North Texas, and George Krause, University of South Carolina, reviewed our proposal and made helpful suggestions at that crucial early stage. Allison Hansen, Erika Germer, and Nadia Khawaja, students at the Georgetown Public Policy Institute, provided skillful research assistance. Hal Wolman and the George Washington Institute of Public Policy also provided welcome research support. At CQ Press, Charisse Kiino played a key role in getting the project off the ground, and Michael Kerns offered lots of excellent suggestions and shepherded the book through development. Nancy Geltman saw the book through production and provided graphical assistance with the book's tables and figures. Jarelle Stein served very ably as the copy editor. Finally, we would be remiss without acknowledging the Aditi Restaurant in Washington, D.C., the site of many enjoyable lunches during which we made great progress in turning our abstract ideas into the book you hold in your hands today.

Of course, it goes without saying that we could not have made any of this happen without the considerable love, patience, and nurturing of our families. In particular, Bill would like to thank his wife, Rosie, for her stimulating ideas and warm support and for decorating the study in which he did most of his writing. Steve would like to thank his parents, Steve and Carol, for their lifelong sacrifices and encouragement; his wife, Desi, for her never-ending companionship; and his children, Julie and Zoli, for their love of both him and Smokey Bear (the bureaucracy touches even the youngest among us!).

BUREAUCRACY AND DEMOCRACY

1 | Bureaucracies as Policymaking Organizations

For DECADES, POLICYMAKERS HAVE confronted three interrelated challenges in elementary and secondary education: (1) finding a way to render public schools more accountable to parents, taxpayers, and other vital constituencies; (2) determining how to improve the performance of public school so that the confidence of a long-disillusioned citizenry is at last restored; and (3) determining how public schools can best help narrow the achievement gap between whites and minorities, the latter of whom depend especially heavily on the school system for advancement and success.

One potential solution that has generated considerable interest in recent years is student testing, sometimes in combination with organizational report cards and financial rewards and punishments. Today, virtually every state issues annual grades for schools and school districts. In many states, the law requires that such report cards be released to parents and the general public.[1] A related approach involves linking test scores to financial bonuses or penalties, an approach sometimes referred to as "high-stakes testing." In South Carolina, for example, schools that experience larger than expected gains in reading and mathematics scores receive monetary awards as well as trophy flags for display and greater flexibility in administering state regulations.[2]

These approaches are embodied in policy at the federal level as well. In 2002 President George W. Bush and a bipartisan coalition in Congress enacted landmark legislation aimed at enhancing educational accountability and performance through a combination of testing requirements and financial inducements. The No Child Left Behind Act includes the following provisions:

- Every state must require annual tests in reading and mathematics for every public school child in grades three through eight, though states are free to design their own testing instruments.
- Public schools whose test scores fail to improve two years in a row are eligible for additional federal aid. However, schools whose scores continue to stagnate or decline must provide low-income students with a variety of educational options, such as money for tutoring and transportation to a higher-performing school. Personnel changes can be required if a school fails to improve for six years.
- Public schools must develop report cards showing how their test scores compare with those of other schools.
- Public schools must narrow the gap in test scores between white and minority students and between financially advantaged and disadvantaged students.
- Every state must participate in the National Assessment of Educational Progress, which periodically assesses the performance of a random sample of public school students in selected subjects.

Most observers agree that this law constitutes the most significant revision of the nation's education policy since the Elementary and Secondary Education Act of 1965. Philosophically, it is rooted in the premise that instruments such as high-stakes testing will promote accountability, which in turn will improve the performance of public schools.

Questions remain about how the law will be interpreted and implemented over time by fifty state governments and thousands of local school systems. For example, there is no guarantee that states will choose suitable testing instruments. Nor is it clear that states will be willing and able to disaggregate test scores by student characteristics. At the time the law was passed, only four states collected and reported achievement data broken down by race, ethnicity, income, disability, and English proficiency.[3] And prior to the law's passage, the **General Accounting Office**—the audit, evaluation, and investigative arm of Congress—found that many states were not complying with assessment requirements already in effect, requirements much weaker than those mandated in No Child Left Behind.[4]

Other observers question the very wisdom of the law's unprecedented emphasis on accountability and performance in education. For example, the sharp turn toward standardized testing may inadvertently undermine good teaching and real learning, as when teachers "teach to the test" and pay scant attention to the fostering of creativity, problem solving, and other important abilities in their students.[5] Competition may also lead to dysfunctional incentives and behaviors, as epitomized by the example of a math teacher at one high-minority school whose principal discouraged her from helping math teachers at a similar school, saying, "Maybe we don't want their scores going up." [6]

Despite such concerns, tangible improvements in the achievement of students, especially those from minority families, may be worth the risks inherently raised by high-stakes testing and similar policies. As Education Secretary Rod Paige put it shortly after the passage of No Child Left Behind:

> Students should make substantial progress every year, in every class, and annual assessments will ensure that they do. Every time they do not, we are not just wasting time, money, and opportunities; we are making students more discouraged, despondent, and disenfranchised.[7]

In this book, we evaluate the operation of public bureaucracies—such as schools, school districts, and education departments— as policymaking organizations in the American democratic system. In this opening chapter, we provide an introduction to the book's basic approach, which is to use several social scientific theories to guide an inquiry into accountability and performance, two key standards by which agencies are judged. This introduction is organized around three *core questions:*

- *WHY ARE ACCOUNTABILITY AND PERFORMANCE IMPORTANT IN UNIQUE WAYS IN PUBLIC BUREAUCRACIES?* Although accountability is vital in all sectors of society, it takes on distinct meanings when authority is exercised by teachers and other public servants. Such decision makers are empowered to serve not shareholders or boards of directors but families and the public.

- *WHAT ARE THE DIFFERENT FORMS OF ACCOUNTABILITY, AND HOW HAVE THEIR USE AND EFFICACY CHANGED OVER TIME?* In recent years, elected officials at all levels of government have sought to make school systems more accountable to political, as opposed to professional, concerns. The imposition of such external standards has important implications for teacher quality, satisfaction, and retention, all of which are in turn linked closely with student achievement.

- **WHY HAS PERFORMANCE BECOME SUCH AN IMPORTANT STAN-
  DARD BY WHICH TO EVALUATE PUBLIC BUREAUCRACIES?** Outputs,
  such as the amount of instructional time devoted to reading, and
  outcomes, such as student performance on standardized tests
  and high school graduation rates, have long been vital to education policy. But measuring these facets of performance is difficult, and it is even harder to demonstrate an unambiguous link
  between specific school activities and the growth and development of different types of children.

In addressing these questions, the chapter lays the foundation for a systematic inquiry into public bureaucracies, organizations where some of society's most fundamental decisions are made.

The Contours of Public Bureaucracy

As the uncertainty surrounding the ultimate effects of No Child Left Behind
so vividly demonstrates, many of the policy decisions that most deeply affect
people's lives are made within public bureaucracies. A **public bureaucracy** is
an organization within the executive branch of government, whether at the
federal, state, or local level. Such organizations run the gamut from the Federal Energy Regulatory Commission to the South Dakota Department of
Game, Fish and Parks to the Integrated Waste Management Department of
Orange County, California.

As Figure 1.1 illustrates, the federal executive branch consists of dozens
of public bureaucracies. Fifteen of these bureaucracies are **cabinet departments,** including the Department of Homeland Security, the first addition to
the cabinet since 1989. Some noncabinet bureaucracies are referred to as **independent agencies** as they are structured to operate with relative autonomy
from White House authority. The Federal Reserve System, with its powerful
chairman Alan Greenspan, is a prominent example of such an organization.
Despite their designation, however, not all independent agencies actually
enjoy such autonomy. For example, presidents of all political stripes closely
monitor and influence the priorities and decisions of the Environmental
Protection Agency (EPA).

The Department of Transportation (DOT) has emerged as a particularly salient bureaucracy since the terrorist attacks of September 11, 2001.
Figure 1.2 provides an overview of its organization. A secretary appointed
by the president and confirmed by the Senate heads the DOT, overseeing a

workforce of more than 100,000 employees and a budget exceeding $50 billion. Many of the employees are located in subagencies, such as the Federal Aviation Administration and the National Highway Traffic Safety Administration, that are devoted to enhancing the efficiency and safety of particular modes of transportation. In the aftermath of September 11, the government created a new DOT subagency, the Transportation Security Administration, to shore up the protection of the nation's transportation system. One of its first tasks was to develop a protocol for screening all checked baggage for explosives. As anyone who travels by air would undoubtedly attest, the agency's policymaking efforts in this area have a very real effect on a fundamental aspect of life in the twenty-first century. On March 1, 2003, the Transportation Security Administration was moved to the Department of Homeland Security.

Accountability and Performance in Public Bureaucracies

Because of the importance of their decisions, bureaucracies from the DOT to local school systems are accountable to a variety of individuals and organizations throughout government and society. These parties include political overseers, such as the president and city council members, as well as constituencies—air carriers, parents, and countless others—who are regulated or served by the agencies.

Public bureaucracies are not unique in this regard. Business firms such as ExxonMobil and Home Depot must also answer to supervisors and clients, including their boards of directors and shareholders. Likewise, nonprofit organizations, such as the American Red Cross and the Ford Foundation, are held accountable to their boards of directors and to the beneficiaries of their services. Unlike these other organizations, however, government agencies also bear the burden of being institutions of American democracy. In democratic institutions, accountability to the American public and its elected representatives is a vital and unique concern. It would be troubling, in other words, if policy were made by officials with little or no connection to the public.

Accountability in democratic policymaking is often viewed through the lens of **fairness.** According to this viewpoint, all parties desiring to participate in particular decision-making processes should be given the opportunity to make their preferences known.[8] This principle is embodied in the **Administrative Procedure Act,** the statute governing the process through

Figure 1.1 The Government of the United States

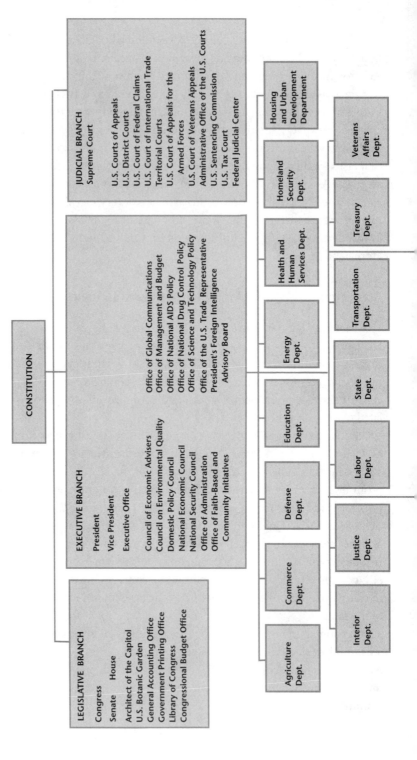

CONSTITUTION

LEGISLATIVE BRANCH

Congress

Senate   House

Architect of the Capitol
U.S. Botanic Garden
General Accounting Office
Government Printing Office
Library of Congress
Congressional Budget Office

EXECUTIVE BRANCH

President

Vice President

Executive Office

Council of Economic Advisers
Council on Environmental Quality
Domestic Policy Council
National Economic Council
National Security Council
Office of Administration
Office of Faith-Based and
    Community Initiatives
Office of Global Communications
Office of Management and Budget
Office of National AIDS Policy
Office of National Drug Control Policy
Office of Science and Technology Policy
Office of the U.S. Trade Representative
President's Foreign Intelligence
    Advisory Board

JUDICIAL BRANCH

Supreme Court

U.S. Courts of Appeals
U.S. District Courts
U.S. Court of Federal Claims
U.S. Court of International Trade
Territorial Courts
U.S. Court of Appeals for the
    Armed Forces
U.S. Court of Veterans Appeals
Administrative Office of the U.S. Courts
U.S. Sentencing Commission
U.S. Tax Court
Federal Judicial Center

Agriculture Dept.

Commerce Dept.

Defense Dept.

Education Dept.

Energy Dept.

Health and Human Services Dept.

Homeland Security Dept.

Housing and Urban Development Department

Interior Dept.

Justice Dept.

Labor Dept.

State Dept.

Transportation Dept.

Treasury Dept.

Veterans Affairs Dept.

INDEPENDENT ESTABLISHMENTS AND GOVERNMENT CORPORATIONS

African Development Foundation
Central Intelligence Agency
Commodity Futures Trading Commission
Consumer Product Safety Commission
Corporation for National and
  Community Service
Defense Nuclear Facilities Safety Board
Environmental Protection Agency
Equal Employment Opportunity
  Commission
Export-Import Bank of the U.S.
Farm Credit Administration
Federal Communications Commission
Federal Deposit Insurance Corp.
Federal Election Commission
Federal Emergency Management Agency
Federal Housing Finance Board
Federal Labor Relations Authority
Federal Maritime Commission
Federal Mediation and Conciliation Service

Federal Mine Safety and Health
  Review Commission
Federal Reserve System
Federal Retirement Thrift Investment Board
Federal Trade Commission
General Services Administration
Inter-American Foundation
Merit Systems Protection Board
National Aeronautics and Space Administration
National Archives and Records Administration
National Capital Planning Commission
National Credit Union Administration
National Foundation on the Arts and
  the Humanities
National Labor Relations Board
National Mediation Board
National Railroad Passenger Corp. (Amtrak)
National Science Foundation
National Transportation Safety Board
Nuclear Regulatory Commission

Occupational Safety and Health Review
  Commission
Office of Government Ethics
Office of Personnel Management
Office of Special Counsel
Panama Canal Commission
Peace Corps
Pension Benefit Guaranty Corporation
Postal Rate Commission
Railroad Retirement Board
Securities and Exchange Commission
Selective Service System
Small Business Administration
Social Security Administration
Tennessee Valley Authority
Trade and Development Agency
U.S. Agency for International Development
U.S. Commission on Civil Rights
U.S. International Trade Commission
U.S. Postal Service

Source: United States Government Manual, 2002–2003 (Washington, D.C.: Office of the Federal Register, GPO, June 1, 2002), 2.

Figure 1.2 Organizational Chart of the U.S. Department of Transportation

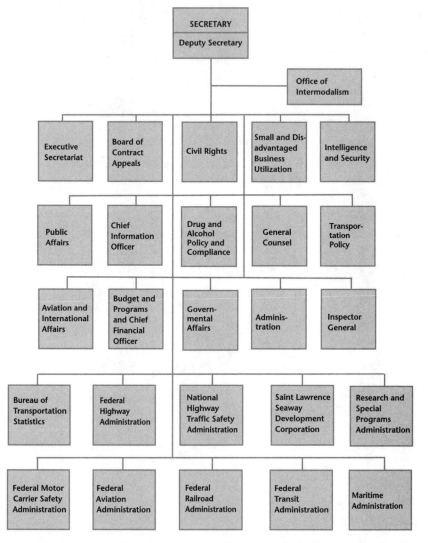

Source: Department of Transportation; http://www.dot.gov/chart.html, April 24, 2003.

Note: The Coast Guard and Transportation Security Administration were moved to the Department of Homeland Security on March 1, 2003.

which agencies formulate many of their most important policy decisions. This statute generally requires agencies to allow interested parties the opportunity to comment on proposed courses of action.

Like democracy itself, this approach to bureaucratic policymaking often proves cumbersome and untidy. Many agency proposals are highly controversial, take an exceedingly long time to develop, and are ultimately met with vociferous opposition.[9] These difficulties raise a second fundamental standard that agencies are called upon to meet—performance.

As with accountability, performance in democratic institutions often means something very different than it does in the context of other types of organizations. In the business world, performance is tracked through well-established indicators such as market shares and stock prices. Appropriate indicators also exist in the nonprofit sector, where the performances of foundations, hospitals, and colleges and universities are routinely measured and compared with those of similar institutions.

Yet such indicators are not always as useful as we would like them to be. As we have already highlighted, performance in education policy is difficult to assess, even with instruments such as report cards and standardized tests. Similar difficulties hold in other policy areas. How is the performance of the DOT to be judged when it comes to airport security? By the speed with which agency employees move passengers through checkpoints? By the rate at which checkpoints are breached? To make matters even more vexing, these questions must be answered in an environment in which the public brings to the agency a series of challenging, and sometimes contradictory, demands—air travel should be convenient, airlines should enjoy financial stability, and airplanes must never again be used as terrorist weapons.

Although it may be tough to judge accountability and performance in public bureaucracies, this task is crucial given the vital role agencies play in the policymaking process. Equally crucial is the need to carry out this evaluation in a systematic manner. With this in mind, we approach the bureaucracy from four distinct perspectives, which deal with the people who work inside executive branch agencies, the political actors who serve as the bureaucracy's supervisors, the clients agencies regulate and serve, and the conflict and cooperation that occur both within the bureaucracy and between agencies and other types of organizations. To better understand these facets of bureaucracy and their implications for accountability and performance, we draw on insights from four prominent social scientific frameworks—bounded rationality, principal-agent theory, interest group mobilization, and network theory. Before applying these frameworks to particular aspects of bureaucratic policymaking, we first lay out in greater detail what accountability and performance mean in the context of the executive branch so that the nature of the task at hand becomes fully apparent.

Accountability and Its Many Faces

Accountability, like peace and motherhood, is one of those wonderful words that instantly evoke all sorts of positive images. But what exactly does it mean? In thinking about accountability within the executive branch, it is useful to distinguish between the source of control over agencies—internal or external—and the degree of control over agency actions—high or low.[10] As Figure 1.3 illustrates, there are four possibilities: **bureaucratic accountability,** where effective control emanates from within the executive branch; **legal accountability,** where control from the outside is effective; **professional accountability,** where internal structures and processes produce low levels of control; and **political accountability,** where control is external and limited. These distinctions can be summed up in this way:

> Under the bureaucratic system, expectations are managed through a hierarchical arrangement based on supervisory relationships; the legal accountability system manages agency expectations through a contractual relationship; the professional system relies on deference to expertise; while the political accountability system promotes responsiveness to constituents as the central means of managing the multiple expectations.[11]

In practice, these distinctions are not always borne out. For example, political control via instruments such as legislative oversight is not necessarily less potent than legal control through statutory requirements.[12] In the early 1990s, in a not uncommon chain of events, the Health Care Financing Administration made significant changes to its rules on Medicare physician payments after its administrator was dressed down at a congressional committee hearing.[13] It is also not always the case that professional norms and standards exert less influence over agency behavior than hierarchical supervision within the bureaucracy.[14] Over the past several decades, the influx of economists into the federal workforce has had a dramatic effect on how

Figure 1.3 Forms of Executive Branch Accountability

Source of Control over Agency

		Internal	*External*
Degree of Control over Agency	*High*	Bureaucratic accountability	Legal accountability
	Low	Professional accountability	Political accountability

Source: Barbara Romzek and Melvin Dubnick, "Accountability in the Public Sector: Lessons from the Challenger Tragedy," *Public Administration Review* 47 (May/June 1987): 227–238. Used with permission.

agencies assess the impact of their regulations, socially as well as economically.

Because of such complications, policymakers must think very carefully when promoting a particular form of accountability. A decision to emphasize one form of accountability over another can have significant consequences. At times it can even spell the difference between life and death. On January 28, 1986, the National Aeronautics and Space Administration defied the views of engineers who warned that the Space Shuttle *Challenger* was not fit to be launched that day. Despite concerns that O-rings, or seals, would fail to function properly if temperatures were too low, the agency succumbed to political pressure to launch the vehicle more or less on schedule. The *Challenger* exploded not long after takeoff, and its seven-member crew, including schoolteacher Christa McAuliffe, perished in the accident. By substituting political accountability for professional accountability in a situation in which technical judgments were absolutely crucial, the agency made a fatal mistake.[15]

The Evolution of Accountability

During the latter half of the twentieth century, accountability emerged as a dominant concern among both policymakers and those outside government. Some bureaucracies, such as the now-defunct Interstate Commerce Commission, were viewed as runaway agencies, beyond the control of elected officials and ordinary citizens. In 1966, in response to such concerns, Congress passed the **Freedom of Information Act,** aimed at making the government's information more readily available to the public. Ten years later the **Government in the Sunshine Act** specified that most federal commission meetings must be open to interested parties from outside government. Congress did not stop there. It also created inspectors general in most cabinet departments to serve as internal watchdogs over agency officials and passed "whistle-blower" legislation to protect federal employees who expose illegal or inappropriate behavior by others in the bureaucracy. While all of this was going on, congressional oversight of the executive branch was becoming more frequent and more intense.[16]

At the state level, similar developments were under way.[17] Many states passed their own freedom of information acts and sunshine laws. Across the country, states enacted legislation requiring the appointment of a public or consumer representative to occupational licensing boards. Most states created offices of consumer counsel to act as advocates for ratepayers in public utility commission proceedings. The overwhelming majority of states established a nursing home ombudsman's office to represent residents before governmental and nongovernmental organizations. Furthermore, many states enacted legislative veto provisions that facilitated political oversight of administrative rules and sunset laws that terminated relatively small agencies on a fixed date unless the legislature intervened.

The overall thrust of these reforms was to make the executive branch more accountable to politicians and to citizens or their surrogates. These reforms, in other words, emphasized external sources of control over bureaucratic and professional approaches. Whereas the Progressives had sought to insulate the bureaucracy from politics during the early days of the twentieth century, reformers in the 1960s, 1970s, and 1980s saw insulation as the problem to be solved. To put it differently, these three decades saw an era of "watchful eye" reforms aimed at curbing the bureaucracy.[18] Other reform movements, such as scientific management in the early twentieth century and liberation management in the 1990s, placed greater faith in bureaucratic discretion and internal sources of control.

The Limits of Accountability

Just as the quest for particular forms of accountability has ebbed and flowed over the years, it has also varied across agencies, depending especially on the complexity of the issues the agency must resolve. For agencies dealing with highly complex issues, both politicians and judges have been more willing to delegate authority and defer to the agency's technical expertise.[19] For instance, financial regulatory agencies, such as the Federal Reserve System and the Securities and Exchange Commission, enjoy more autonomy than most agencies in part because of the arcane nature of their jurisdictions.

Such independence enables skilled, creative leaders to manage their agencies more effectively. For example, during the 1990s, Alan Greenspan was widely credited with using his extraordinary influence over the nation's monetary policy to help propel the economy into one of its most robust periods of growth ever.[20] Although Greenspan's effectiveness was derived in no small part from his personal credibility and experience,[21] his agency's independence from Congress and the president enabled him to pursue his vision of sound monetary policy without interference and distraction.

Complexity alone does not account for the enormous power vested in some agencies. Political factors play a central role as well. The interests regulated by the Securities and Exchange Commission—brokerage firms, investment banks, mutual funds, and stock exchanges, to name a few—are quite diverse and are generally at odds with one another.[22] Given this conflict, members of Congress find it desirable to empower the agency and, in the process, avoid the inevitable wrath of those parties that come out on the losing end of securities policy. If the agency's political environment were less contentious, then Congress might insist on a greater measure of political or legal, as opposed to professional, accountability.

A final factor to consider is the tradeoff between accountability today and accountability in the future.[23] In democratic politics, the majority is never more than an election away from being banished to minority status. When such a shift occurs, the bureaucracy naturally falls under the domain of a new majority. Fearful that this shift will bring about a fundamental change in the political pressure exerted on the executive branch, the existing majority has an incentive to insulate agencies from outside sources of control. This incentive is especially strong when the existing majority has only a tenuous grip on the reins of power. During such times, great emphasis is placed on bureaucratic and professional accountability, and agencies are loaded with cumbersome structures and procedures. For example, some agencies are given restrictive mandates and are located within the executive branch in places relatively impervious to external influence. In the end, the lack of political and legal accountability decried by officials from across the ideological spectrum owes its existence not only to factors internal to the bureaucracy but to the dictates of electoral politics as well.

The Push for Performance

In the 1990s the concept of **performance** came to rival accountability as a standard for evaluating executive branch agencies. On its own merits, performance is important in democratic institutions, as the public is well served by government organizations that operate effectively and produce generally acceptable results. Performance is also of concern because it is intimately connected with accountability. To take one example, agencies subjected to particularly strict forms of political accountability may find it difficult to take sufficient advantage of their expertise and specialization. In recent years, scores of teachers have expressed deep dissatisfaction with an ongoing erosion in their classroom autonomy, arguing that this erosion stifles not only their instructional efforts but also the learning possibilities of many of their students.

Like accountability, performance can be defined and measured in a variety of ways. One approach is to focus on the activities, or **outputs,** over which agencies exert direct control. For an organization such as the EPA, outputs include the number of inspections conducted and the amount of monetary fines imposed. Another approach is to pay attention to the results, or **outcomes,** that agencies seek to bring about. Examples include cleaner air, lower poverty, safer workplaces, less disease, and more employment. A third approach is to focus on the effects of agency outputs on societal outcomes, controlling for other factors—economic growth, to name one—that play an important role in shaping such outcomes.

In fact, just as accountability is multidimensional, so too is performance. Consider, by way of example, the distinction between routine performance and behavior during a crisis. A given agency may do well when handling routine tasks but may stumble when called upon to confront a novel challenge or situation. Most observers acknowledge that the U.S. Postal Service is a remarkably efficient and productive organization.[24] In part, the agency's success derives from the nature of its fundamental task, which is unambiguous and easy for all to see. When it comes to delivering the mail under normal, relatively favorable conditions, then, letter carriers and clerks perform well.

But what about when the agency suddenly found itself confronting mail contaminated by potentially deadly anthrax spores? On October 15, 2001, a letter that had passed through a District of Columbia postal processing facility, on its way to the office of Sen. Tom Daschle, D-S.D., tested positive for anthrax. When postal workers expressed concern and asked if they should take antibiotics, their supervisors told them antibiotics would not be necessary.[25] At a press conference, Postmaster General John Potter offered reassurances that the contaminated letter posed little, if any, threat to postal or congressional employees. Tragically, however, two postal workers died within a week, and many others found themselves potentially at risk.[26] In fairness to the postmaster general, he got much of his advice from the Centers for Disease Control and Prevention, whose scientists drew inappropriate conclusions from the limited evidence available to them. Regardless, the decision not to administer antibiotics proved to be a fatal error in a time of crisis for a normally effective organization.

A related distinction exists between **policymaking** and **implementation.** An agency such as the Social Security Administration (SSA) may perform well because its central task is routine—distributing checks to retirees and other program recipients. When performing roles such as this one, agencies implement policies established elsewhere in government. An agency can, without too much difficulty, develop procedures for effectively delivering resources to beneficiaries. If Congress specifies social security legislation in sufficient detail, then the SSA need not fret about bigger, more difficult policy concerns.

Other agencies make policy all the time, a much harder task to perform well. For example, the EPA takes many important actions each year. In 2001 alone the agency issued fifty-two rules considered particularly significant.[27] These rules, which have the full force of law, ultimately determine the cleanliness of air and water, as well as who bears the costs of providing these public goods. Although the agency's enforcement practices have their own difficulties, it is generally easier to conduct an inspection or even to organize a cluster of inspections than to develop a rule from scratch.

Distinguishing between **efficiency** and **equity** as operational manifestations of performance is also important. For decades, state welfare agencies were free to set benefit levels but were not free to deny services to eligible clients. With the passage of the Personal Responsibility and Work Opportunity Reconciliation Act of 1996, these agencies were, for the first time, granted the discretion to decide who gets services and who does not. Such judgments, which determine how equitable welfare policies will be, require agency officials to make the tough decisions previously made by state legislators and other elected politicians. To further complicate matters, equity can be defined in many different ways. The distinction between equality of opportunity and equality in outcomes is just one dimension that must be considered. The end result of all of this is that it is tougher to measure equity than to gauge efficiency, and it is exceedingly difficult to reconcile competing views of how resources should be allocated across society. As this discussion implies, performance cannot be meaningfully separated from the values that make up the core of American democracy.

The Government Performance and Results Act

Given the centrality of performance in democratic policymaking, the federal government has for some time experimented with management reforms aimed at rationalizing the allocation of scarce resources. These experiments—with names such as "management by objectives" and "zero-base budgeting"—have been roundly criticized as fads long on symbolism and short on substance.[28] Despite these reforms, critics have contended, federal budgeting continues to be incremental in nature, with powerful interests blocking any significant departure from the status quo.

The enactment of the **Government Performance and Results Act** (GPRA) in 1993 struck some observers as a more promising development. Unlike other management reforms, put forth by the executive branch alone, GPRA was a law with bipartisan support from both the legislative and executive branches. GPRA also differed from previous reform efforts in that it allowed agencies several years to develop and implement strategic plans and performance measures and reports. After the initial incubation period, these documents were to be used by the executive and legislative branches in making budgetary decisions. According to one interpretation, agencies that performed poorly would get less, while agencies that performed well would get more. According to another interpretation, performance measures and reports would help policymakers redesign failing programs and learn from successful ones.

In implementing GPRA's early requirements, most agencies were successful in meeting congressional deadlines for producing various documents, but few were successful in actually measuring results. For example, the Department of Housing and Urban Development collected and reported data on uncollected rents but not on housing quality, thus severely limiting its ability to measure the performance of its public housing program. Other agencies, such as the Forest Service, struggled with conflicting goals (producing timber versus sustaining wildlife, for example), which made it difficult to measure overall success. Four years after GPRA's enactment, the General Accounting Office (GAO) characterized the law's implementation as "uneven."[29]

Two years after this characterization, in 1999, the GAO concluded that "moderate" improvements had been made but that "key weaknesses" remained.[30] A few agencies, such as the Department of Transportation, the Department of Education, and the Department of Justice, had assembled credible performance information. But most agencies still struggled with conceptual and methodological issues.

Some of the biggest challenges arose at agencies with significant intergovernmental relationships. The EPA, for example, depends on states to implement numerous programs aimed at reducing water pollution. Because states measure water quality in many different ways, it is difficult for the agency to know how much progress has been made over time and across different areas of the country. Even within the same region, states use different sampling methods to determine water quality. Within New England, Rhode Island samples all of its waters every two years, while New Hampshire focuses its efforts on problematic waters. Other states sample one-fifth of all their waters annually.

Similarly, the Department of Health and Human Services relies upon states to measure progress in areas such as welfare reform, child support enforcement, and access to health care services. For such programs, the data the agency supplies to Congress are only as good as the data generated by the states. Definitional variations present problems here as well. For example, the Centers for Medicare and Medicaid Services allows states to define what constitutes "full immunization" for a two-year-old child when reporting such data to the federal government. Focusing on New England again, states differ from one another in how many shots they require for children

Table 1.1 "Full Immunization" of Two-Year-Old Children, New England States

	Diphtheria, Tetanus, and Pertussis	Injectable or Oral Polio Vaccine	Mumps, Measles, and Rubella	Hemophilus Influence Type B	Hepatitis B Vaccine	Varicella Zoster Vaccine
Connecticut	4	3	1	3	2	0
Maine	4	3	1	1	2	0
Massachusetts	4	3	1	1	3	0
New Hampshire	4	3	1	3	3	0
Rhode Island	4	3	1	4	3	0
Vermont	4	3	1	4	0	0

Source: Centers for Medicare and Medicaid Services, "Government Performance and Results Act: Immunization of Medicaid Two-Year-Old Children" (Baltimore, Md.: CMS, July 2002). Also Karen Halverson, Vermont Department of Health, e-mail communication with Gormley, July 23, 2002.

Note: The numbers indicate how many shots or other forms of immunization are required for two-year-olds to satisfy the state's definition of what constitutes "full immunization."

to be considered fully immunized. As Table 1.1 illustrates, Vermont does not require two-year-olds to receive the hepatitis B vaccine, while Massachusetts, New Hampshire, and Rhode Island call for three such immunizations.

Although the GAO has criticized the executive branch for implementing GPRA in a poor and uneven fashion, the truth is that Congress deserves at least some of the blame. With few exceptions, legislators have ignored performance data, even from agencies that have produced relatively useful and complete information. In the end, congressional appropriators continue to pay little or no attention to GPRA reports when making resource allocations.

The commitment of the president is also a factor to consider when evaluating the performance of GPRA. For the most part, the Clinton administration's support for GPRA was perfunctory at best. In contrast, President George W. Bush has exhibited a keen interest in linking performance measures to budgetary decisions. As part of the fiscal year 2003 budget process, the **Office of Management and Budget** (OMB), which helps the president oversee the preparation of the federal budget, rated 126 federal programs as effective, moderately effective, ineffective, or unknown. In putting together these ratings, OMB sought to explicitly incorporate performance measures into its budgetary decision making.[31] The infancy of this effort underscores how much work there is to be done in gauging and enhancing the performance of executive branch agencies, even in the context of a management reform as heralded as GPRA.

Agency Reputations in the Real World

Although the quest for systematic measures of performance has developed considerable momentum in recent years, perceptions of bureaucratic performance still depend more on soft judgments than on hard data, more on intuitions than on indicators. To put it differently, a revolution in data generation does not guarantee a revolution in data utilization. Sometimes a vivid story matters more than a well-designed chart or graph. Sometimes a clever phrase or a lovable mascot proves more effective than a thick document chock full of statistics.

In a world where bureaucratic reputations are at times only loosely linked to actual performance, several points should be made about how agencies are perceived. First, perceptions vary dramatically. Those who must pay taxes have a rather different view of the Internal Revenue Service (IRS) than those who prepare tax returns for a living. Among the latter, 61 percent believe the IRS does a good or excellent job. Among the former, only 40 percent give the IRS such a rating. To cite another example, 68 percent of environmental advocates believe the EPA does a good or excellent job. In contrast, only 41 percent of business managers give the agency such a rating.[32]

Second, perceptions change, sometimes very quickly. As Frank Sinatra sang, you can be "riding high in April, shot down in May." Consider the case of the Securities and Exchange Commission (SEC), once regarded as the crème de la crème of federal regulatory agencies.[33] In 2002, following accounting scandals at Enron and other corporations, some observers accused the SEC of being "asleep at the wheel."[34] They singled out its chairman, Harvey Pitt, for meeting with corporate executives whose firms were being investigated for securities fraud and for requesting that the SEC be elevated to cabinet status. Congress rejected, and even President Bush disavowed, this request, which would have boosted Pitt's salary by nearly $30,000.[35] Not long after these episodes, Pitt stepped down as SEC chairman under great pressure from an administration embarrassed by his missteps and bent on shoring up perceptions of its ability to manage the economy effectively.

Bureaucratic reputations can also change for the better. For example, the Federal Emergency Management Agency (FEMA) used to be regarded as one of the weakest agencies in the federal bureaucracy. When a natural disaster struck—an earthquake, a hurricane, a flood—FEMA, it seemed, responded with too little, too late. The agency's assurances were not to be trusted; its paperwork was more impressive than its support. Crushed by the disaster itself, victims felt betrayed by the one agency supposed to help them. All of this changed, however, with the 1993 arrival of James Lee Witt, who transformed FEMA into a proactive, responsive agency with a reputation for efficiency and caring.

Third, perceptions can be manipulated. Many agencies have their own publicity machines and work hard at generating both diffuse and specific support. A century ago, the Forest Service was particularly successful at generating political support. By mailing out more than 9 million circulars annually, the Forest Service created a highly favorable image for itself in the public's mind.[36] The agency then helped sustain this image by conjuring up a marvelous "spokesman"—the legendary Smokey Bear, who is depicted in action in Figure 1.4. In similar fashion, state health agencies have recently generated popular support for the Children's Health Insurance Program by linking their programs to popular local symbols, such as the badger (Wisconsin) or the husky (Connecticut).

Fourth, perceptions matter. By winning the support of most Progressive magazines and newspapers, the U.S. Postal Service was able to convince Congress to establish a postal savings system in 1910.[37] For years the Federal Bureau of Investigation enjoyed a reputation for no-nonsense, vigorous law enforcement that enabled the agency to augment its budget and staff. Movies and television shows celebrating G-men and their crusade against gangsters such as Al Capone enabled the agency to fare well on Capitol Hill, even when times were tight. For example, J. Edgar Hoover received congressional authorization to establish a Division of Identification and Information in 1930, right in the heart of the Great Depression.[38] More recently, the positive image of the Food and Drug Administration (FDA) helped that agency win passage of user fee legislation, which requires pharmaceutical and biotechnology companies to pay the agency to review new drug applications.[39] As this example illustrates, perceptions are not wholly separate from actual performance, as the user fees collected by the FDA played a key role in helping the agency cut its average approval time nearly in half during the mid-1990s.

Figure 1.4 1956 Poster of Smokey Bear

Source: Forest Service, USDA. The name and character of Smokey Bear are the property of the United States, as provided by 16 U.S.C. 580p-1 and 18 U.S.C. 711, and are used with the permission of the Forest Service, U.S. Department of Agriculture.

Accountability and Performance: Theories and Applications

Thus far the discussion has emphasized that accountability and performance are multifaceted concepts of fundamental importance when it comes to evaluating the place of executive branch bureaucracies in the American democratic system. A number of questions remain, however: *How are accountability and performance best judged, given their significance and complexity? Are there theories of politics and organizations that might provide particular insight into various aspects of accountability and performance? In the end, what general lessons can be learned about the determinants of both bureaucratic successes and failures?* These questions motivate the chapters that follow.

Our basic orientation is to evaluate accountability and performance not through impressions and anecdotes, however telling these may sometimes be, but through systematic analysis. As summarized in Table 1.2 (and noted earlier in the chapter), we consider the bureaucracy from four different perspectives, in each instance drawing on a well-known social scientific theory especially well equipped to shed light on at least one facet of accountability and performance. We then apply the lessons learned from this exercise to case studies of particular agencies to bring the implications of the disparate frameworks together in the context of actual agency experiences. We conclude by offering some general rules of thumb about the prospects for bureaucratic accountability and performance in light of the unique place occupied by administrative agencies in American democracy.

Chapter 2 focuses on the bureaucracy's people, from the secretaries who head cabinet departments to the teachers and other public servants with whom citizens have direct contact. We approach the behavior of these officials through the lens of **bounded rationality.** The basic premise holds that although individuals in organizations are rational, they do not comprehensively assess the benefits and costs of all, or even most, of their possible courses of action. Rather, decision makers seek to "satisfice"—that is, to arrive at outcomes that, while not necessarily ideal, are nonetheless quite satisfactory. Bounded rationality draws our attention to shortcuts, such as problem disaggregation and standard operating procedures, that are routinely a part of bureaucratic decision making.

Chapter 3 turns our attention to the bureaucracy's bosses, from the president all the way down to local officials. All of these actors routinely delegate policymaking authority to the bureaucracy. Delegation is essential given the

Table 1.2 Evaluating Bureaucratic Accountability and Performance

Aspect of Bureaucratic Accountability and Performance	Theoretical Framework			
	Bounded Rationality	*Principal-Agent Theory*	*Interest Group Mobilization*	*Network Theory*
Aspect of Bureaucratic Accountability and Performance	The bureaucracy's people	Bureaucratic supervisors	Agency clients	Conflict and cooperation
Form of Accountability Emphasized	Bureaucratic and professional	Political and legal	Political	Bureaucratic
Key Performance Value	Problem solving	Policymaking and implementation	Responsiveness to constituents	Coordination and influence across organizations
Some Important Structures and Processes	Specialization, standard operating procedures, authority, socialization	Institutional design, oversight, appropriations, appointments	Direct lobbying, grassroots, legislative support	Grants-in-aid, public-private partnerships, interagency meetings
Social Science Roots	Psychology, public administration	Economics, political science	Political science	Sociology, public administration

scope and complexity of contemporary government, yet it also raises the possibility that the agencies charged with making and implementing public decisions may serve their own interests rather than those of the citizenry and its elected representatives. According to **principal-agent theory,** the key for the bureaucracy's bosses is to design agencies wisely and to carefully monitor the behavior of executive branch actors. Although there are a variety of ways in which these tasks can be accomplished, no particular strategy is foolproof in limiting agency freedom.

Chapter 4 also focuses on actors external to the bureaucracy—the individuals and organizations that agencies regulate and protect. For these actors, the consequences of bureaucratic policymaking vary over time and across issues. Importantly, the distribution of benefits and costs affects the mobilization of interest groups and the general public. At times, benefits accrue to small segments of society, such as specific businesses and industries, while costs are spread widely across the population. In these situations, organized interests, but not broad societal forces, are compelled to bring their influence to bear on government agencies through **interest group mobilization.** Although it is widely thought that the prevalence of such situations has declined in recent decades, interest groups certainly continue to play a central role in shaping public policy.

In chapter 5 we return to the bureaucracy itself and consider how agencies interact with one another, and with other organizations, through a variety of networks. These networks include intergovernmental partnerships in areas such as environmental protection, collaborations between agencies and nongovernmental organizations, and interagency structures such as the president's cabinet. By linking network theory to what is sometimes known as the tools approach, we gain an understanding of how networks actually operate. In general, the use and efficacy of networks are topics of emerging importance for understanding accountability and performance in the executive branch.

Chapter 6 assesses the utility of the four theoretical perspectives by applying each of them to a series of agencies. These case studies focus on two federal agencies—the Federal Trade Commission and the Centers for Medicare and Medicaid Services—and two state agencies—the Florida Department of Environmental Protection and the Maryland Department of Health and Mental Hygiene. Once again, the aim of these applications is to explore the joint power of the theories in accounting for agency experiences in the real world.

Finally, in chapter 7 we consider the factors, including accountability, that account for variations in executive branch performance. In doing so, we rely on evaluations of more than two dozen federal agencies that have been carried out in recent years. These ratings are used to support a series of general propositions regarding the root causes of bureaucratic successes and failures.

As we view bureaucratic accountability and performance from all of these perspectives, it will become apparent that the executive branch is a dynamic collection of organizations that perform, in some instances better than others, innumerable vital functions in the American political system. Along the way we will hear directly from four well-known public servants—James Baker III, Dan Glickman, Donna Shalala, and Dick Thornburgh—who have run federal agencies under several presidential administrations. Through their stories, the bureaucracy will be brought to life in a way that complements our effort to think systematically about the internal and external workings of executive branch organizations.

Key Terms

Accountability, 10
Administrative Procedure Act, 9
Bounded rationality, 22
Bureaucratic accountability, 10
Cabinet department, 4
Efficiency, 16
Equity, 16
Fairness, 5
Freedom of Information Act, 12
General Accounting Office, 2
Government in the Sunshine
    Act, 12
Government Performance and
    Results Act, 16

Implementation, 15
Independent agency, 4
Interest group mobilization, 24
Legal accountability, 10
Office of Management and
    Budget, 18
Outcome, 14
Output, 14
Performance, 14
Policymaking, 15
Political accountability, 10
Principal-agent theory, 24
Professional accountability, 10
Public bureaucracy, 4

2 | Bureaucratic Reasoning

When a state childcare inspector visits a day care center and finds some routine problems, it is relatively easy to know what to do. Consider, for example, the following hypothetical scenario presented to state childcare inspectors in Colorado, North Carolina, Oklahoma, and Pennsylvania:

> You visit the Little Flower Day Care Center for a renewal visit and discover that one of the toilets is overflowing onto the bathroom floor. The center director is already aware of the situation and has called a plumber. Before you leave, the plumber has arrived and fixed the problem.

A majority of childcare inspectors in all of the four states would talk with the director; a majority in three of the four states would place a record in the center's file.[1] For this particular problem, there is a strong consensus on how to proceed. Childcare regulators in all four states have developed similar standard operating procedures to follow when they encounter an isolated code violation that does not pose a serious threat to the health and safety of children.

Many other kinds of agencies have also developed standard operating procedures for dealing in a consistent way with situations regularly encountered. One goal in the use of such procedures is equitable treatment. In Detroit, Michigan, for instance, the Environmental Enforcement Division, which deals with problems of debris and overgrowth and closely follows a set of bureaucratic rules, has a policy of responding to every citizen contact referred to them. The Sanitation Division is also organized around an egalitarian principle—"pick up garbage from each residence once a week, every week." [2] The resulting patterns of service delivery are relatively apolitical and relatively predictable.

But standard operating procedures, helpful in routine circumstances, may fail when dealing with an unprecedented situation. Consider the horrible events of September 11, 2001. Responding to the shocking news that the World Trade Center had been hit by an airplane (later, two airplanes), New York City's police officers and firefighters converged on the scene. Despite the chaos, they did their best to follow standard operating procedures, encouraging an orderly evacuation of the imperiled buildings. Unfortunately, there were no manuals to guide the heroic civil servants in those specific circumstances, to warn them about the imminent danger of collapse and the need for speed.

These examples illustrate important differences between the handling of routine problems and the handling of crisis situations. With routine problems, the reliance on standard operating procedures usually serves the bureaucrats and us reasonably well. When a crisis occurs, the use of standard operating procedures, while it may still prove very useful, may not be enough to avoid disaster.

These cases also illustrate another important point: bureaucratic decisions are a function of both the task environment (in this case, the provocation or threat) and the decision maker (in this case, civil servants). In the first three examples, the task environment was simple, familiar, and determinative; in the fourth example, the task environment was complex, unusual, and ambiguous. The World Trade Center crisis also reveals how decision makers may affect the outcome of events.

Recent reports suggest that there was a difference between how the police departments and how the fire departments responded to the crisis. Police officers, equipped with high-tech radios and trained in their use, received the highly useful information that the North Tower was glowing red. This helped them to save others and themselves through a swift evacuation. Although 37 New York Port Authority police and 23 New York Police Department officers did die, casualties could have been much worse. In contrast, the New York Fire Department, which had purchased such radios, had not trained its firefighters to use them. Cut off from vital intelligence, 343 firefighters perished in the disaster. The decisions made about training were thus significant.[3]

Communication matters, especially in a crisis; bureaucrats need to be in touch with other bureaucrats and with their superiors. A full analysis of decision making requires that one pay attention to both the problem to be solved and the persons who have been asked to solve it. This critical insight can be traced to the writings of Herbert Simon, an important figure in political science, economics, and cognitive psychology and a Nobel Prize winner.[4]

In this chapter, we try to understand how individual bureaucrats think and how they behave within an organizational setting. The core questions we will explore are:

- *HOW DO BUREAUCRATS MAKE DECISIONS?* We consider some strategies for simplifying problems and note how these strategies differ from those employed in a rational choice model.

- *DO BUREAUCRATS MANAGE TO APPROXIMATE RATIONAL BEHAVIOR?* We argue that they do, and we highlight the concept of satisficing as a key explanation for bounded rationality.

- *WHAT MOTIVATES BUREAUCRATS?* We discuss empathy and commitment and attitudes toward risk. We do not denigrate bureaucrats, but neither do we romanticize them.

- *HOW DO ORGANIZATIONS PROMOTE COHESION?* Here we consider the roles of training, information, and professionalism.

More broadly, we consider the consequences of bounded rationality for organizational performance.

The Bounded Rationality Model

Herbert Simon, a leading figure of public administration, helped to explain bureaucratic decisions by developing a model of **bounded rationality.**[5] According to Simon, individuals who work within organizations, such as bureaucrats, face at least three difficulties. First, their knowledge of the consequences of possible choices is fragmentary. Given time constraints and the limits of the human mind, knowing all the consequences that will flow from a given choice is impossible. For example, if you close a day care center, some children may be relocated to a better center, but others may be placed with relatives who really would prefer to be doing something else. Thus the quality of care the children receive may not improve. Second, values can be only imperfectly anticipated because the experience of a value differs from the anticipation of that same value. By this Simon means that when we experience something (a vacation, a dessert, a public policy), the actual experience may cause us to rethink how valuable the goal was in the first place. If parents pay 20 percent more for a better day care center, they may or may not conclude that the additional expense was worthwhile. Third, only a few alternatives can be considered. In the case of a bad day care center, a childcare inspector might pursue literally dozens of options. In practice, however, inspectors tend to zero in on only a handful of them.

Simon's model of bounded rationality stands in sharp contrast to what is sometimes called the **rational choice model.** In its purest form, this model assumes that individuals making decisions know their preferences, are able to consider all possible alternatives, and can anticipate the full set of consequences that will flow from each alternative. In short, decision makers **optimize,** that is, they make the best decision. Some versions of the rational choice model do not go quite so far. For example, economists sometimes note the absence of perfect information and how that affects decisions.[6]

In any case, the rational choice model assumes much greater rationality than Simon believes to be possible. According to him, real bureaucrats make decisions through the use of shortcuts that help them to function effectively despite cognitive and situational limits. He refers to this process as **satisficing.** In effect, satisficing means that a bureaucrat, or another decision maker, considers options only until finding one that seems acceptable given what the bureaucrat knows about his or her values and the probable consequences of that option. In Simon's words: "Because administrators satisfice rather than maximize, they can choose without first examining all possible behavior alternatives and without ascertaining that these are in fact all the alternatives."[7] Although satisficing sometimes leads to bad decisions, it is remarkably quick and productive. Think of it this way: Would you rather devote an entire week to getting one decision exactly right or to getting one hundred decisions approximately right? That might be worth the risk of getting a few wrong.

Whatever model might be employed by decision makers in an ideal world, satisficing seems to be the one most of them use in the real world. For example, when urban planners in the San Francisco Bay Area contemplated mass transit options in the 1950s and the 1960s, they considered a relatively narrow range of options. Planners for the five-county Bay Area Rapid Transit (BART) system considered only rail options, ignoring buses and automobiles as means of transportation. In nearby Oakland, planners for the two-county Alameda-Contra Costa Transit Authority (AC) gave initial consideration to a wider range of options but only because they inherited a multimodal system. Following a decision by the California Public Utilities Commission to allow the use of buses instead of trains, AC gave serious consideration to bus options only. The systems ultimately developed by these two sets of planners reflected these circumscribed alternatives: BART evolved as a rail system, while AC evolved as a bus system.[8]

The U.S. Customs Service's response to the problem of "port running" also illustrates satisficing behavior. Port running is a particularly bold form of smuggling in which the driver of a vehicle carrying illegal contraband proceeds brazenly to an inspection booth. If challenged by the inspector, the driver attempts to escape with little regard for life or property. When port running between Mexico and the United States became a serious problem in the mid-1990s, the Customs Service actively considered approximately five solutions.[9] Eventually, the agency chose to arrange concrete barriers in a zigzag pattern just behind the inspection booths. Drivers leaving the inspection booth had to maneuver slowly through the barriers before they could drive away. If they tried to run, they could be stopped without putting other people at great risk. There is no way of knowing whether this was the best possible solution. For the Customs Service, it was sufficient that this policy seemed to reduce the number of port running incidents and contributed to a substantial increase in the black market price of running an illegal load (a good sign that smugglers regarded the new policy as an effective one).

Simplified Problem Solving

Over the years, bureaucracies have developed several familiar techniques to help solve difficult problems. These include problem disaggregation, the use of standard operating procedures, attention to sunk costs, and the use of simulations, or tests. The purpose of these techniques is to simplify problems and the search for solutions. If these techniques work, bureaucracies can save time and money and make some progress toward important goals. In short, bureaucratic performance improves.

Problem Disaggregation

Most problems are multifaceted or multidimensional. By breaking such problems down into their component parts—**problem disaggregation**— bureaucrats can transform a daunting megaproblem into an assortment of soluble miniproblems.

Consider, for example, the problem of pollution. In 1970 the newly created U.S. Environmental Protection Agency (EPA) attacked the problem by breaking it down in several ways. First, the agency distinguished pollution by medium—air versus water versus land. Second, it distinguished between pollution from **point sources** (such as power plants) and pollution from **nonpoint sources** (such as runoff from farms). Third, the EPA distinguished between pollution in **attainment areas** (relatively good environmental quality) and pollution in **nonattainment areas** (relatively poor environmental quality).

With these distinctions in mind, and with considerable guidance from Congress and the federal courts, the EPA was able to zero in on problems based on several factors—severity, visibility, and tractability. Initially, the agency tackled air pollution from point sources, especially in nonattainment areas. Next, it focused on water pollution from point sources. Eventually, it would make considerable progress in both areas. For example, the amount of lead in the atmosphere declined sharply (see Table 2.1),[10] and several major waterways became fishable and swimmable again. Other pollution problems, such as hazardous waste disposal, nonpoint pollution, and global climate change, proved more vexing and initially received little attention. But over time they, too, would receive more attention. Had the EPA attempted to address all these problems at once, the outcome would probably have been much frenetic activity with few positive results.

Efforts to solve the drug problem have also yielded some progress, following critical decisions on how to disaggregate the problem and how to allocate scarce resources. The Department of Justice, for example, has distinguished between domestic and international cases, between major and

Table 2.1 Changes in Air Quality and Emissions, 1986–1995

Pollutant	Air Quality Change	Emissions Change
Carbon Monoxide	–37%	–16%
Lead	–78%	–32%
Nitrogen Dioxide	–14%	–3%
Ozone	–6%	–9%
Particulate Matter	–22%	–17%
Sulfur Dioxide	–37%	–18%

Source: Clarence Davies and Jan Mazurek, *Pollution Control in the United States* (Washington, D.C.: Resources for the Future, 1998), 60.

minor cases, and between arrests (which generate favorable statistics in the short run) and breaking up the drug cartels (arguably more important in the long run).

Standard Operating Procedures

Habits and routines are excellent devices for coping with familiar problems. In Simon's words: "Habits and routines may not only serve their purposes effectively, but also conserve scarce and costly decision-making time and attention." [11] Within the bureaucracy, the routines are often called **standard operating procedures,** norms designed to suit specific circumstances, available to organization members when situations resembling those circumstances occur. Standard operating procedures arise from many sources. When environmental agency officials prepare an environmental impact statement before approving a major project it is because they are required by law to do so. When welfare caseworkers insist on receiving a social security number before endorsing a welfare application, it is because they are required by law to do so. Many standard operating procedures originate with the political executives who run the bureaucracy. And some procedures originate with bureaucrats on the frontlines—**street-level bureaucrats,** as Michael Lipsky would call them.[12]

A particularly interesting standard operating procedure emerged within the military during World War I. Much of the warfare in France and Belgium occurred in or near trenches, where opponents were pinned down in close proximity to each other. After a pitched battle, sentries patrolled each side's perimeter, placing themselves and their enemy counterparts at great risk. Re-

"Our principal focus was on drug organizations. We collated all the information we had on drug trafficking organizations and put it all together so that the size of the problem was made evident. We concentrated on major cases and came to concentrate on the international investigations and prosecutions. There's not a single gram of heroine or cocaine made in this country. It all comes from outside the country. We knew we had to go to the source. I spent a lot of time traveling, meeting with my counterparts, and impressing upon them the necessity of cooperation. Shortly after President Bush took office, I went to Peru, Colombia, and Bolivia to meet with our counterparts there to deliver a message on the need for cooperation. We also had some difficulties with Mexico and constant back and forth there because of their large transshipment area. And then we enlisted European and Asian counterparts, all the time delivering a consistent message that drug cartels don't observe national borders and law enforcement can't do so either. We developed some pretty good relationships with those folks and brought them around to our point of view about the need to concentrate not just on arresting people or seizing drugs but [also on] breaking up major organizations, hitting them where it hurts."

markably, an unspoken agreement emerged over time that neither side would shoot at the other, giving everyone a breather from the stresses and strains of warfare. This "live-and-let-live" system evolved without the approval of higher authorities and persisted despite efforts to control it.[13] It is a good example of a standard operating procedure developed by street-level bureaucrats.

Though standard operating procedures do tend to persist over time, they can be changed. For instance, some state childcare agencies have opted for **differential monitoring,** linking the frequency of inspections to past performance, giving more attention to the worse facilities, less to the better ones.[14] Similar changes have occurred in child protection agencies and in occupational safety and health agencies. For example, as a result of legislation passed in 1994, Missouri's child protective services agency developed a

Table 2.2 Workers' Compensation Claims, Maine

Year	Workers' Compensation Claims (Injuries with 1 Lost Workday or More)	Incidence Rates (Lost Workday Cases per 100 Full-Time Workers)
1991	8,923	49.43
1992	7,090	43.39
1993	5,808	37.43
1994	4,695	37.48

Source: Maine Area OSHA Office, "Annual Report on the Maine Top 200 Program, 1995." Data supplied by Dr. John Mendeloff, Graduate School of Public and International Affairs, University of Pittsburgh.

differential response system calibrating the agency's response to fit the severity of the provocation: more serious cases continued to trigger an investigation by child protection personnel and police; less serious cases were referred to family assessment personnel, who provided assistance rather than punishment.[15] In Maine, the regional office of the Occupational Safety and Health Administration (OSHA) discovered that 200 firms were responsible for approximately 44 percent of the state's workplace injuries, illnesses, and deaths. OSHA gave each of the 200 firms a choice: conduct a comprehensive hazard assessment, correct all hazards identified, and develop an improvement plan for the future or face a traditional comprehensive inspection. An overwhelming majority of the firms opted for the former, and worker compensation claims dropped dramatically thereafter (see Table 2.2).[16]

Sunk Costs

Although procedural changes do occur, bureaucrats become invested in a certain way of doing things because any new procedure or strategy requires upfront costs that may turn out to be considerable. In Simon's words: "Activity very often results in 'sunk costs' of one sort or another that make persistence in the same direction advantageous." [17] In effect, **sunk costs** refer to the investment already made in a particular strategy that renders the pursuit of other strategies less attractive.

The phenomenon of sunk costs helps explain why it is so difficult to create a new agency or cabinet-level department. To bureaucrats, the status quo means established cubicles in familiar buildings at convenient subway stops; established relationships with familiar personnel whose quirks and foibles are well understood; and an established mission that flows from a familiar statute whose nuances are well known. Occasionally, the sunk costs argument can be overcome. But it takes a national emergency (such as those that led to the Department of Energy and the Department of Homeland Security) or a strong constituency (such as those involving the Department of Education and the Department of Veterans Affairs) to do so.

Simulations and Tests

When familiar problems arise, bureaucrats can rely on standard operating procedures. But what are they to do when unfamiliar problems arise? The question has become even more pressing in recent times because new technological developments have accelerated the generation of new problems. For example, in the late 1990s government officials began to fret that massive computer failures would occur when the year 2000 arrived because computers had been programmed with two-digit codes for year (00–99), making them ill-equipped to cope with the transition from 1999 to 2000. From a human point of view, the transition was a logical progression from one year to the next; from a computer's point of view, however, it was a backward shift of ninety-nine years. To the computer, 00 meant 1900, not 2000. Without appropriate corrections, this reading could result in enormous calculation errors, malfunctions, and shutdowns. Imagine, for instance, how someone's Social Security check might be deflated in keeping with a retroactive cost-of-living adjustment of nearly a century.

To anticipate the transition to the year 2000 (or Y2K), companies, agencies, and others ran **simulations,** or tests, to discover what might happen. The Chrysler Corporation, for instance, turned all of its clocks to December 31, 1999, at its Sterling Heights automobile assembly plant. The security system shut down and would not let anybody out! A Florence, Arizona, prison conducted a similar test and got the opposite result: the security system opened all its doors.[18] Not a good outcome for a prison! Fortunately, it was a test. Such simulations can be very helpful to bureaucrats (and to private employers) as a way of confirming that real problems do exist. Eventually, government agencies (and private employers) were able to correct the computer problems. When Y2K arrived, few problems developed. A serious crisis was thus averted.

Implications for Policy Analysis

An important development in the history of bureaucratic decision making has been the creation of policy analysis bureaus within administrative agencies. The purpose of such bureaus is to provide a cabinet secretary or other agency head with valuable information on the probable consequences of choices under active consideration. In Simon's words, such bureaus recognize important limits to individual and organizational rationality and seek to overcome them.

If Simon is correct, policy analysis within the bureaucracy differs from the rational choice model of neoclassical economics, which assumes a world of perfect information and unlimited time. According to one version of the rational choice model, the decision maker specifies some values or goals, considers a wide range of alternatives, gathers evidence on the expected consequence of each alternative, and chooses the one that best maximizes the values of overriding importance.[19] Simon assures us that decision making in the real world cannot be so comprehensive.

At the same time, Simon believes that bureaucrats are *trying* to be rational. In a brief discussion of firefighting, for example, the problem is not that some neighborhoods are whiter than others or more affluent than others or represented by a more powerful alderman than others but rather that bureaucrats cannot know the likelihood that a fire will break out in one section of the city rather than another.[20]

If Simon sees less rationality in policy analysis than some economists, he sees more rationality than some political scientists. Deborah Stone, for example, argues that policy analysis is inherently political.[21] Instead of trying to clarify their values, decision makers try to disguise them. For example, Alan Greenspan, the head of the powerful Federal Reserve Board, is known for his cryptic utterances. He once said before the Senate Banking Committee, "If I say something which you understand fully in this regard, I probably made a mistake." [22] The search for alternatives may also be less public spirited than Simon suggests. Instead of a good faith search for interesting alternatives, we sometimes see a deliberate effort to keep threatening alternatives off the agenda.

From yet another perspective, policy analysis within the bureaucracy tends to be inconsistent with both economic rationality and bounded rationality. Based on research at the Department of Energy (DOE), Martha Feldman contends that policy analysis is usually not intended for a specific decision, that it rarely addresses a well-specified problem, and that it seldom is completed in time to have an impact. For example, she notes that of twelve policy papers prepared by DOE policy analysts within a three-month period, only one could be clearly linked to a pending decision. According to Feldman, policy analysts do not help to solve problems, as Simon suggests; rather, they produce interpretations of issues, which help policymakers to gain a better understanding of the world around them.[23]

Despite these objections, some forms of policy analysis conducted by bureaucrats are strikingly consistent with bounded rationality. One is **cost-benefit analysis.** Rooted in microeconomics, cost-benefit analysis attempts to place a monetary value on both the costs and the benefits of proposed policy alternatives. To the extent that it is successful, this type of analysis helps to render bureaucratic decision making more rational by supplying decision makers with benefit-cost ratios that facilitate easy comparisons across policy options. Thus if a dam in Mississippi has a benefit-cost ratio of 6/1, while a dredging project in Louisiana has a benefit-cost ratio of 2/1, the Army Corps of Engineers ought to prefer the dam.

At first, it might appear that cost-benefit analysis is more consistent with pure rationality than with bounded rationality. After all, the basic idea is to monetize all costs and benefits and to produce a single number comparing the two. In the real world, however, cost-benefit analysis always suffers from incomplete and imperfect information. Benefits are notoriously difficult to measure, and discount rates, which convert future costs into current dollars, are controversial. Though animated by a vision of pure rationality, cost-benefit analysis resembles bounded rationality in practice.

Motivation

In a pure rational choice model, self-interest motivates bureaucrats. In advancing their self-interest, they seek to maximize utility. A number of scholars have questioned whether this perspective adequately characterizes bureaucrats, politicians, or voters.[24] They would agree with Peter Clark and James Q. Wilson, who argue that **purposive incentives** (such as the pursuit of the public interest) and **solidary incentives** (such as the respect of one's peers) are powerful motivating forces for some bureaucrats.[25] Even some economists acknowledge that many bureaucrats have "mixed motives," combining self-interest and altruistic support for certain values. Anthony Downs, for instance, asserts that **zealots, advocates,** and **statesmen,** not just **climbers** and

Table 2.3 Types of Bureaucrats

Climbers consider power, income, and prestige as nearly all-important in their value structures.

Conservers consider convenience and security as nearly all-important. In contrast to climbers, conservers seek merely to retain the amount of power, income, and prestige they already have, rather than to maximize them.

Zealots are loyal to relatively narrow policies or concepts, such as the development of nuclear submarines. They seek power both for its own sake and to effect the policies to which they are loyal. We shall call these their sacred policies.

Advocates are loyal to a broader set of functions or to a broader organization than zealots. They also seek power because they want to have a significant influence upon policies and actions concerning those functions or organizations.

Statesmen are loyal to society as a whole, and they desire to obtain the power necessary to have a significant influence upon national policies and actions. They are altruistic to an important degree because their loyalty is to the "general welfare" as they see it. Therefore statesmen closely resemble the theoretical bureaucrats of public administration textbooks.

Source: Adapted from Anthony Downs, *Inside Bureaucracy* (originally published by Little, Brown & Co., Boston, Mass., 1967, p. 88). Copyright ©1967 RAND Corporation, Santa Monica, Calif. Reprinted with permission.

conservers, populate the bureaucracy (see Table 2.3).[26] It is difficult to reduce the behavior of zealots, advocates, and statesmen to self-interest alone.

Empathy and Commitment

Empathy represents one departure from pure self-interest. Certain bureaucrats identify with disadvantaged constituents, such as the poor or the disabled. Other bureaucrats identify with regulated firms, perhaps because they interact so often with the firms' representatives. Still other bureaucrats, who belong to a particular ethnic group, identify with members of that group. Gender is another source of empathic bonds.

Technically, empathy and self-interest can be reconciled. If a bureaucrat's concern for others directly affects his or her own welfare as well, then one can argue that this is just a subtle manifestation of self-interest. As Amartya Sen notes, however, some people "commit" themselves to a principle that clashes with self-interest.[27] When a bureaucrat fights for a principle or cause that puts his or her career at risk, such commitment suggests that purposive incentives are at work. When a white bureaucrat fights prejudice against blacks in a school or firm, the underlying motivation may well be commitment rather than empathy.

A study of bureaucratic motivation during the Reagan administration found considerable evidence of self-interested behavior, where bureaucrats complied with questionable directives from above for fear of losing their jobs. This proved especially true at the National Highway Traffic Safety Administration and the Food and Nutrition Service. In contrast, bureaucrats at the Civil Rights Division of the Justice Department and the EPA were more willing to place their jobs at risk. A strong sense of professionalism motivated some rebellious bureaucrats; ideological aversion to President Reagan's policies motivated others.[28]

Attitudes toward Risk

Observers often assert that bureaucrats are risk averse. In fact, most people are risk averse most of the time. Most of us wear seatbelts when we drive, don't smoke, stay home during a bad snowstorm, and avoid crime-ridden neighborhoods after dark. Once the dangers of Pinto fuel tanks were exposed, consumers switched to other cars; once the dangers of Firestone tires were exposed, consumers switched to other tires. Our collective investment in homeland security after September 11 suggests a collective aversion to risk. Thus the question is not whether bureaucrats are risk averse but whether they are more risk averse than the rest of us.

Foreign Service officers, within the State Department, are sometimes depicted as unusually risk averse. Specifically, some observers claim the officers are more cautious and timid than the political appointees who run the department. Chester Bowles, who believed this, argued that Foreign Service officers, being less prepared to take risks and less likely to think creatively, made poor candidates for top positions at State.[29]

Not everyone would agree. Charles Bohlen, who served as U.S. ambassador to the Soviet Union during the 1950s, argued that Foreign Service officers "were just as willing, in fact more so, to stick their neck out than were political appointees."[30] More broadly, it appears that, while attitudinal differences between bureaucrats and politicians do exist, they are less striking in the United States than in other countries.[31]

In thinking about risk, bureaucrats and politicians alike seem to be guided by what cognitive psychologists call the **availability heuristic.** Rather than considering all existing examples of some phenomenon and then reaching a conclusion, people tend to judge a situation based on the most readily available case, oftentimes the most recent case.[32] In the wake of an accident or a disaster, we become more cautious, more risk averse because that accident or disaster is more readily available to us, more easily called to mind. This helps to explain why bureaucrats and politicians reacted with strong rhetoric and tough policies to the Three Mile Island accident of 1979, which threatened the possibility of a meltdown of a nuclear power plant reactor core. Although this kind of bounded rationality might seem perverse, it has its advantages. In addition to saving time and effort, it takes into account the psychological costs of certain choices. In Charles Perrow's words, the availability heuristic recognizes that "the public's fears must be treated with respect, and a way found to bring them into policy considerations."[33]

Organizational Advancement

For many bureaucrats, the welfare of the bureaucracy itself comes to rival the individual bureaucrat's welfare in importance. Bureaucracy's defenders and critics alike have observed a striking tendency for bureaucrats to identify with their organizations and the organizations' goals. As Herbert Simon put it, "The common claim that economic self-interest is the only important human motivation in the workings of a society is simply false, for it is an easily observable fact that, within organizations, organizational identification requires at least equal billing with self interest." [34]

A key advantage of organizational identification is that it enables the bureaucracy to socialize its members to pursue organizational goals that have been duly authorized by elected officials. In this sense, organizational identification promotes *legal accountability*. By ensuring that civil servants and political executives promote the same organizational goals, it also promotes *bureaucratic accountability* (see chapter 1). But what if political exec-

Inside Bureaucracy with	James Baker III *Secretary of the Treasury (1985–1988)* *Secretary of State (1989–1992)*

"You have in the Foreign Service a higher degree of career employees than at other bureaucracies. They come from a very prestigious source: the Foreign Service exam. It's different in that respect from other bureaucracies. Sometimes it affects them beneficially and sometimes negatively. As with anybody else, you've got good apples and bad apples.

"Some people think that cabinet secretaries are here today, gone tomorrow. I'm not saying that all Foreign Service officers are that way. More than anything else, they want to be players. When I took office, I said I was going to be the White House's man at the State Department instead of the State Department's man at the White House. There were mumblings and grumblings, but that all went away when it became clear that the State Department was going to be the main agency implementing George Herbert Walker Bush's foreign policy. Bureaucrats relate warmly and well to strong secretaries. And I was one because I was a close friend of the president. Nobody was going to get between me and the president. I think the same thing happened in the Kissinger years at State."

utives or politicians sacrifice organizational goals for political self-promotion? A potential disadvantage of organizational identification is that bureaucrats who simply do what their bosses tell them may lose sight of the broader goals the organization is supposed to promote. If the bureaucracy veers substantially from its legitimate goals, individual bureaucrats may veer with it, rather than challenging the organization from within (what Albert Hirschman would call **voice**) or resigning in public protest (what Hirschman would call **exit**).[35]

Promoting Organizational Cohesion

How do bureaucracies and their political appointees promote the kind of organizational cohesion Simon and others have noticed and applauded? One strategy is to train bureaucrats so they know exactly what is expected of them. When a new recruit arrives, it is customary to have a probationary period, during which the new arrival learns the ropes from a mentor or a cluster of mentors. At some agencies, the probationary period is relatively long and the training process relatively rigorous. Police departments, for example, rely on police academies to ensure the learning of proper techniques.

A second strategy is to ensure that information flows up and down the organization. Regular meetings offer one opportunity for superiors and subordinates to exchange information and ideas. Organizers hope that by the meeting's end, all personnel will be on the same wavelength. Memos are also important tools for feedback from below and guidance from above.

A third strategy is to rely upon professions to socialize individuals and to certify both skills and values. By hiring members of a profession whose tenets and norms match its own, a bureaucracy can save itself a good deal of time and effort. In his classic study of the Forest Service, Herbert Kaufman noted how bureaucrats used this technique to counter centrifugal tendencies inherent in an agency whose employees work, for the most part, in remote locations and with limited supervision. By hiring professional foresters for numerous jobs, including personnel management, administrative management, and budgeting positions that actually could have been filled by persons with different credentials, the Forest Service helped to ensure a common outlook that lessened the need for close supervision.[36] By rotating these professionals on a regular basis, the Forest Service also helped to ensure that tendencies toward **capture** and **localism** would be overcome. Capture occurs when regulatory agencies adopt the thinking of the interests they should be regulating; localism occurs when clientele agencies adopt the thinking of local clients.

Although some agencies rely heavily on one profession, as the Forest Service did, most recruit individuals with diverse professional backgrounds. Such practices help agencies to perform varied and complex tasks by taking

Inside Bureaucracy with	Dan Glickman *Secretary of Agriculture (1995–2001)*

"By and large I found the Forest Service personnel to have an esprit de corps. I used to call it my little Marine Corps. They were out there. They were pretty much on their own. They felt they had this historic sense of mission. They wear uniforms. There's hierarchy. They directly interface the public. The Food and Nutrition Service is just a totally different animal, much more of a classic regulatory operation. Some of them are out there interfacing the public but not a lot. Most of them are designing regulations. They would be much more as classic government employees or bureaucrats."

advantage of people with different professional norms and skills. For better and for worse, these professionals are like the tiger whose stripes remain well after being placed in a zoo.

Consider, for example, the Federal Trade Commission (FTC), which has recruited both lawyers and economists to handle antitrust matters. The lawyers, with a relatively short time frame and a penchant for litigation, prefer to pursue lots of antitrust cases, including small ones, at once. The economists, with a longer time frame and a preference for restructuring industries, would rather wait for a blockbuster case to come along.[37] While conflicts between economists and lawyers who work for the same agency may require managers to spend some time arbitrating disputes, those conflicts between the two professions can also be constructive. For example, the FTC pursues a good mix of difficult and easy cases, thanks to the combined input of economists and lawyers.

Consequences of Bounded Rationality

Is bounded rationality a virtue, a vice, or a necessary evil? Simon's perspective is clear. Although bounded rationality underscores the limits of organizational decision making, Simon was not pessimistic about either individual or organizational behavior. Rather, he believed that individuals have the ability to adapt to formidable challenges through satisficing and other shortcuts. Furthermore, he believed that organizations can help ensure that individuals make decisions roughly consistent not only with their personal preferences but also with their organizations' most important goals. In Simon's words: "The rational individual is, and must be, an organized and institutionalized individual. If the severe limits imposed by human psychology are to be relaxed, the individual must in his decisions be subject to the influence of the organizational group in which he participates." [38] In short, Simon was optimistic about bounded rationality.

Is such optimism justified? To answer that question, it is useful to reconsider some of the essential elements of bounded rationality: a narrow search, problem disaggregation, approximations, and standard operating procedures.

A Narrow Search

A hallmark of bounded rationality is its explicit willingness to limit the decision-making process to a relatively narrow range of options. We saw that planners for the BART system limited their choices to rail initiatives, while planners for the nearby AC system limited their choices to bus routes. One can easily imagine that these pragmatic decisions, understandable in the short run, might prove disastrous in the long run. Yet a careful analysis reveals quite the opposite. Thanks to a circumscribed range of options, the two mass transit systems developed independently as **parallel systems,** or organizations with similar goals but with very different strengths and weaknesses. When strikes afflicted one of the systems, the other could absorb a sudden spike in demand. When bad management plagued one of the systems, the other could keep running smoothly. When technical breakdowns undermined one of the systems, the other could help out. The result, though serendipitous, was far better than two blended systems would have been. As Jonathan Bendor concluded, "Taken together, AC and BART form a more flexible response to long-term problems than does either one taken separately." [39] Chalk one up for satisficing.

Problem Disaggregation

In an essay Anne Lamott describes a childhood scene etched in her memory: her brother, a procrastinator, had put off writing a lengthy report on birds until the night before it was due. Frustration led to fear, then to panic. How could he possibly finish the assignment on time? Their father, calm and reassuring, put his arm around his son's shoulder and shared one of the secrets of writing (and problem solving): "Bird by bird, buddy. Just take it bird by bird." [40]

Like Lamott's brother, bureaucratic decision makers have learned that they need to break big problems down into digestible chunks. That is how NASA managed to put a man on the moon. That is how Robert Moses transformed the landscape of New York City. That is how Jaime Escalante enabled disadvantaged students from a Los Angeles barrio to excel in mathematics and pass the Advanced Placement calculus exam. And that is how environmental bureaucrats have combated pollution.

Yet the bird-by-bird approach has a down side. In the case of environmental protection, the EPA's decision to tackle pollution medium by medium has been reinforced by structural arrangements that mimic this approach. Thus the EPA has an Air and Radiation Division, a Water Division, and a Solid Waste and Emergency Response Division (see Figure 2.1). Unfortunately, the Air and Radiation Division focuses so obsessively on air that it pays limited attention to water and land impacts; the Water Division focuses so obsessively on water that it pays limited attention to air and waste impacts. Because most pollution transcends a single medium, a **stovepipe mentality**, in which problems are disaggregated and compartmentalized, may inhibit a more **holistic perspective**. Although some state environmental agencies have attempted to take crossmedia transfers into account—for example, through streamlined permitting systems—this remains a serious problem, at both the state and federal levels.[41]

Approximations

Another feature of bounded rationality is its willingness to settle for approximately correct answers rather than precise answers. Perhaps it is this sort of thinking that gave us the Leaning Tower of Pisa! But in most instances, approximations serve us rather well.

Consider the problem of tips earned by waiters and waitresses at restaurants and similar establishments. Because these are often cash transactions, some employees underreport their earnings, thus failing to meet their tax obligations and imposing a burden on the rest of us. Instead of counting tips at every restaurant in the United States—a herculean task—the Internal Revenue Service (IRS) decided in 1994 to calculate probable tip revenue based on business volume. By the end of 1996 the IRS had introduced this system at more than 22,000 establishments, and reported tip income had increased by more than $2 billion.[42] Estimates of tip revenue were sufficiently conservative that no one, or almost no one, paid more than he or she owed.

For the reasons discussed earlier, cost-benefit analysis, which seeks considerable precision, nevertheless falls short much of the time. In some instances, the imperfections of cost-benefit analysis result in bad decisions. For example, in evaluating the Dickey-Lincoln School hydroelectric power project in Maine, the Army Corps of Engineers estimated the benefit-cost ratio to be 2/1, when in fact the ratio was more like 0.8/1 or 0.9/1.[43] Luckily, the mistake was discovered, and Congress terminated funding for the project. More often, cost-benefit calculations fall well beyond the boundary of 1.0, thus reducing the policy implications of calculation error. For example, a cost-benefit analysis of the EPA's proposal to reduce the amount of lead in gasoline yielded a benefit-cost ratio higher than 10/1, although it was impossible to measure all the benefits.[44] In this instance, as in many others, the policy implications were clear. Even if the true benefit-cost ratio was 11/1 or 12/1—or

Figure 2.1: EPA Organizational Structure

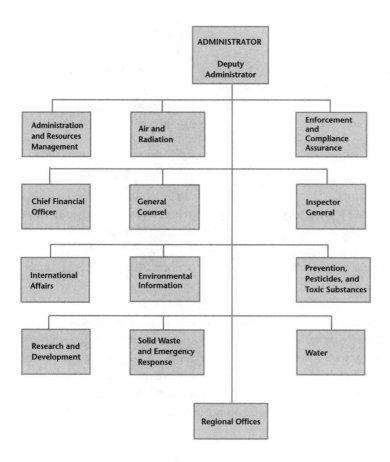

Source: Environmental Protection Agency; http://www.epa.gov/epahome/organization.htm, May 10, 2003.

even 9/1—the EPA was fully justified in proceeding with its lead reduction plan.

Standard Operating Procedures

In the television series *Judging Amy*, Tyne Daly plays the part of a zealous social worker, Maxine Gray, who works for the Department of Family Services in Hartford, Connecticut. Not known for "going by the book," Maxine often gets into trouble with her superiors for departing from standard operating procedures. Her retort is that when children's lives are at stake, standard operating procedures are less important than good outcomes.

It is possible to identify cases where standard operating procedures, designed to rationalize bureaucratic decision making, produce questionable results. Regulatory inspectors who always go by the book sometimes behave unreasonably.[45] Policy analysts who become preoccupied with routines sometimes waste time and lose sight of broader goals.[46] Adherence to standard operating procedures does not always prevent accidents from occurring.[47] Standard operating procedures may be useless in a novel situation.

Nevertheless, standard operating procedures help street-level bureaucrats to process cases and resolve routine problems quickly. These procedures also help managers to control those street-level bureaucrats. In addition, standard operating procedures help to prevent police officers from abusing suspects, inspectors from playing favorites, and IRS auditors from targeting individuals for political reasons. Furthermore, they help bureaucracies to devote more resources to novel problems because bureaucrats need not reinvent the wheel when a familiar problem appears.

One of the simplest, but most compelling, examples of a standard operating procedure that works well is the emergency response calling system. Over time, most adults and even some young children have learned that in an emergency they should dial 911. This arrangement has helped to save hundreds, perhaps thousands, of lives. It is particularly interesting because it involves a standard operating procedure for nonroutine situations. Even in the middle of a crisis, standard operating procedures can be extremely helpful.

Conclusion

Bounded rationality is a useful starting point for an in-depth discussion of bureaucratic politics because it is much more realistic than a rational choice perspective. With limited information, limited alternatives, and limited time, real bureaucrats make decisions as best they can. They learn from experience, relying on standard operating procedures to make their tasks more manageable. They simplify problems by disaggregating them, or breaking them into bite-size chunks. In Simon's words, they satisfice because they cannot optimize.

Simon's perspective distinguishes him from Charles Lindblom, another decision theorist. According to Lindblom, individuals and organizations typically rely upon **incrementalism** as a decision making tool.[48] Instead of beginning with a range of choices, as Simon posits, Lindblom believes that decision makers begin with the status quo. They then deviate from the status quo cautiously, yielding policies that differ only incrementally from previous policies. Incrementalism as an outcome is entirely possible under Simon's model of bounded rationality (recall, for example, the concept of sunk costs), but it is not preordained because incrementalism as a procedure is not the only way for decision makers to cope with limited time and information. As studies have shown, incrementalism is not always the best way to describe the policymaking process.[49] Nor is it always the best way to describe bureaucratic decision making.

Despite its strengths, bounded rationality is not the only useful way to think about bureaucratic decision making. In a sense, the world described by Simon resembles a planet populated by *Star Trek's* Vulcans, beings such as Spock, known for his iron logic, his capacity for independent thought, and his incorruptibility. What is missing from Spock, and from Simon's bureaucrats, is not just emotion but politics. In the real world, pressure from legislators, chief executives, judges, interest groups, journalists, and citizens constrains bureaucratic decision making. These actors do not appear in Simon's account.

In our next chapter, we focus on some of these actors—the politicians and the judges authorized to tell bureaucrats what to do. We introduce an alternative theoretical perspective, known as principal-agent theory, which pays much closer attention to the bureaucracy's sovereigns. Bureaucrats do not make decisions in a vacuum, as Simon sometimes implies. Yet, as we shall see, the bureaucracy's principals experience many of the same limitations that bureaucrats do. As they seek to control the bureaucracy, politicians and judges are constrained by limited information, limited options, and limited time.

Key Terms

Advocates, 37	Conservers, 38
Attainment area, 31	Cost-benefit analysis, 37
Availability heuristic, 40	Differential monitoring, 33
Bounded rationality, 28	Differential response, 34
Capture, 43	Exit, 42
Climbers, 37	Holistic perspective, 46

3 | The Bureaucracy's Bosses

IN THE WANING DAYS OF THE Clinton presidency, the Occupational Safety and Health Administration (OSHA) issued a rule designed to protect workers against injuries caused by repetitive motion. This rule was a major policy action in that hundreds of thousands of Americans, in settings as diverse as corporate offices, meat-cutting plants, and medical facilities, miss work each year because of "ergonomics-related" injuries. The rule was also highly controversial. Analysts projected that collectively businesses would incur costs in the billions of dollars to comply with OSHA's requirements, which included reviewing employee complaints, redesigning problematic workstations, and providing compensation for disabilities.

Shortly after George W. Bush assumed the presidency, the controversy surrounding the ergonomics rule erupted on Capitol Hill. Most Republican legislators, as well as some Democrats, vehemently opposed the rule, preferring either a less expansive approach or no regulation at all. Seeking to overturn OSHA's action, these lawmakers resorted to an obscure parliamentary maneuver. Under the **Congressional Review Act** of 1996, agency rules can be nullified if both chambers of Congress enact a **resolution of disapproval**. Because such resolutions cannot be subjected to committee hearings, extensive debate, and other standard features of the lawmaking process, they are easier to pass than normal legislation. On March 21, 2001, barely two months after it took effect, the ergonomics rule became the only agency action ever to have been repealed in this way when President Bush signed into law a resolution disapproving the standards established by OSHA.[1]

The ergonomics controversy illustrates the power that policymakers outside the bureaucracy can wield over an agency. They usually exercise this power more subtly, however. Efforts by legislators to influence bureaucracies often take, for example, the form of informal staff communications and requirements that agencies give advance notice of their intended actions.

Despite the ubiquity of such efforts, bureaucracies retain considerable autonomy over policymaking, even in the face of open hostility from elsewhere in government. In the aftermath of the September 11, 2001, terrorist attacks, Congress enacted an aviation and transportation security law with great fanfare. This law gave the Department of Transportation (DOT) sixty days to devise a system for screening all checked baggage for explosives. Not only did the agency publicly resist this deadline, but it also simultaneously established a policy—moving passengers through security checkpoints in ten minutes or less—that many observers decried as contrary to the law's primary aim of making air travel safer.[2]

Episodes such as these are commonplace in the American political system. They are also vitally important. The interactions of agencies with their external political environments determine which public decisions will be made in bureaucracies and which will be made in other institutions of government. Put differently, the outcomes of these interactions establish the very boundaries of bureaucratic authority.[3]

As illustrated by the ergonomics and explosives examples, these boundaries are sometimes, but not always, set with an eye to democratic principles such as accountability and performance. Congress and the president took away OSHA's authority to make ergonomics policy not long after control of the White House shifted from one political party to the other, a particularly blunt imposition of political accountability. In the case of DOT, it is not clear that outputs such as screening baggage and moving passengers quickly are effective in bringing about the outcomes—safety and convenience in air travel—desired by policymakers and their constituents. In the end, the boundaries of bureaucratic authority are best understood as manifestations of the ongoing contest between government agencies and their political supervisors for control over the policymaking process.

With these issues in mind, this chapter provides a detailed examination of the relationship between agencies and the outside political world. It is organized around the following core questions:

- *UNDER WHAT CONDITIONS IS POLICYMAKING RESPONSIBILITY DELEGATED TO THE BUREAUCRACY?* For years elected officials entrusted OSHA with the authority to make ergonomics policy, only to severely limit this authority when the political environment was transformed.

- *IN WHAT WAYS DO OTHER GOVERNMENT ACTORS SEEK TO INFLU-ENCE THE MANNER IN WHICH AGENCIES EXERCISE THEIR RESPON-SIBILITIES?* The Aviation and Transportation Security Act not only gave DOT the authority to screen baggage but also attached a strict timetable to this authority, thereby limiting the agency's flexibility in making and implementing policy in this area.

- *TO WHAT EXTENT ARE EFFORTS AT POLITICAL CONTROL SUCCESS-FUL, IN LIGHT OF THE FACT THAT AGENCIES CAN, AND DO, TAKE STEPS TO PRESERVE AND EXTEND THEIR AUTHORITY?* Facing stiff resistance from DOT and a variety of other sources, Congress ultimately extended the baggage screening deadline, allowing airports a significant amount of additional time to get explosives detection systems up and running.

The chapter approaches these core questions primarily from the perspective of principal-agent theory, an approach widely used to understand the origins and implications of delegated authority. It is particularly appropriate in that it places bureaucratic policymaking in its broader context. Agencies do not operate in a vacuum but rather in an environment where public decisions can be, and often are, made in alternative venues. As will become apparent, this environmental reality has fundamental consequences for both bureaucratic accountability and performance.

Delegation, Adverse Selection, and Moral Hazard

Delegation is a common feature of modern life. Clients grant attorneys the authority to provide legal representation, patients rely on doctors to treat illnesses, and employers hire workers to perform tasks of all sorts. These types of relationships share fundamental characteristics. Clients, patients, and employers all face difficulties in choosing and monitoring those to whom they delegate authority. Principal-agent theory is an approach to understanding the causes and consequences of these difficulties.[4]

A **principal** is an actor who enters into a contractual relationship with another actor, an **agent.** The agent is entrusted to take actions that lead to outcomes specified by the principal. For example, doctors act as agents when they prescribe medicines and perform procedures to enhance the duration and quality of the lives of their patients (that is, principals), and lawyers act as agents for persons accused of a crime. These arrangements arise when principals lack the ability to achieve their goals by themselves. Self-representation is not advisable, in most cases, for defendants seeking to minimize the likelihood of a guilty verdict!

A key assumption of principal-agent theory is that self-interest primarily motivates both principals and agents. In general, principals and agents face divergent incentives, and this divergence means that purely self-interested behavior on the part of agents may not produce the outcomes desired by principals. For instance, the owners of business firms are concerned first and foremost with maximizing profits. Although rank-and-file employees certainly share a stake in company performance, their subordinate status shapes their actions in important ways. The workers on assembly lines may have little reason to work at top speed if the benefits of their efforts accrue solely to corporate executives and shareholders.

Principals face two specific difficulties when dealing with agents. The first is known as **adverse selection.** This difficulty arises when principals cannot directly observe important characteristics of agents but must rely on rough indicators. Defendants cannot easily discern the true motivations and skills of attorneys and therefore must select legal representation on the basis of factors such as reputations and caseloads. Although such proxies may have merit, they are not foolproof. In the end, principals run the risk of hiring agents not ideally suited for the task at hand.

The second difficulty is known as **moral hazard.** This difficulty stems from the fact that agents, once selected, cannot be readily evaluated in their work environments. As a result, principals must make inferences about the degree to which agents are effectively securing the outcomes they were hired to bring about. Potential patients often judge doctors who perform laser eye surgeries by their success rates. Such measures, however, prove to be far from perfect. It may be hard to discern the individual performance of a doctor who works as part of a team of laser eye surgeons. To further complicate matters, the outcomes of surgeries are affected not only by the doctors' actions but also by the patients' presurgery eyesight conditions (such as how nearsighted or farsighted they were). Because of these uncertainties, agents may find it possible to shirk their duties, or even to undermine the goals sought by principals, without being detected.

Can principals overcome the difficulties caused by adverse selection and moral hazard? One of the main lessons of principal-agent theory is that delegation almost invariably leads to **agency loss.** Agency loss occurs when the behavior of agents leaves principals unable to achieve their goals in an efficient manner or realize them at all. Agency loss, however, can be limited under the right circumstances. For principals, then, the key task is to take steps that help bring such circumstances about.[5]

Perhaps the most common way to mitigate the agency loss associated with adverse selection is the use of **screening mechanisms.** Basically, principals must get agents to reveal their motivations and skills before hiring them. For example, employers routinely judge the qualifications of applicants through apprenticeships and examinations. The problem of moral hazard can be ameliorated in two distinct ways. The first is **institutional design.** Here, principals place agents in situations in which they find it in their self-interest to work toward outcomes favored by the principals. Corporations, for instance, commonly provide workers with a financial stake in company performance through devices such as stock options. The second approach is **oversight** of agent actions. By monitoring agents at work, principals aim to identify and redirect behavior inconsistent with their objectives. Principals can also use oversight as a deterrent. The mere possibility of being monitored may induce agents to forego activities that do not serve principals well.

Principal-agent theory can easily be applied to policymaking in the bureaucracy. Administrative agencies are agents to whom policymaking authority is delegated. This authority originates with principals such as chief executives, legislatures, and judiciaries. The act of delegation brings each of these principals face-to-face with particular manifestations of adverse selection and moral hazard. For example, legislators have relatively little influence over the selection of agency officials, as personnel matters fall largely under the domain of the chief executive and the civil service system. Given such difficulties, why do principals empower agencies in the first place? Put differently, what are the benefits of policymaking in the bureaucracy?

Why Bureaucracy?

One obvious rationale for bureaucracy is the scope of modern government. Early in its history, the federal government performed only a handful of functions, such as setting duties on foreign goods. Figure 3.1 illustrates that as the government's reach extended, the size of the bureaucracy grew as well.

Figure 3.1 The Size of the Federal Bureaucracy, 1821–1999

Number of civilian employees

Year

Sources: U.S. Bureau of the Census, *Historical Statistics of the United States, Colonial Times to 1970,* bicentennial ed., part 1 (Washington, D.C.: Government Printing Office, 1975). U.S. Census Bureau, *Statistical Abstract of the United States: 2000,* 120th ed. (Washington, D.C.: Government Printing Office, 2000).

During the New Deal, perhaps the most ambitious expansion of government power in American history, the number of civilian employees in the executive branch nearly tripled, from about half a million to close to 1.5 million. Another indication of bureaucracy's growth is the number of pages the *Federal Register* (the executive branch's official daily publication) consumes. The documents published in the *Federal Register* include agency regulations, proposed rules, and notices, as well as executive orders and proclamations and other presidential materials. As indicated in Table 3.1, the size of the *Federal Register* has grown more than fourfold since 1960.

Contemporary government addresses issues not only wide ranging but often quite complex as well. In formulating the ergonomics rule, OSHA had to synthesize knowledge from fields as diverse as economics, engineering, medicine, and management. Policymaking efforts such as this one are simply beyond the existing capabilities of other government institutions. Congress,

Table 3.1 Number of Pages in the *Federal Register,* 1960–1999

Year	Number of Pages
1960	14,479
1965	17,206
1970	20,036
1975	60,221
1980	73,258
1985	50,502
1990	49,795
1995	62,645
1996	64,591
1997	64,549
1998	68,571
1999	71,161

Source: Office of the *Federal Register,* National Archives and Records Administration.

even with hundreds of members and thousands of staffers, possesses a mere fraction of the specialized expertise found in the bureaucracy.

Bureaucracies are also valuable to government actors pursuing specific, self-interested goals. Legislators build their cases for reelection in part by helping constituents overcome bureaucratic "red tape." [6] An example of such **casework** is the assistance commonly offered to retirees whose Social Security checks have been lost in the mail. On a broader scale, elected officials can use agencies to avoid the blame that comes with controversial or difficult decisions.[7] By placing responsibility for aviation security in the hands of DOT, Congress has distanced itself from culpability should there be a catastrophic breakdown in the system.

Importantly, the motivation behind the delegation of authority to the bureaucracy cannot be meaningfully separated from agency effectiveness. For example, agencies called upon to perform contradictory tasks may find it particularly difficult to succeed. Despite the recent emphasis on aviation security, Congress still expects DOT to look after the financial stability of air carriers and other traditional concerns that may be jeopardized by antiterrorism measures. In a similar vein, OSHA's mission—to save lives, prevent injuries, and protect workers' health—does not mention consideration of the costs imposed on businesses, even though it is central to the agency's often contentious decision-making processes. In general, the efficacy of agencies as institutions of democratic policymaking is in part a product of the politics surrounding the bureaucracy's supervisors.

Why Delegation Varies

Although delegation to the bureaucracy is widespread, it nevertheless varies considerably across issue areas, as laid out in Figure 3.2. When issues are low in salience, politicians are more likely to delegate authority to the bureaucracy. Occupational licensing and childcare regulation usually fall into this category. When issues are high in salience, as in the case of civil rights disputes and environmental policy, delegation is less viable because citizens and organized interests expect elected officials to act decisively.[8] Complexity also matters, especially for highly salient issues. When issues are high in salience and low in complexity, politicians often seek to control the bureaucracy by specifying the substance of policy in great detail. Antidiscrimination edicts exemplify this approach. When issues are high in both salience and complexity, elected officials are more likely to exert leverage over policymaking through procedural instruments, such as the requirement that agencies conduct environmental impact assessments before adopting rules likely to have a major impact.[9]

For similar reasons, delegation also varies within issue areas. It is thought that congressional control of the Environmental Protection Agency (EPA) is greatest when both legislative preferences and capabilities are

Figure 3.2 Explaining Variation in Delegation

Complexity

		Low	High
Salience	**Low**	Delegation	Delegation
	High	Substantive controls	Procedural controls

Source: William Gormley Jr., "Regulatory Issue Networks in a Federal System," *Polity* 18 (summer 1986): 607.

strong, as when issues are high in salience and low in complexity. Among the key provisions of the Clean Air Act Amendments of 1990, those pertaining to acid rain best fit this description. The acid rain portion of the law has a much higher concentration of detailed substantive provisions than the sections addressing air toxins, mobile sources, and chlorofluorocarbons.[10] Here is one example of this type of provision:

> The Administrator shall not allocate annual allowances to emit sulfur dioxide pursuant to section 405 in such an amount as would result in total annual emissions of sulfur dioxide from utility units in excess of 8.90 million tons.[11]

When congressional preferences and capabilities are less developed, Congress is less likely to provide such precise instructions.

Issue characteristics alone do not determine whether delegation occurs and what form it takes. Partisan control of the legislative and executive branches affects these determinations as well. When divided government exists—one party controls the legislature and the other the office of chief executive—delegation becomes less likely.[12] Understandably, Democratic legislators are less trusting of bureaucracies headed by Republicans, and Republican legislators less trusting of bureaucracies run by Democrats.

In the end, political principals evaluate policymaking in the bureaucracy against its alternatives. The critical question is, *Would these principals be better served by making policy themselves or by delegating authority to bureaucratic agents?* As we have seen, principals sometimes eschew delegation altogether. The benefits of delegation, however, often prove too irresistible to pass up. For principals, then, the trick is to capture these benefits without being unduly harmed by the actions of self-interested agents.

Implementing Childcare Legislation

To more fully appreciate the politics of the delegation decision and the boundaries of bureaucratic authority, consider the implementation of a pair of federal childcare laws passed in 1990 and 1996. In both instances, Congress approved childcare subsidies to be distributed by state governments to families with relatively low incomes. The first law created a new Child Care and Development Block Grant, while the second consolidated a number of different funding streams, including the block grant, under the rubric of a new Child Care and Development Fund.

As Table 3.2 indicates, the 1990 legislation, sometimes known as the ABC bill, delegated considerable discretion to the Department of Health and Human Services. In addition to appropriating a certain amount of money for the program, thereby placing a ceiling on how much could be spent, Congress stressed the importance of parental choice, indicating that it wanted children to be enrolled with the provider preferred by parents "to the maximum extent practicable." In interpreting this provision, the agency specified that a state could not exclude certain categories of care (such as family childcare), certain types of providers (such as church-based centers), or "significant numbers of providers" in any category or type of care. As for payment rates, Congress specified that the agency must take the costs of different settings and age groups into account and that there should be separate rates for children with special needs. But Congress left it up to the agency to determine whether states should be free to pay providers more for providing higher-quality services. After wrestling with this issue, the agency decided to allow such differentials but to limit these differences to 10 percent. In effect, Congress established basic guidelines for administration of the block grant but left a lot of the specific operational decisions to the agency.

Table 3.2 Implementation of the 1990 Child Care Law

Issue	Provision of the Law	Agency Implementation
Parental choice	The child will be enrolled with the eligible provider selected by the parent "to the maximum extent practicable."	State and local rules cannot have the effect of excluding certain categories of care, certain types of providers, or "significant numbers of providers" in any category or type of care.
Payment rates	Payment rates must take into account variations in the costs of providing childcare in different settings, for different age groups, and for children with special needs.	States may distinguish between higher-quality and lower-quality providers within a category of care in setting payment rates, but such rate differentials may not exceed 10 percent.
Administrative expenses	States must spend 75 percent of their childcare allotments to improve the quality and availability of childcare, and a "preponderance" of the 75 percent must be spent on childcare services.	For the first two years at least 85 percent of the 75 percent share must be spent on childcare services, as opposed to administrative expenses.

Source: Adapted from House Ways and Means Committee, Subcommittee on Human Resources, *Regulations Issued by the Department of Health and Human Services on Child Care Programs Authorized by Public Law 101-508* (Washington, D.C.: GPO, September 13, 1991).

When revisiting the program in 1996 Congress decided to reiterate its strong commitment to parental choice and to payment rates that would promote equal access. For its part, however, the agency decided to lift the 10 percent ceiling on rate differences within a category of care. In addition, for the first time the agency decided to recommend that states imposing a copayment requirement on parents restrict that copayment to 10 percent of the total fee. Table 3.3 provides a summary of these new provisions.

Table 3.3 Implementation of the 1996 Child Care Law

Issue	Provision of the Law	Agency Implementation
Copayments	Rates should be designed in a way that facilitates parental choice.	It is recommended that no state require a copayment greater than 10 percent; copayments, if required, can be waived for children in protective services or for families with incomes at or below the poverty level.
Payment rates	Rates should be designed in a way that promotes equal access.	States should be free to set differential payment levels within categories of care, to reward providers who offer higher quality; a prior limit of 10 percent for differential payment levels within a category is rescinded.
Market rate survey	Payment rates established by states should be comparable to those paid by families who are not eligible for subsidies.	States must conduct a biennial market rate survey to ensure that payment rates reflect changing market conditions.

Source: Adapted from U.S. Department of Health and Human Services, Administration for Children and Families, "Child Care and Development Fund; Final Rule," *Federal Register,* July 24, 1998, 39935–39998.

A comparison of these decisions helps clarify both the constraints that legislation imposes on the bureaucracy and the discretion that agencies can use to promote their own policy preferences. The Department of Health and Human Services (HHS) under President George H. W. Bush, headed by Louis Sullivan, imposed limits on state childcare agencies to promote parental choice and keep costs down. In contrast, the HHS under President Clinton, headed by Donna Shalala, sought to foster improvements in childcare quality and to limit the financial contributions parents would have to pay. Together these episodes demonstrate that the preferences of elected officials fundamentally shape bureaucratic decisions and that the influence of these political principals is invariably limited when policymaking authority is delegated.

Managing Delegation

Given the persistence of agency loss, political principals not only make delegation decisions with an eye to strategic considerations but also think carefully about managing the authority vested in agencies. Principals differ in the tools they can call upon as they set about this exceedingly difficult task. Some principals find themselves better equipped to cope with adverse selection issues than with moral hazard concerns, while others find the reverse to be true.

Presidential Power

When cataloging the efforts of principals to limit agency loss, a logical place to start is with the president, the formal head of the federal bureaucracy. The presidency is a unique institution in American politics. Only the president has a national constituency and a strong desire to build a legacy that will be remembered fondly in history. For these reasons, the president, more so than others in government, has an incentive to bring the bureaucracy under **coordinated control**.[13] A bureaucracy that functions well as a unit, rather than as an uncoordinated batch of agencies, will be a valuable asset for a president seeking grand policy achievements. But does the president possess the capabilities necessary to bring such coordination about?

The ambiguity of Article II of the Constitution is widely viewed as important in determining the president's ability to command the bureaucracy. Historically, the relative dearth of enumerated powers has been taken as a sign of presidential weakness. With little formal authority, presidents must generally rely on their interpersonal skills to persuade other policymakers to go along with White House initiatives.[14] This lack of authority holds even within the executive branch, where the president is the "chief" in name only.[15]

Recently, Article II's ambiguity has come to be seen by some analysts in a fundamentally different light.[16] Presidents have, throughout history, taken **unilateral actions** not explicitly permitted by the Constitution. Famous examples include the Louisiana Purchase, the Emancipation Proclamation, and the creation of the EPA. Such actions are unilateral in that they are not subject to congressional or judicial approval. In fact, it is difficult for Congress and the courts to stand in the way of presidential unilateralism, even when such behavior expands and consolidates the power of the White House. The ability of the president to control the nation's policymaking apparatus, including the federal bureaucracy, has accumulated over time and continues to accumulate to this day.

APPOINTMENTS. In terms of formal authority, the president is uniquely well equipped to address the problem of adverse selection. Presidents have the power to appoint—subject to Senate confirmation—cabinet secretaries, regulatory commissioners, administrators of independent agencies, and a host of subordinates to these top-ranking officials. All in all, political appointees fill approximately three thousand positions in the executive branch bureaucracy.[17]

Appointments are powerful instruments that can be used to influence the scope and content of bureaucratic policymaking. For example, outputs in agencies ranging from the Food and Drug Administration (FDA) to the Equal Employment Opportunity Commission have shifted noticeably as a direct response to changes in leadership. To take the case of the FDA, product seizures declined by more than 50 percent after the Reagan White House tapped Arthur Hull Hayes—a champion of regulatory relief for business— to lead the agency.[18]

Despite such successes, appointees are inherently limited in their ability to shape bureaucratic decisions. The average agency head has a tenure of less than three years. With such a short time horizon, appointees must move quickly if they want to leave a significant mark on their organizations. The fact that most appointees are not personal associates of the president, and therefore do not enjoy open, regular access to the White House and its resources, makes this task more difficult. Hence appointees are largely left to their own devices in dealing with their subordinates, the vast majority of whom were at the agency long before the current administration came to power and will continue in their positions well after the presidency has again changed hands. For all these reasons, the utility of appointments as a way of managing delegated authority is highly variable across administrations, agencies, and appointees themselves.

On the last point, what separates effective leaders from appointees who run into difficulties in dealing with their agencies and the administration?

Instructive is the case of Paul O'Neill, President George W. Bush's first secretary of the treasury. Less than two years into his tenure, O'Neill became the first cabinet member to leave the administration. Several months of criticism about his handling of an economy in the midst of a prolonged slump preceded O'Neill's departure. Despite his experience as the chairman and chief executive officer of aluminum giant Alcoa, O'Neill did not enjoy the confidence of Wall Street, an absolutely critical constituency for any treasury secretary. In addition, O'Neill did not demonstrate the flair for publicity that successful appointees so often bring to their positions. Even on a made-for-TV trip to Africa, alongside rock star Bono, O'Neill came off as a wooden leader who did not fully understand and appreciate the plight of debt-ridden countries in the developing world. In the end, O'Neill did not possess the combination of personal and professional skills necessary to be an effective appointee for President Bush.

CIVIL SERVICE REFORM. Through much of the nation's history, presidents have sought to enhance their control over the bureaucracy by reforming the rules that govern civil servants, those executive branch officials not subject to presidential appointment and Senate confirmation. In 1905 President Theodore Roosevelt formed the Keep Committee to investigate ways of improving the organization and effectiveness of the federal government.[19] Franklin Roosevelt oversaw passage of the **Reorganization Act** of 1939, establishing the **Executive Office of the President,** which provides the White House with an apparatus for directing and coordinating policy in areas particularly central to the president's agenda. The Council of Economic Advisors and the National Security Council have both been a part of the Executive Office for many years. Under President George W. Bush, the

Executive Office also includes the Office of Faith-Based and Community Initiatives.

In 1978 the **Civil Service Reform Act** brought significant changes to the personnel system of the executive branch. For example, the act established the **Senior Executive Service,** a group of top-level civil servants with less job security than that of their colleagues but more of an opportunity to earn bonuses based on productivity and other performance measures. The idea behind this reform was to create a senior management system under the president that could meaningfully compete with the private sector in recruiting and retaining individuals of exceptional talent. In terms of enhancing the president's capacity to influence decision making inside executive branch agencies, that act and similar reform efforts have garnered mixed reviews.

At first glance, career bureaucrats—who number in the millions—would seem unlikely to be very responsive to presidents and politics more generally.[20] Consider, however, that from the early 1970s to the early 1990s—a period in which Republicans controlled the White House for all but four years—top-level civil servants became increasingly conservative and Republican as a group.[21] In 1970 President Nixon faced a civil service leadership that favored Democrats by a three-to-one margin. By the first Bush administration, Republicans enjoyed an 11 percent edge among these officials. This change occurred for a variety of reasons, including Civil Service Reform Act provisions that gave presidents the authority to move top-ranking careerists around the bureaucracy in ways advantageous to the administration.

The potency of personnel management is illustrated by the debate over the creation of the Department of Homeland Security.[22] In 2002 President Bush proposed merging twenty-two agencies and 170,000 employees into a single organization aimed at protecting the American homeland from terrorist threats. The president's proposal ran into difficulty in the Senate, then under Democratic control. The key stumbling block was presidential prerogatives in managing the department's civil servants. President Bush requested the authority to hire, demote, and transfer employees for national security reasons. A majority of Senators opposed this request on the grounds that it represented too significant an erosion in the collective bargaining rights usually held by federal employees. Not until Republicans gained control of the Senate following the November 2002 elections did the administration muster the congressional support necessary to secure a personnel system with the flexibility and control Bush sought.

REGULATORY REVIEW AND THE OFFICE OF MANAGEMENT AND BUDGET. As the scope and complexity of bureaucratic policymaking have grown, presidents have taken steps to enhance their ability to observe and evaluate agency decisions. One tool modern presidents have used to cope with moral hazard is the **Office of Management and Budget** (OMB). Created in 1970, OMB is a White House organization whose mission includes the development and implementation of policies governing the regulatory process.

In the early 1980s Congress established a new organization, the **Office of Information and Regulatory Affairs** (OIRA), within OMB. OIRA, a bureaucracy in itself, serves as a kind of "counterbureaucracy," overseeing executive branch agencies to ensure that regulations will not be unnecessarily costly.[23] During the Reagan administration, OIRA grew increasingly tough on agencies. From 1981 to 1989 the percent of agency rules reviewed by OIRA that remained unchanged declined from 87.3 to 70.9.[24] During this period, the EPA withdrew two asbestos rules under pressure from OIRA, and OSHA drastically modified a rule reducing worker exposure to ethylene oxide, a chemical used to sterilize hospital equipment. Other agencies, including the Department of Housing and Urban Development, the Department of Education, and HHS, fought their own skirmishes with OIRA.[25]

Because the head of OIRA is a political appointee serving at the president's pleasure, the agency can be a powerful tool for administrations looking to leave their marks on government regulations. As a case in point, the

EPA is more likely to reduce industries' compliance costs if the president expresses probusiness sentiments in the midst of a rulemaking and OIRA's review of the agency's proposal. OIRA, however, has proved an imperfect instrument of control, often acting in ways not explicitly specified, or desired, by the president. Industry compliance costs also decline as a result of OIRA pressure, beyond the influence of presidential statements.[26] In short, OIRA acts not only as an agent of the president but also, at times, as an agent of firms targeted by government regulations.

Congressional Control of the Bureaucracy

Due to its orientation as a lawmaking and investigatory body, Congress is best equipped to manage the bureaucracy through institutional design and oversight. Congress enacts, usually with presidential approval, the statutes that create and assign tasks to executive branch agencies. These statutes provide legislators with opportunities to place structural and procedural constraints on bureaucratic policymaking. For example, the Occupational Safety and Health Act of 1970 permits OSHA to regulate only those hazards specified by researchers at the National Institute of Occupational Safety and Health.[27] Congress also bears responsibility for keeping a watchful eye on the policies and programs formulated and operated within the executive branch. It carries out these responsibilities through channels such as oversight hearings and investigations into allegations of waste, fraud, and abuse.

Toward what ends do legislators typically utilize these instruments? With hundreds of different constituencies enfranchised in the Senate and House of Representatives, congressional control of the bureaucracy is fundamentally uncoordinated in its orientation.[28] In other words, specific committees and subcommittees—such as the Ways and Means Committee's Subcommittee on Health—may influence what goes on in particular agencies—such as the Centers for Medicare and Medicaid Services—but the bureaucracy as a whole does not operate under the direction of Congress as an institution. In the end, no matter how potent Congress and its members may be, the control exercised by the legislative branch is particularistic rather than generalized (that is, aimed at furthering general societal and political interests).

THE POLITICS OF BUREAUCRATIC STRUCTURE. At times, agencies seem designed to fail, or at least to operate in ways not even their most ardent supporters could appreciate and understand. Consider, as an example, the Consumer Product Safety Commission. Created in 1972, the commission is an independent regulatory body charged with reducing the risk of injury and death associated with consumer products. Reluctant to champion the burgeoning consumer movement, the Nixon administration originally proposed placing the commission within the Department of Health, Education, and Welfare, where it would have had relatively little power and could have been easily monitored by the White House.[29] Congress, however, rejected

Inside Bureaucracy with	Donna Shalala *Secretary of Health and Human Services* *(1993–2001)*

"Members of Congress would call and ask us to see people. We tried to be accommodating as long as it wasn't illegal. We made sure it was legal. Members of the Congress intervened most often on waivers. They would say, 'We hope you'll approve the waiver.' Usually, they wouldn't have a clue what it was about! When we got a waiver request, if we were giving them flexibility, we wanted to be sure that they were protecting certain groups, such as the disabled. We wanted to make sure they were expanding services and improving quality."

this proposal and structured the commission so it would be well insulated from presidential control. Importantly, this insulation was not complete in that, among other things, the commission was forced to rely on the Justice Department to carry out most legal actions against violators of safety standards. Over time such requirements have served to weigh the commission down and inhibit its ability to carry out its mission effectively.

Why do legislators structure agencies in ways that all too often undermine bureaucratic accountability and performance? Two features of the democratic process are particularly salient when considering these structural choices.[30] The first is **political uncertainty.** Thanks to elections and other mechanisms, powerful politicians and their favored constituencies cannot count on controlling the institutions of government into the indefinite future. Inevitably, at some point opposing ideological and partisan forces will take over the reins of power. This uncertainty has important implications for bureaucratic design as agency benefactors have incentives to protect their creations from meddling by unkind political authorities. In the case of the Consumer Product Safety Commission, such protection came through the appointment of commissioners to fixed, staggered, seven-year terms, which effectively distanced the commission from presidential control, even administrations with consumerist sentiments. In the end, political uncertainty leads agency supporters to "purposely create structures that even they cannot control." [31]

The second key feature of the democratic process is **political compromise.** Under the separation of powers system, opponents of legislative action are usually granted concessions. At times, these concessions prove to be of great consequence, severely limiting the ability of legislative advocates to achieve their objectives. The creation of the Consumer Product Safety Commission was not a total loss for business interests. In addition to Justice Department enforcement, these interests secured the right to judicial review of commission decisions and a guarantee that the commission would come up for reauthorization in three short years. In other words, Congress gave business and other commission foes the leverage necessary to immediately set about the task of undermining the agency and abolishing it completely before it became too entrenched in the executive branch. In general, as Terry M. Moe has argued, the dictates of political compromise imply that agencies are designed "in no small measure by participants who explicitly want them to fail." [32] The lessons of political uncertainty and political compromise, taken together, reveal that if Congress has difficulty in managing delegated authority, this difficulty springs not only from bureaucratic behavior but from the nature of the legislative process as well.

ADMINISTRATIVE PROCEDURES. Within the constraints imposed by bureaucratic structure, Congress can influence what the executive branch does by manipulating the **administrative procedures** under which agencies operate. Administrative procedures specify the steps agencies must follow when making decisions and formulating policies. These steps typically include gathering certain types of information and consulting with stakeholders in particular ways. The **National Environmental Policy Act** requires agencies to prepare environmental impact statements for rules with potentially significant ecological consequences. These statements lay out the likely effects of the rule and the steps the agency will take to minimize environmental harm.[33] Sometimes, administrative procedures target specific agencies or decisions. For example, statute requires the Federal Railroad Administration (FRA) to hold public hearings during all of its rulemakings.[34]

In what ways do administrative procedures potentially enhance congressional control over the bureaucracy? Administrative procedures can create bureaucratic environments that mirror the politics that occurred in Congress when it delegated authority to the agency.[35] In 1996 Congress amended the Safe Drinking Water Act. While working on the amendments, legislators heard from three distinct types of stakeholders—utilities and other water producer interests, state and local regulators, and environmental and consumer organizations.[36] The amendments delegated great authority to the EPA to set standards for contaminants, such as arsenic, that pose a threat to drinking water. The amendments also specified very carefully the composition of the National Drinking Water Advisory Council, a stakeholder organization with which the agency consults when crafting drinking water regulations. Specifically, the advisory council must be composed of an equal number of water producers, state and local government officials, and representatives of the general public. This membership requirement ensures that the agency will hear from the interests that participated in the congressional debate over the amendments. In other words, the pattern of participation in drinking water rulemakings will resemble in important ways the participatory environment that had characterized the lawmaking process.

Administrative procedures can also stack the deck in favor of particular constituencies. Over time, the National Environmental Policy Act has brought ecological considerations more to the fore than they would otherwise have been in agency proceedings. For example, environmentalists have used the act to stop construction projects initially endorsed by the Army Corps of Engineers. These successes have led to a noticeable change in the types of projects the corps is willing to propose.[37]

Finally, administrative procedures can place bureaucratic policymaking on autopilot. In other words, as the preferences of enfranchised constituencies change, agency decisions change correspondingly. During the 1970s the cable television industry emerged as a powerful political force in Congress. Shortly thereafter, the industry became the beneficiary of a major deregulation effort by the Federal Communications Commission. This deregulation occurred without any direct congressional intervention but via changes in the set of interests represented in commission proceedings.[38] In general, well-designed administrative procedures obviate the need for constant legislative attention to agency behavior.

Thus administrative procedures vary in important ways in the leverage they give members of Congress over the management of delegated authority. Some administrative procedures, such as the requirement that FRA hold public hearings, serve to place hurdles in front of agencies.[39] These hurdles increase the costs to agencies of doing their day-to-day business. Other administrative procedures increase the costs of taking particular courses of action. The National Environmental Policy Act, for example, makes it difficult for agencies to give short shrift to the environment in cases where the ecological stakes are relatively pronounced. With this variation in mind, it is difficult to make blanket claims about the efficacy of administrative procedures in promoting congressional control of the bureaucracy.

OVERSIGHT. Traditionally, legislators have sought to reduce their moral hazard problem through oversight of the bureaucracy. Oversight occurs in a variety of forms, including committee hearings and scandal-induced investigations.[40] For a long time, most observers thought that members of Congress neglected oversight in favor of other activities,[41] such as bringing federal projects and other forms of "bacon" home to their constituents. In recent decades, however, there has been a noticeable increase in oversight activity.[42] Among other things, this increase is a reflection of Congress's growing incentive and capacity to keep tabs on agency doings.

When engaging in oversight, members of Congress can pursue one of two basic strategies. The first is **police patrol oversight.** In police patrols, legislators search for bureaucratic actions that fail to conform to congressional expectations, much in the way that officers on the beat seek to ferret out criminal activity. In contrast, **fire alarm oversight** places much of the burden of monitoring the bureaucracy on citizens and organized interests. Like firefighters, legislators swing into action after someone sounds the alarm, using their policymaking apparatus to bring recalcitrant agencies under control. Given that police patrols require a relatively significant investment of congressional time and resources, it is widely presumed that the fire alarm approach dominates oversight.[43]

This presumption is not necessarily accurate, however. By some accounts, committee hearings, a particularly common and important form of oversight, more often than not prove to be police patrol in their orientation.[44] In 1995, for example, 86.1 percent of the House Judiciary Committee's hearings consisted of routine, ongoing legislative activities, as opposed to reactions to crises and other types of galvanizing events. These activities included consideration of the reauthorization of the Administrative Conference of the United States, an organization charged with studying agency processes and making recommendations to Congress regarding how to improve these processes. Several months after this hearing, Congress voted to terminate the agency's funding. All of this occurred with very little outside involvement or even awareness. Rather, Congress's oversight of the Administrative Conference took place within the context of the agency's regularly scheduled reauthorization process.

In all forms, oversight is inherently limited in its ability to constrain agency behavior. Once they identify transgressions, legislators must have the incentive and capacity to sanction and redirect agencies. Each set of the tools that might be used for such purposes—appointments, budgets, and legislative actions—can be problematic in important respects.[45] For example, Congress, with its dispersion of authority across chambers and committees, has difficulty passing legislation of any kind. Even if Congress enacts legislation targeting an agency, there is no guarantee that the new law will succeed where previous efforts failed in bringing about compliant behavior. Although oversight occasionally produces dramatic results, more often than not it is most useful as a way of deterring agencies from running too far afoul of congressional legislators.

Judicial Review

The judicial system, like the presidency and Congress, is appropriately viewed as a principal to the bureaucracy's agents. Judges routinely oversee and review the work of executive branch agencies. In this vein, one of the most common judicial tasks is ensuring that bureaucrats act in accordance with the law. A somewhat less common task is ensuring that bureaucratic actions are consistent with the Constitution. If an agency takes steps deemed illegal or unconstitutional, then its work can be overturned in the judiciary. When this happens, the court in question will often remand the action to the bureaucracy, with specific instructions as to how the agency's legal or constitutional mistakes might be rectified. How, then, do the courts go about dealing with their moral hazard difficulties?

JUDGES V. POLITICIANS. Judicial review has several characteristics that distinguish it from instruments of presidential and congressional control. First, whereas politicians can engage in either police patrol or fire alarm oversight, the latter alone is available to judges. Courts can only hear cases brought to their doorsteps by plaintiffs. Put differently, judges must wait for individuals or organizations to pull a fire alarm indicating that they have been injured or aggrieved by some agency action. Thus in its basic orientation toward the bureaucracy the judiciary is more passive than either the executive or legislative branch.

Second, judges place greater emphasis than politicians on procedural irregularities. One of the hallmarks of judicial review is an acute awareness of the procedural requirements the Administrative Procedure Act imposes on agencies. The courts sometimes overturn bureaucratic actions because agencies have failed to provide adequate notice of a proposed rulemaking. Likewise, an agency that fails to provide interested parties with an adequate opportunity to comment on a proposed rule or fails to adequately explain the reasoning behind a final rule may find itself prohibited from completing or implementing the action at hand.

Third, because the judiciary is subject to numerous legal and traditional constraints, interactions between judges and agencies tend to be more formal and less frequent than those between politicians and agencies. The nature of these interactions can lead to both negative and positive results. On the one hand, formal, infrequent interactions discourage flexible problem solving by agencies and stifle negotiations between judges and bureaucrats. On the other hand, these arrangements make it somewhat more difficult for agencies to shirk judicial orders. Unlike politicians, who express themselves through laws, hearings, executive orders, informal meetings, and telephone conversations, judges express themselves solely through official decisions and decrees. Agencies can at times deflect informal pressure from one politician by contending that informal pressure from elsewhere imposes obligations to the contrary. Pressure from judges is far more visible, much easier to document, and ultimately more difficult to resist.

These characteristics can be observed in the reactions of federal agencies to Supreme Court decisions that reversed or remanded executive branch actions. From 1953 to 1990 there were 229 such decisions. Although uncommon relative to the total number of cases handled in that time, these decisions provoked a significant response on the part of the bureaucracy. Major policy change occurred in response to 72.7 percent of the decisions, while moderate and minor alterations followed 14.1 and 5.9 percent of them, respectively. Only 7.3 percent resulted in a complete absence of policy change.[46] As these episodes indicate, the coercive power of the Supreme Court and other judicial bodies is rather potent. What remains an open question is whether this coercion serves to enhance bureaucratic performance as well as accountability.

CIRCUIT COURTS AND ADMINISTRATIVE LAW. Within the federal judiciary, most lawsuits challenging agency decisions originate in district or trial courts. By law, however, some agency decisions may be appealed directly to a circuit court of appeals. Regardless of where a case originates, circuit courts of appeals are particularly important in the field of administrative law. Prominent among them is the U.S. Court of Appeals for the District of Columbia—or the **D.C. Circuit**—because a disproportionate number of appeals are filed in the city, where most agencies are headquartered. Indeed, legal analysts sometimes refer to the D.C. Circuit as the second most important court in the land, behind only the Supreme Court.[47] Whether or not that assessment is true, it is indisputable that the D.C. Circuit "enjoys an unmatched reputation as a leader in determining the substance and content of administrative law." [48]

As a general rule, circuit courts of appeals affirm decisions made by administrative agencies. During the 1970s circuit courts affirmed, on average, more than 60 percent of all agency decisions subjected to challenges. During the 1980s this affirmation rate rose to more than 70 percent. The D.C. Circuit, however, has been consistently less deferential than other circuit courts. During the 1970s and 1980s the D.C. Circuit sustained agencies only 57 and 56 percent of the time, respectively. [49]

The greater judicial activism of the D.C. Circuit can be traced back to the 1970s, especially to the thinking of Judge Harold Leventhal. In *Greater Boston Television Corp. v. the Federal Communications Commission,* Leventhal first articulated the **hard look doctrine** of judicial review, which called for judges to take their supervisory responsibilities seriously. In that decision, Leventhal wrote that a court must intervene if it "becomes aware, especially from a combination of danger signals, that the agency has not really taken a 'hard look' at the salient problems, and has not genuinely engaged in reasoned decision-making." [50] In a series of subsequent decisions, Leventhal and other judges on the D.C. Circuit struck down a variety of major bureaucratic actions based on tough scrutiny of the agencies' substantive reasoning in complex cases. For example, in *International Harvester Co. v. Ruckelshaus,* the D.C. Circuit invalidated the EPA's emission standards under the Clean Air Act by challenging the agency's underlying methodology. [51]

Another prominent D.C. Circuit judge, David Bazelon, supported Leventhal's call for tough scrutiny but preferred strong procedural review over strong substantive review. In the *International Harvester* case, for example, Bazelon argued that the agency's refusal to grant a one-year suspension of its 1975 emission standards was procedurally flawed because the agency had not allowed the petitioners a general right of cross-examination during the rulemaking proceedings. [52] Ultimately, the Supreme Court curbed the D.C. Circuit's penchant for strong procedural review in the *Vermont Yankee* case in 1978. In that decision, the Supreme Court held that a federal court may not impose procedural requirements on an agency above and beyond those specified in the Administrative Procedure Act. [53] Importantly, this decision left strong substantive review untouched and may have even encouraged it. [54]

Although the D.C. Circuit enjoys considerable prestige, the Supreme Court does not automatically defer to it or to any other court. The *Vermont Yankee* decision aptly illustrates this point, but there are other examples as well. [55] In 2001 the Supreme Court overruled a 1999 decision by the D.C. Circuit that had overturned a soot and smog rule adopted by the EPA. In *American Trucking Associations v. EPA,* the D.C. Circuit had reversed the agency's rule by reviving a moribund doctrine of administrative law known as the **nondelegation doctrine.** This doctrine states that Congress may not delegate legislative authority to the executive branch of the government. In effect, the doctrine implies that congressional standards must have some teeth, some specificity. In *American Trucking,* the Supreme Court unanimously upheld the agency's authority to set new and tougher clean air standards without first considering the potential economic impact of these standards on the trucking industry. The Supreme Court also explicitly declined to invoke the nondelegation doctrine, thus repudiating the D.C. Circuit.[56]

THE SUPREME COURT. Like circuit courts of appeal, the Supreme Court is more likely to defer to agencies than overturn them.[57] While the outcome of any Supreme Court case depends on many factors—the legal merits of the case, the skills of the attorneys, and so forth—political ideology also plays a role in the Court's decision making. The more liberal Warren Court (1953–1969) supported liberal agency decisions 85.7 percent of the time, while the more conservative Burger Court (1969–1986) supported liberal agency decisions only 69.1 percent of the time. Similarly, the Warren Court supported conservative agency decisions 63.4 percent of the time, a rate nearly 20 percent lower than that of the Burger Court. Although the Supreme Court, and courts more generally, often hesitate to rule against agencies, this does not mean judicial review is ineffectual. Agencies undoubtedly craft their decisions with an eye to the possibility that their procedures and substantive reasoning may at some point be subjected to judicial scrutiny.

Principal-Agent Theory and the Bureaucracy's Clients

Consistent with principal-agent theory, chief executives, legislatures, and judiciaries all find themselves in positions where they can limit the loss associated with the delegation of policymaking authority to the bureaucracy. None of these political principals, however, can completely eliminate the problems raised by adverse selection and moral hazard. When setting about the task of managing delegation, each principal faces unique difficulties, from the judiciary's inherently reactive nature to the president's ambitious desire for coordinated control of a sprawling bureaucracy.

An approach common to all of these principals is enlisting the help of third parties in the use of screening mechanisms, institutional design, and oversight. For many years the White House has relied on organized interests to put forth and evaluate presidential appointees. In fact, President George W. Bush stoked a mild controversy when he broke from precedent by declining to consider the recommendations of the American Bar Association in filling federal judgeship vacancies. In Congress, the essence of fire alarm oversight is the empowerment of citizens and groups to keep a watchful eye on agency proceedings and decisions. To keep their dockets full, the courts rely on litigants to press claims about the illegality and unconstitutionality of bureaucratic actions.

All of this raises the question of whether principal-agent theory can provide insight into the role and influence of agency clients in bureaucratic policymaking. Strictly speaking, clients are not bureaucratic principals as they are neither the hierarchical supervisors of agencies nor the wellsprings of delegated authority. As a result, clients are only as potent as the public officials whose backing they enjoy.

For such backing to materialize, clients must possess attributes of significant value to political principals. For example, members of Congress have a never-ending need for information about the views of their constituents, the predispositions of their colleagues on pending legislation, and the outcomes likely to follow from their policy choices.[58] Clients who can meet these information needs are naturally advantaged in the lawmaking process. These advantages carry over into the bureaucracy when legislators structure agencies, design administrative procedures, and conduct oversight in ways targeted to ensure that policymaking in the executive branch does not stray too far from deals struck in Congress.

Who then are the clients best positioned to serve as powerful third parties in the principal-agent hierarchy? The key consideration here is mobilization. For some time it has been clear that not all parties with a stake in government activity organize in pursuit of their policy preferences. Likewise, the extensiveness of client mobilization varies greatly across the issues that fall under the domain of the executive branch. In the end, principal-agent theory points not only to the unique position of clients in the policymaking hierarchy but also to the need for a close examination of the factors affecting the mobilization of both the beneficiaries and targets of agency actions.

Principals and Principles

As this chapter has demonstrated, the bureaucracy has no shortage of bosses. At times they exercise extraordinary influence over what agencies can and cannot do. With one vote Congress nullified OSHA's ergonomics rule, a major policy action years in the making. Such highly visible cases aside, the bureaucracy's bosses usually exercise their authority in much subtler and more conditional ways. A year after Congress ordered that all checked baggage be screened for explosives, DOT had not yet completed the task. When the agency pressed for a year's extension, Congress granted it.[59]

If the power of those who serve as the bureaucracy's principals is conditional, then what specific conditions determine the contours of agency discretion? Part of this story deals with the tools principals possess, and do not possess, to combat adverse selection and moral hazard. Although the Constitution provides the presidency with few formal advantages vis-à-vis the bureaucracy, presidents are powerful in ways difficult to measure. When the president puts the full authority and prestige of the White House behind an initiative, as George W. Bush did with the Department of Homeland Security, it is often difficult for other policymakers, including bureaucrats, to resist. Yet from the perspective of these policymakers, presidential agendas are usually rather limited in scope. As a result the president exercises power on only an occasional basis.

The judiciary is also a potent principal that gets involved in agency decision making under a limited set of circumstances. For most agencies most of the time, judicial review undoubtedly represents an unpleasant prospect, but one they experience only occasionally. The same cannot be said when it comes to legislative principals. Legislators have their hands on everything from agency design to oversight of the bureaucracy. Although these instruments give Congress and other such principals strong leverage over the problem of moral hazard, this leverage by no means eradicates agency loss, as the following example illustrates.

The Resource Conservation and Recovery Act of 1976 empowers the EPA to issue standards for the treatment, storage, and disposal of hazardous wastes.[60] The act requires the agency to adhere to a variety of analytical, disclosure, and participation procedures when setting these standards. Importantly, the agency has found a way to get around these requirements when it so desires. In cases where it wishes to evade congressional scrutiny, the EPA eschews the issuance of formal rules and makes policy instead through

guidance documents. Although guidance documents (statements agencies produce to flesh out their stances on particular issues) lack the full force of law, regulated firms routinely comply with them. Thus, despite Congress's efforts, hazardous waste policy is often made beyond the reach of the tools legislators normally use to limit bureaucratic discretion.

To put it differently, part of the story of the boundaries of bureaucratic authority concerns the willingness of agency officials to respond to their bosses' cues. In the broadest sense, the bureaucracy's bosses include not only chief executives, legislatures, and judiciaries but the public—the very society within which agencies operate—as well. With this in mind, many bureaucrats try to represent the public interest as best they can determine it. When viewed in this way, agencies appear to be populated for the most part with officials who are **principled agents.**[61] That is, agency officials are hard workers who are highly professional, devoted to the mission of their organizations, and only rarely driven to shirk or sabotage the policy aims of their bosses. In the end, control of the bureaucracy emanates not only from political principals but also from other sources inside and outside of agencies.

Key Terms

4 | The Bureaucracy's Clients

IN THE SUMMER OF 2000 wildfires of historic proportions raged across the American West. One of the most devastated areas was Montana's Bitterroot National Forest, where more than 355,000 acres of ponderosa pines burned. From one of these trees state wildlife officials dramatically rescued a malnourished, orphaned black bear cub. The cuddly cub, with his singed paws wrapped in bandages, enthralled the nation and came to epitomize nature's resiliency in the face of horrific destruction.[1]

A year and a half later, resiliency of a different sort sparked a political firestorm. On December 18, 2001, the Forest Service announced a plan to make more than 46,000 acres of burned timber available for logging. According to the agency, the removal of this charred lumber would promote the forest's revitalization by reducing the fire threat posed by thousands of dead and dying trees. The agency's plan was heartily endorsed by the logging industry and other local economic interests, all of which stood to benefit greatly from the harvest. Environmentalists staunchly opposed the recovery operation on two ecological grounds: one, it would interfere with the decomposition that naturally occurs after forest fires; two, it might produce runoff harmful to bull trout and other fish already threatened by abnormally high sediment levels.[2]

The controversy surrounding Bitterroot's revitalization put the Forest Service in a difficult, yet not uncommon, position. By law, the agency must pursue "sustainable multiple-use management" of the land under its domain.[3] This mission means that the agency must serve the interests of both environmentalists seeking to conserve natural resources and parties seeking to foster rural economic development.

The two constituencies flexed their political muscles during the debate over Bitterroot. Groups such as the Montana Wood Products Association pressured the agency not only to open the forest up to timber removal but also to act without delay. Within two years burned trees dry and crack, losing their commercial value. Responding to this concern, the Forest Service waived the public appeals process that usually takes place before the agency finalizes logging decisions.

On the day the recovery operation was announced, two environmental groups—the Wilderness Society and American Wildlands—went to court to block the Forest Service's action. Within hours a federal judge issued an order prohibiting the agency from moving ahead with the harvest. The order castigated the agency for failing to provide the public with an opportunity to contest the logging plan, vividly noting that "trees cannot be returned to their stumps." [4]

Several weeks later, with time for a profitable and environmentally sound harvest running short, the same judge ordered the Forest Service, logging interests, and environmentalists to work out a compromise. Within days environmental groups agreed to drop their appeal and let the recovery operation begin immediately. In return the agency and the timber industry promised not to harvest trees located in the most environmentally sensitive, roadless areas of Bitterroot. Under the terms of this settlement, the industry ultimately removed a little less than 15,000 acres of charred lumber from the forest, not quite a third of the acreage it had originally hoped to log. [5]

The court's intervention in the dispute over Bitterroot's future illustrates just how important, and difficult, it is for agencies to cultivate their constituencies. Organizations and citizens regularly wield enormous influence over policymaking in the bureaucracy. This power, however, does not necessarily direct agencies toward noncontroversial and widely supported actions. Nor does the public necessarily pressure agencies in ways that foster effective decision making.

This chapter focuses on the bureaucracy's **clients,** those interests in society that agencies are charged to regulate and protect. It is organized around three core questions:

- *WHAT TYPES OF CLIENTS ARE MOST ACTIVE IN BUREAUCRATIC POLICYMAKING?* Although both economic and environmental interests made their voices heard on Bitterroot's recovery, it is often the case that important clients remain silent on matters being weighed by agencies.

- *THROUGH WHAT VENUES DO CLIENTS PARTICIPATE IN AGENCY POLICYMAKING?* Organizations and citizens can access the bureaucracy in a multitude of ways. Denied an opportunity to offer comments on the Forest Service's logging plan, environmentalists exercised their input via the legal system.

- *HOW MUCH INFLUENCE DO CLIENTS EXERT OVER AGENCY DECISIONS?* In the end the Forest Service was swayed not only by the logging industry's plea for rapid action but also by environmentalist arguments about the need to protect and restore Bitterroot's most treasured resources. Agencies, however, are not always responsive to clients and are sometimes accused of being out of control.

On the last two points it may sound as if the politics of the Bitterroot harvest are not indicative of agency-client relations in general. In fact, the theoretical perspective adopted in this chapter—interest group mobilization—is based on the notion that client activism and influence vary systematically across time and policy areas. Characteristics of the issues at hand have important implications, in ways described in the next section, for both the behavior of clients and agency accountability and performance.

The Benefits, Costs, and Politics of Public Policy

Public policies affect citizens, organized interests, and society itself in a plethora of ways. For example, the Federal Highway Administration allocates funds for road construction that benefit virtually all Americans, the Social Security Administration oversees the transfer of income from workers to retirees, and the Environmental Protection Agency (EPA) regulates the operation of firms that discharge pollutants into the air and water. One common feature of these policies and all others is that they deliver benefits and impose costs. The way in which these benefits and costs are distributed across agency clients varies, however.[6]

Benefits and **costs** can be **concentrated** or **diffuse** in their effects. Concentrated effects occur when benefits or costs accrue to specific segments of

Figure 4.1 The Benefits, Costs, and Politics of Public Policies

Benefits of Public Policy

		Concentrated	Diffuse
Costs of Public Policy	Concentrated	Interest group politics	Entrepreneurial politics
	Diffuse	Client politics	Majoritarian politics

Source: From *Bureaucracy: What Government Agencies Do and Why They Do It* by James Q. Wilson. Copyright © 1989 by Basic Books, Inc. Reprinted by permission of Basic Books, a member of Perseus Books, L.L.C.

society, such as individuals with certain characteristics (for example, retirees) or firms doing business in particular industries. Effects are diffuse when broad swaths of the population feel the benefits or costs (for example, highway drivers).

Importantly, the benefits and costs of policies affect the mobilization of societal interests and ultimately the politics of the bureaucracy. Figure 4.1 summarizes these effects. When benefits are concentrated and costs diffuse, **client politics** characterizes policies. Specific constituencies mobilized by the prospect of reaping significant rewards dominate such issues. Society in general subsidizes the rewards. With costs so widely spread, little incentive exists for broad public involvement in the policymaking process.

Nuclear power policy in the middle of the twentieth century offers a classic example of client politics.[7] At that time public utility companies and other economic interests pressed the Atomic Energy Commission to promote the production of nuclear power by readily approving the construction and operation of plants throughout the country. These efforts proved successful in part because they faced little opposition. The economic costs of building up the nuclear power industry were to be distributed widely across society, and the environmental consequences were not yet publicly apparent (the Three Mile Island accident and the Chernobyl disaster lay well in the future).

When both the benefits and costs of policies are concentrated, however, the mobilization of societal interests is not so one-sided. **Interest group politics** characterizes such policies. Once again the general public is not actively engaged in, nor perhaps even aware of, the contest over the direction of policy. Rather, this contest is fought among specific constituencies whose interests are at odds with one another. Early in the twentieth century, the trucking industry emerged as a serious competitor to railroads as a way of moving goods and services around the country. In the decades that followed, each set of interests continually lobbied the Interstate Commerce Commission for regulations that would profit its mode of transportation and cripple the other. Over time this battle became a mismatch as the agency went from being accommodating to the railroads to being controlled by motor carrier organizations such the American Trucking Association.[8]

Interest groups do not dominate the political process when the benefits of policies are diffuse. The combination of diffuse benefits and concentrated costs instead produces **entrepreneurial politics.** Policy entrepreneurs are individuals, from inside and outside government, who take on organized interests in the name of the general public. In 1965 public interest advocate Ralph Nader published *Unsafe at Any Speed,* a book about the dangers of cars as they were then designed. This book, and Nader's efforts in general, galvanized the consumer movement and ultimately provided the impetus for the adoption of many automotive safety features, such as air bags and antilock brakes, that Americans now take for granted.[9]

Finally, when both the benefits and the costs of policies are diffuse, **majoritarian politics** results. With little stake in the policymaking process, specific interests and organizations do not mobilize in support of, or opposition to, government actions. Rather, the political debate centers on broad, often ideological, considerations that cut across society, such as the proper role of government in economic and social matters. Some of the most significant policies in U.S. history fall into this category, including the Sherman Antitrust Act of 1890, a seminal moment in the trust-busting movement. At that stage of the industrial revolution, public sentiment was turning against large corporations and the power they increasingly wielded over the lives of everyday Americans. The Sherman Act, however, did not target specific firms and industries but monopolistic practices in general. As a result, opposition

Figure 4.2 The "Iron Triangle" of Politics

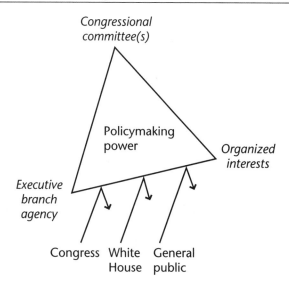

to the act was diffuse and grounded in the constitutional argument that the federal government has no authority to break up industrial trusts or, more broadly, to foster economic competition.[10]

To sum up, the theoretical perspective adopted in this chapter suggests that organized interests can dominate policymaking in the bureaucracy but only under certain conditions. A key question then becomes, *How often do these conditions materialize?* Interestingly, the answer to this question has changed quite a bit over the past four decades.

The Rise and Fall of Iron Triangles

A favorite pastime of journalists and pundits is bemoaning the fact that organized interests, especially business and industrial, have captured the U.S. government. In 2001 the collapse of Enron, a once high-flying energy company, brought such criticism to bear on both the Clinton and Bush administrations. People accused officials in agencies such as the Department of the Treasury of doing the company's bidding over the years by failing to regulate some of its more controversial practices, practices that eventually contributed to Enron's downfall.[11] Although episodes such as this one are no doubt telling, they are often used to exaggerate the influence of special interests in contemporary American politics.

To be sure, interest groups have historically played a fundamental, and at times dominating, role in the political process. A half-century ago many observers noted that public policy was at times the handiwork of **iron triangles.**[12] Figure 4.2 summarizes the essence of this observation. Iron triangles are issue-specific coalitions that consist of (1) the congressional committee of jurisdiction, (2) the relevant executive branch agency, and (3) those interests most directly affected by government actions in the area. These three parties jointly control policymaking by determining what issues make it onto the political agenda and how these issues will be resolved. Put differently, other interested parties, such as Congress as a whole, the White House, and the general public, are afforded very little influence over the scope and content of public policy. A prime example is agriculture policy. Legislators from farming areas secure seats on Congress's agriculture committees and work closely with the Department of Agriculture (USDA) and organized representatives of farming interests, such as the National Farmers Union, to produce profarmer policies. Largely shut out of this process are the tens of millions of Americans who consume agricultural products; so, too, are their elected representatives.

The grip of iron triangles over policymaking began to loosen in the 1960s for two principal reasons. One is that the number and nature of inter-

Figure 4.3 Positive and Negative Images in Media Coverage of Nuclear Power

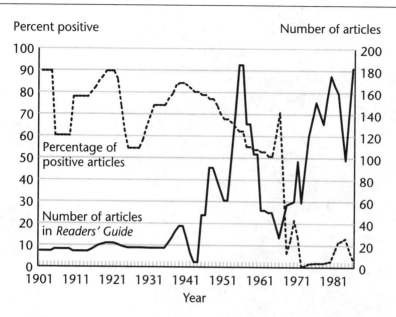

Source: Policy Agendas Project, Center for American Politics and Public Policy, University of Washington, http://depts.washington.edu/ampol.aihome.shtml, February 28, 2003.

Note: The lines provide information about (1) the number of articles in the *Readers' Guide to Periodical Literature* on Nuclear Power and (2) the percentage of these articles that conveyed positive policy images.

est groups active in the political process underwent a dramatic transformation. In 1960 there were 523 advocacy organizations with offices in Washington, D.C. By 1980 this number had grown more than tenfold, to 5,769.[13] A significant part of this growth came in the form of **public interest groups,** organizations promoting broad societal causes rather than the material gain of their members. Examples include environmental groups such as the World Wildlife Fund, founded in 1961, and consumer groups such as Public Citizen, which got its start a decade later.

The rise of public interest groups in and of itself was not enough to overcome the entrenched presence of iron triangles. One reason iron triangles were often successful in protecting their political turf was that they took great care to envelop themselves in positive **policy images.**[14] For decades the nuclear power industry promoted itself as a clean, cheap source of energy. As time went by, however, this positive policy image gave way to a far more negative one. Environmental groups and other opponents of nuclear power emphasized the dangers posed by mishaps at reactors and the difficulties associated with the storage of waste. Figure 4.3 illustrates that these tactics, no doubt strengthened by catastrophic and near-catastrophic events in the nuclear industry, proved largely successful. Media coverage of nuclear power went from overwhelmingly positive through the 1950s to decidedly negative in later decades. Just as telling is the fact that the Nuclear Regulatory Commission, the successor to the Atomic Energy Commission, has not ordered a new nuclear power plant since 1979.[15]

The shift in the locus of power in the area of nuclear energy is not unusual in that iron triangles of all sorts have lost their political monopolies. Today policymaking is often the domain of what might be called **sloppy hexagons**[16] or, less colorfully, **issue networks.**[17] A constant flow of participants in and out of the decision-making arena, not limited access, characterizes issue networks. Some of these participants are traditional power brokers such as business and industry, while others include public interest advocates, economic and technical experts, and representatives of state and local governments. Because of this diversity, high levels of conflicts among participants, rather than strict agreement, typify these networks. These conflicts encompass not only the question of how best to resolve policy problems but also more fundamental questions such as, *What is the nature of the problem? Is there a problem at all?*

A great example of an issue network comes from the area of embryonic and fetal research, one of the most controversial areas of public policy at the dawn of the twenty-first century.[18] When it first came onto the national agenda in the 1970s, this issue was dominated by a small set of actors, most notably the scientific community. Researchers in universities and medical schools worked closely with the National Institutes of Health to establish a positive policy image grounded in the benefits of scientific autonomy and progress. Ultimately, the aim was to ensure a constant flow of government funding for research that some scientists believe holds the key to unlocking the mysteries of many of the world's most painful and deadliest diseases. Today this image, and the iron triangle it helped sustain, does not enjoy the monopoly it once did. Embryonic and fetal research raises fundamental moral concerns, such as the value of different forms of human life and the role of medical science in creating, enhancing, and destroying such life. These concerns are now being vigorously debated by ethicists, religious authorities, and activists on both sides of the abortion issue. Executive branch officials all the way up to the president have been involved in making decisions that generally serve to heighten, rather than diminish, the level of disagreement embodied in this issue network.

The rise and fall of iron triangles illustrate three central points with respect to the benefit-cost approach to understanding societal mobilization and bureaucratic politics. The first is that the benefits and costs of policies vary not only across issues but over time as well. A closely related lesson is that perceived, as well as actual, benefits and costs play a critical role in determining the nature of the politics surrounding a policy area. Although the benefits and costs associated with nuclear power and embryonic and fetal research have undoubtedly evolved over the years, the demise of these long-standing iron triangles was in no small part a product of seismic shifts in the images through which potentially contentious issues were appraised and acted upon. Finally, such developments suggest there are now far fewer instances of client politics, and perhaps even interest group politics, than in years past. Although powerful interests and organizations still can, and do, exert extraordinary influence over the political process, the exercise of this power is not nearly as prominent as before.

The Venues of Client Participation

Thus far this chapter has focused on the types of clients generally most active in bureaucratic policymaking as well as on how patterns of client activism have changed over the past several decades. Little has yet been said about the specific venues through which clients make their views known to agency officials. These venues run the gamut from commenting on proposed agency policies to prevailing upon politicians to intervene in bureaucratic proceedings. As will become apparent, venues are distinct in terms of the resources clients must be able to bring to bear if they wish to participate regularly and effectively through these channels.

The Notice and Comment Process

One of the central ways in which agencies make policy is through **rulemaking,** the bureaucratic equivalent of legislative lawmaking.[19] When engaged in rulemaking, agencies craft decisions that allocate governmental resources, redistribute these and other resources across segments of society, and regulate the behavior of particular societal actors. As an example, on October 9, 2002, the Customs Service issued a rule granting duty-free treatment for certain beverages processed in Canada and made with Caribbean rum. This action was one of twelve rules promulgated that day by federal agencies, an indication of just how common rulemaking is within the executive branch.

For more than half a century, rulemaking at the federal level has been governed by the Administrative Procedure Act (APA).[20] The APA generally requires agencies to provide public notice of their intention to take action by publishing a proposed rule in the *Federal Register.* The act also instructs agencies to offer interested parties the opportunity to comment on proposals. The **notice and comment process,** as this participation venue is known, is one of the most common ways in which clients come into contact with agency decision makers.

For any given rulemaking, the number of comments submitted usually turns out to be rather modest. During the summer of 2002 agencies issued

Inside
Bureaucracy
with

Donna Shalala
Secretary of Health and Human Services
(1993–2001)

"Implementation was everything. When we were in the midst of a rule-making process, we rarely saw anyone."

seventeen rules considered "major." [21] **Major rules** are actions projected to have particularly pronounced consequences, such as annual effects on the economy of at least $100 million.[22] Despite their elevated significance, many of these seventeen actions generated few, if any, comments. For example, on June 28, the Centers for Medicare and Medicaid Services (CMS) issued a rule updating its payments for home health services. CMS received only two comments during the course of this rulemaking.

On occasion, agencies are inundated with comments on their proposed rules. CMS received 1,196 comments on a hospital-related action it took in the summer of 2002. In 1995 the Food and Drug Administration stirred up great public controversy by proposing to regulate the advertising, labeling, and sale of tobacco products to juveniles. This proposal precipitated the submission of about 700,000 comments, a volume that has rarely, if ever, been matched by other rulemakings.[23]

Although the notice and comment process provides a solid foundation for client participation, it has its shortcomings. Rules sometimes take years to develop and are regularly subjected to litigation after being promulgated.[24] These difficulties are traceable in part to the inherently adversarial nature of notice and comment rulemaking, a result of two factors. Under the APA, clients never come into direct contact with one another, participating solely via written comments, which contributes to the adversarial atmosphere. In addition, these comments routinely stake out extreme positions and focus on pointing out flaws in agency proposals rather than identifying solutions to difficult problems. With these limitations in mind, there has been a movement over the past two decades to augment the notice and comment process with a variety of collaborative approaches to client participation.

Advisory Committees and Other Venues of Collaboration

In the early 1980s the Federal Aviation Administration (FAA) set about updating its rules on the maximum flight and duty time of pilots and other air carrier personnel.[25] As part of this process, the agency published several proposed rules in the *Federal Register*. These proposals elicited serious stakeholder objections, and the agency found itself unable to complete the rulemaking via the notice and comment process.

At this point the FAA turned to an advisory committee to help resolve the impasse. This advisory committee consisted of seventeen members, including representatives of the National Air Carrier Association, the Aviation Consumer Action Project, Southwest Airlines, and the International Brotherhood of Teamsters.[26] The agency charged these representatives with jointly developing a course of action that would garner the support of aviation stakeholders of all stripes.

Advisory committees are commissioned for such tasks all the time. About 1,000 advisory committees operate within the federal executive branch.[27] Advisory committees comprise clients who share a stake in specific policy areas. These clients receive the opportunity to offer their input in a variety of ways, such as by helping agencies set their policymaking agendas, drafting reports on specific issues that arise during rulemakings, and commenting jointly on agency proposals. Examples of advisory committees include the National Environmental Justice Advisory Council, the Advisory Committee on Nuclear Waste, and the Advisory Council on Children's Educational Television.

The **Federal Advisory Committee Act** (FACA) governs the operation of such committees. Under this statute, client representation on advisory committees must be balanced.[28] In other words, advisory committee members must consist of a representative cross section of the clients with a stake in the policy area under a committee's jurisdiction. The idea behind the balance requirement is to prevent a single constituency, such as business interests, from dominating advisory committee proceedings. Thus the National Drinking Water Advisory Council consists of five members from utilities and other water producers, five from state and local governments, and five from environmental, consumer, and other public interest groups. Such arrangements are commonplace among advisory committees.

When these committees operate as envisioned, they embody the application of collaborative techniques to client participation. Clients interact directly with one another in an environment designed to foster the identification of mutually agreeable courses of action. This process paid dividends for the FAA in 1985, when the agency was finally able to revise its flight and duty time rules. This revision, which provided crew members with a nine-hour rest period prior to extended duty shifts, came about in no small part as a result of the input of an advisory committee.

On occasion, the committees are used to facilitate a particular form of collaboration known as **negotiated rulemaking.** In negotiated rulemaking, advisory committees receive the authority to craft policy statements that are then published by agencies as proposed rules. The idea behind negotiated rulemaking is that comment periods and other subsequent venues of participation will proceed relatively quickly and harmoniously as clients themselves have generated proposals with widespread, if not unanimous, concurrence.

Most observers acknowledge, however, that the benefits of negotiated rulemaking are readily attainable only under certain circumstances.[29] For example, bargaining sessions will most likely produce consensus when the number of stakeholders is limited. To put it differently, an auditorium full of people have difficulty engaging in meaningful negotiations. For such reasons negotiated rulemaking has been used on a very limited basis. From 1983 to 1996 federal agencies undertook only sixty-seven negotiated rulemakings.[30] Although these rulemakings addressed a variety of important issues, such as occupational exposure to benzene and asbestos in schools, the relative infrequency of negotiated rulemaking demonstrates the limited applicability of advisory committees as consensus-building instruments.

Advisory committees are not the only venues of collaborative participation. Agencies regularly hold **public meetings** and **public hearings,** where clients have the opportunity to testify and perhaps rebut one another's arguments in front of key executive branch officials. From March to May of 2000 the Federal Railroad Administration held a series of ten hearings at locations around the country.[31] These hearings addressed the use of locomotive horns at highway-rail grade crossings. This issue is important from a public safety perspective in that trains collide with highway vehicles about 4,000 times during the course of a year. At these hearings the agency discovered that there is a human cost to the sounding of warning whistles, especially in the vicinity of communities normally characterized by peace and quiet. Tearful testimony was provided by residents linking sleep deprivation, and even the loss of livelihood, to horn blowing by trains passing nearby in the dark of the night. Railroad conductors, too, recounted tales of personal trauma. One stated simply: "My ears have been harmed from too many train whistles."[32]

Political Intervention

Another way in which clients seek to influence bureaucratic policymaking is by securing friendly interventions by prominent politicians. Such interventions have enabled Florida developers and business groups, for instance, to win concessions in environmental policy from federal, state, and local agencies. A key battleground in this area has been the Florida Everglades, an assortment of swamps and forests vital to southern Florida's water supply and home to many endangered species, including the greatly revered Florida panther.

In the early 1990s, when a prominent Florida developer, Ben Hill Griffin III, proposed the construction of a new institution of higher education—Florida Gulf Coast University—on 760 acres of donated land, biologists at the Fish and Wildlife Service expressed strong reservations. Griffin's plan, these scientists warned, would trigger "unprecedented" development for miles around the proposed campus, demolishing precious wetlands in the process.[33]

In the face of this warning, a Griffin lobbyist persuaded Sen. Bob Graham, D-Fla., to intervene on the developer's behalf. After a meeting between this lobbyist and Fish and Wildlife Service officials in Atlanta, the agency backed down from the confrontation. Next Griffin supporters won the allegiance of Florida's other senator, Republican Connie Mack. Mack contacted the Florida commander of the Army Corps of Engineers, urging the agency to approve a permit so the project could proceed expeditiously. Despite their reservations, corps officials issued the permit, and the university, an "ecological disaster" according to critics, admitted its first student—Mariana Coto—in 1997.[34]

The story of Florida Gulf Coast University is not unique. Clients of all types appear to make their views known to executive branch officials via legislators and other politicians. For example, firms located in districts represented on House committees with jurisdiction over the Federal Trade Commission are less likely to be sanctioned by the agency than firms lacking such representation.[35] The assumption is that this linkage is due to the fact that business groups apply pressure on particularly influential members of

"If I got a call from the president himself I'd call him back, but if I got to the office and they said the White House called, Congressman Obey called, and Senator Stevens called, I would usually call Obey and Stevens first. In my case it was probably cultural. I grew up in the Congress. I also knew that my career in the department and my success were probably more directly related to how I related to Congress than anything else. I mean, they can make you or break you. Also the White House chiefs of staff—Panetta and Podesta—were students of Congress. (Panetta had spent most of his life working in Congress.) So they were also hypersensitive to members of Congress. I had a deep and healthy respect for that, and for that reason I had a much better relationship with Congress as an institution than probably most of my cabinet-level colleagues. On the other hand, some of the cabinet folks had never spent any time in the Congress, so they didn't have the same frame of reference."

Congress, who in turn are inclined to communicate their constituents' preferences to the agency.

It would be a mistake to assume that business organizations are the only clients engaged in what might be called "political meddling." Regulated firms face tougher enforcement by the Occupational Safety and Health Administration, as well as its state-level counterparts, in locations represented by congressional delegations sympathetic to labor interests.[36] The assumption here is that unions and other labor organizations urge like-minded legislators to insist that the agency be vigilant when enforcing worker safety laws, at least within specific geographic jurisdictions. As long as reelection-oriented legislators consider these organizations to be important constituencies, such urgings are not likely to go unheeded.

Client Participation and the Internet

As the twentieth century came to a close, the FAA broke new ground in the use of the Internet, a technology that promises to reshape the way in which agencies and their clients communicate. For the first time ever, the agency held a public forum that took place entirely in cyberspace.[37] This forum focused on licensing requirements for small-scale rockets, the kind launched by amateurs for recreational or educational purposes. For two weeks interested parties engaged in near real-time discussions about various aspects of amateur rocketry and what actions the agency might take to regulate this increasingly sophisticated hobby.

One of the forum's primary purposes was to elicit the participation of as diverse a collection of stakeholders as possible. On this score the forum proved a smashing success. The agency heard from "hobbyists, educators, rocket organizations, launch companies with developmental or test vehicles, state and local government agencies, private land owners whose land is used for rocket launches, and the general public." [38]

Despite this apparent success, many questions about the benefits and costs of online proceedings have yet to be definitively answered. For example:

- Does the Internet attract new participants or simply provide established participants with an additional way to make their views known?
- Do online proceedings, and the virtually instantaneous communications they foster, reduce the time it takes agencies to make policy?
- What effect does the Internet have on outcomes such as the quality and legitimacy of agency actions and the distribution of benefits and costs among stakeholders?

Although the answers to these questions will become increasingly clear as agencies experiment further with e-participation, it is not too early to make some preliminary assessments. [39] To begin with, agencies from across the federal government are using the Internet to inform the public about planned actions and opportunities to comment on these plans. Some of this notification occurs via the *Federal Register*, available online since 1994 (http://www.access.gpo.gov). The rest occurs through agency Web sites and electronic mailing lists. For example, the home page of the EPA directs interested parties to a link called "Regulations and Proposed Rules." [40] From this link planned actions can be identified by either the date on which they were announced or their subject matter.

Increasingly, agencies are accepting comments on proposed rules via e-mail. In 1999 the EPA and Department of Labor permitted e-comments in more than two-thirds of their rulemakings.[41] By contrast, the Department of Health and Human Services requires paper comments in all but a handful of circumstances.

The Department of Transportation is one of the trendsetters when it comes to providing online access to the full public record of its policymaking activities. The agency's Docket Management System (http://dms.dot.gov) contains *Federal Register* documents, public comments, benefit-cost analyses, transcripts of hearings, records of meetings with stakeholders, and other pertinent materials. These documents make it relatively easy for stakeholders to view, and respond to, information submitted by other parties. The system is also of great value to the agency, which saves more than one million dollars annually in administrative costs.[42]

State and local agencies, too, have begun engaging their constituents via the Internet. Residents of Oregon can log onto http://www.oregon.gov and interact with government officials in a variety of ways. For example, the Department of Environmental Quality posts advance notices of public hearings and lists opportunities for the public to comment on prospective agency actions. Through these venues stakeholders can weigh in on issues such as the awarding and renewal of discharge permits to firms that release contaminants into the air. In a similar vein, the Occupational Safety and Health Division has an e-mail notification service that allows users to receive automatic updates on topics ranging from methylene chloride exposure limits to safety standards in steel erection.

There are some initial indications that the Internet has had an effect on agency policymaking. On December 21, 2000, the USDA issued standards for the production, handling, and processing of organically grown foods.[43] This action was highly salient, as indicated by the fact that the agency received more than 300,000 comments on its proposed standards. The dynamics of these comments were distinct and worth noting. Typically, the bulk of the public's comments arrive at the agency right before the deadline for submission. By waiting until the last minute, commenters deny opposing interests the opportunity to craft and circulate rebuttals. In the organic food case, however, a large number of stakeholders filed comments at the very beginning of the submission period. These stakeholders sought to take advantage of the fact that the agency was experimenting with an interactive process in which comments and other materials were placed online (http://www.ams.usda.gov/nop/) and treated as part of an ongoing dialogue between the agency and outside parties.[44] In this setting early comments proved particularly influential in that they established the fundamental tone and direction of the entire process.

The Internet may alter the behavior of active stakeholders, but is it likely to mobilize new constituencies? One possibility is that the Internet may change the calculations of societal interests that have historically been unwilling to incur the costs of participation. For example, policies where benefits are concentrated and costs diffuse may no longer be the sole province of narrow constituencies searching for, and protecting, particularized gains. In other words, the Internet has the potential to dilute the power of iron triangles and the client politics with which they are associated. Before such outcomes can be realized, however, the **digital divide**—the gap in computer use and skills between wealthy and poor Americans—must be greatly reduced.

At this point, the effect of the Internet on the timeliness and substance of agency policymaking remains uncertain. One reason for this uncertainty is that agencies have largely turned to the most comprehensive and promising forms of e-participation when confronted with especially complicated and contentious issues. It took the USDA more than three years to issue standards for organic foods. Would this process have unfolded more rapidly had the agency not placed such a premium on electronic interactions? Or would it have taken even longer to finalize the controversial standards in the absence of online collaboration? Distinguishing between these scenarios can be difficult at present and will continue to be so until e-participation in all of its forms becomes a regular part of the policymaking process, across both agencies and issues.

Client Influence on Bureaucratic Policymaking

The popular image of clients, particularly organized interests, is that they are enormously resourceful and extraordinarily influential.[45] The overall accuracy of these perceptions, however, may be questioned for a number of reasons. First, interest groups differ dramatically in size, finances, membership, expertise, and credibility. All interest groups are certainly not created equal! According to *Fortune* magazine, the most powerful organized interests in America include the National Rifle Association, the Association of Trial Lawyers of America, and the National Beer Wholesalers Association.[46] Many thousands of organizations fall well short of these groups in terms of personnel and budgetary resources as well as political clout.

Second, interest groups may be more effective in some settings than in others. Whereas Congress is designed to be highly porous and accessible, the bureaucracy, despite a multiplicity of participatory venues, is not fundamentally an institution of representative government. This means that commonplace resources such as campaign contributions and grassroots mobilization may not be directly useful to clients seeking to influence executive branch policymaking. Third, interest groups are far more prominent in some policy debates than in others. To reiterate a central theme of this chapter, the significance of organized interests depends in part on whether the costs and benefits of policies are concentrated or distributed.[47] Fourth, interest group power ebbs and flows over time. Evidence suggests that organizational influence in the federal bureaucracy declined from the early 1970s to the mid-1980s, then rebounded somewhat.[48] Fifth, the influence of particular types of interest groups changes systematically over time. For example, Republican administrations tend to be more responsive to business organizations and conservative advocacy groups, while Democratic administrations tend to be more responsive to labor unions and advocacy groups with a liberal bent.

Despite these qualifications, there is considerable evidence that interest groups influence bureaucratic decision making. Although no cabinet secretary today would come right out and say that "What's good for General Motors is good for the United States," business groups undoubtedly command the attention of executive branch officials. In at least two policy areas—the environment and consumer protection—public interest groups have become increasingly powerful in recent decades. In addition, state and local governments themselves have taken on the role of organized lobbyists, as when the National Governors Association has sought to shape the welfare reform decisions that emanate from federal offices.

Business Organizations

The role of business in the policymaking process is uniquely important. As C. Edward Lindblom has put it: "Businessmen generally and corporate executives in particular take on a privileged role in government that is, it seems reasonable to say, unmatched by any leadership group other than government officials themselves." [49] Because maintaining low unemployment and strong economic growth are high priorities for governments of all stripes, keen sensitivity to business interests is apparent throughout the world. It is especially striking, however, in the United States, where the private sector accounts for a relatively large percentage of the nation's economic productivity.

Business organizations influence the bureaucracy because they possess financial resources, policy expertise, and political clout. Financial resources enable them to hire well-respected, experienced staff members, including former executive branch officials. These resources also enable them to conduct research, finance receptions, and mobilize grassroots support. Policy expertise enhances their credibility when they present arguments to government officials. Political clout helps to ensure their access to key decision makers.

The so-called **revolving door** between government agencies and the private sector offers a particularly important source of business power. Officials at the Federal Communications Commission who used to work in the broadcast industry are more likely to vote in support of the industry when such issues come before the agency.[50] Even agency officials who have not previously worked in a particular industry may behave favorably toward it if they hope to one day secure a job there.

Dan Glickman
Secretary of Agriculture
(1995–2001)

"A lot of top-level bureaucrats at the USDA had been there many years. Some had worked in these commodity groups. It's kind of a small, incestuous community. Everybody knew each other."

Direct lobbying is another useful strategy. In 1998 lobbyists from the sugar industry helped to persuade the Army Corps of Engineers to reconsider its water storage plans in the vicinity of Florida's Lake Okeechobee. Instead of building a large reservoir on sugar lands, as originally intended, the agency agreed to build underground storage systems, as proposed by sugar interests.[51] In exercising this influence "the sugar companies not only survived the battle over Everglades restoration; they guaranteed their future water supply." [52]

Similar conclusions have been reached for other agencies and policy arenas. Consider, for example, the EPA's authority, granted by the Federal Insecticide, Fungicide, and Rodenticide Act, to approve or cancel the registration of specific pesticides. One study found that over a fifteen-year period, the agency was less likely to cancel a pesticide's registration if a grower group intervened in the decision-making process.[53] A decision not to cancel a registration permits growers to use the pesticide despite any environmental concerns.

Business organizations influence not only federal agencies but state agencies as well. A study of public utility commissions in twelve states found that utility companies were moderately influential in one state and very influential in the other eleven.[54] Similarly, a study of environmental regulations in all fifty states found water pollution standards to be relatively weak in states in which the mining industry accounts for a particularly substantial share of economic activity.[55]

In general, business organizations fare better on issues where the glare of publicity is relatively dim. High issue salience generally works to the advantage of groups that can make strong appeals to the general public. Low issue salience, in contrast, generally favors economic interests with much narrower constituencies. The actions of the mass media, which both react to and promote high issue salience, help to explain this pattern. As it has been put, the role of the press is to "afflict the comfortable and comfort the afflicted." [56] In performing this role, journalists and other media officials draw attention to policy arrangements that benefit small numbers of producers at the expense of large numbers of consumers. In the end, however, although the influence of business organizations is mitigated by media coverage and other factors, this influence remains pervasive across agencies and levels of government.

Public Interest Groups

At first glance the bureaucracy would not seem to be fertile territory for public interest groups, organizations such as Common Cause, the Consumers Union, and the Natural Resources Defense Council. Although bureaucratic decision making is surprisingly transparent, it is nonetheless more opaque than decision making in legislatures. This opacity enhances the difficulty for wide audiences seeking to participate in, and exercise influence over, agency proceedings. Moreover, issues addressed in bureaucratic settings tend to be more technical, more abstruse, and remoter than those resolved by legislatures. Such circumstances naturally favor experts, including agency personnel and the kinds of professionals public interest groups often cannot afford to maintain.

Despite these handicaps, public interest groups enjoy advantages today that they did not possess prior to the 1960s. The Freedom of Information Act and the Government in the Sunshine Act make it easier for public interest groups, as well as other interested parties, to obtain important agency documents and to attend meetings where vital policy decisions are being considered. In addition, the National Environmental Policy Act and other statutes have created opportunities for public interest groups to challenge bureaucratic decisions in the courts.

The long saga over the spotted owl illustrates public interest groups' ability to shape bureaucratic decisions with a combination of direct lobbying and indirect intervention through the judiciary. In 1986 a small Massachusetts-based environmental group, GreenWorld, asked the Fish and Wildlife Service to list the spotted owl as an endangered species. When the agency failed to do so, the Sierra Club Legal Defense Fund initiated litigation against the government. In 1989 a federal district court judge issued the first of a long series of rulings that would ultimately compel the agency to designate

Dan Glickman

Secretary of Agriculture (1995–2001)

"Some people believe that the Forest Service for years was so closely tied to timber interests that you had an iron triangle between Western-based senators, the timber industry, and the Forest Service bureaucracy. But during the Clinton administration that wasn't true. The Clinton Forest Service policy was very much more habitat-protection oriented and species-protection oriented. The environmental community was extremely active and was an equal match for the timber community. Frankly, it was one of the healthier areas of public policy because there was genuine debate, not only over legislative but also over regulatory issues. There was a kind of equality of engagement that you certainly did not see in farm policy, for example."

the spotted owl as endangered. Subsequent interventions by environmental groups resulted in decisions sharply curtailing the ability of the government to sell timber in the Northwest's old-growth forests, particularly in the vicinity of spotted owl habitats.[57]

Environmental groups have been particularly influential participants in bureaucratic policymaking. In addition to restrictions on timber sales, they have used their power to promote reductions in livestock grazing and recreational use of national forests. It has been demonstrated that during the late 1980s and early 1990s, an "amenity coalition" of environmental groups and sympathetic government officials was more effective than a "commodity coalition" of ranchers and timber companies in shaping Forest Service planning decisions.[58]

Ultimately, the influence of public interest groups depends a good deal on the policy preferences of the bureaucracies whose behavior they are trying to shape. The Children's Defense Fund and other child advocacy groups fared better in shaping the child care policies of the Clinton administration than in influencing comparable policies during the preceding Bush administration.[59] Olivia Golden, the head of the Administration for Children, Youth, and Families under President Clinton, was a former senior staffer at the fund, demonstrating that the revolving door can at times work to the advantage of public interest groups. In addition, Donna Shalala, the head of the Department of Health and Human Services, was very sympathetic to the fund and its aims. To top it off, first lady Hillary Clinton had once been a fund board member. Interestingly, though these institutional linkages did not exist before President Clinton took office, child advocacy groups had won some modest victories during the administration of George H. W. Bush.[60] These earlier victories testify to the power that public interest groups can now bring to bear on the policymaking process, regardless of the political climate.

State and Local Governments

Governments themselves rank among the bureaucracy's most effective clients. Federal agencies hear all the time from state governments, local governments, and **professional associations** such as the National Conference of State Legislatures, the Association of State Drinking Water Administrators, and the National League of Cities. State and local governments enjoy special deference in the policymaking process because they authoritatively represent citizens in particular parts of the country. This deference is heightened when state and local officials work together, through organizations that allow them to speak with one voice.[61] The National Governors Association, to take one example, has been a particularly powerful force under recent presidents, several of whom had been governors themselves.

It is important to note that state and local governments often target Congress and the White House rather than executive branch agencies. Even working alone, many governors enjoy the stature and prestige necessary to arrange audiences with key members of Congress and the president's closest aides. From the perspective of such officials, why bother with the bureaucracy itself when you can confer with the bureaucracy's bosses?

State and local governments are in regular communication with officials inside the bureaucracy, however. The rulemaking process is a common target for such interventions. For example, state and local governments file more than 1,000 comments per year in EPA rulemakings deemed to be "major" or "significant." [62]

In recent years, state and local governments have repeatedly pressed federal agencies for waivers from rules and regulations. In the area of health care, states have pursued waivers allowing them to substitute managed care for fee-for-service medicine in their Medicaid programs. In education, state governments and local school districts have requested waivers enhancing their flexibility in administering education programs. In welfare policy, state governments have sought to reform their systems in all sorts of novel ways.

In responding to waiver requests, the federal government has generally accommodated the states and localities while satisfying its own legal and political concerns. The Clinton administration was particularly receptive to waiver requests.[63] When President Clinton took office, only one state—Arizona—had received the authority to create a statewide research and demonstration project under Medicaid. By the end of the Clinton administration, eighteen states were operating under such waivers. The Department of Education also responded favorably to state requests, granting 446 waivers from 1995 to 1999.

From time to time federal agencies do deny state and local requests for waivers. In some instances the federal government denies such requests because it lacks the statutory authority to grant particular waivers. In other instances it denies requests because of expressed opposition. For example, the Clinton administration terminated New Mexico's managed care program for mental health after receiving extensive negative commentary from the Bazelon Center for Mental Health Law, a public interest group that enjoyed considerable credibility within the administration. This decision was reversed under President George W. Bush, whose administration was responsive to a different set of mental health interests.[64]

Direct intervention in a federal agency's deliberations is often accompanied by other approaches, such as expanding the scope of conflict.[65] Democratic South Carolina governor Jim Hodges used a variety of strategies in opposing a Department of Energy (DOE) decision to ship plutonium from Colorado to his state. Hodges pleaded with Energy Secretary Spencer Abraham to stop the shipment and also asked Tom Ridge, director of Homeland Security, to intervene on South Carolina's behalf. When these efforts bore no fruit, Hodges ratcheted up the level of controversy by taking the DOE to court and by generating considerable mass media attention. He even threatened to lie down in front of any truck attempting to carry a plutonium shipment across South Carolina's border! Ultimately, Hodges was forced to acquiesce when a federal appeals court ordered him not to interfere with the plutonium shipment.[66] He won an important concession along the way, however. In a written letter, Abraham promised to seek legislation guaranteeing the removal of the plutonium if it could not be processed.[67]

Clients and the Institutions of Government

The squabble between South Carolina and the federal government reinforces one of the central lessons of this, as well as the preceding, chapter. Client participation in bureaucratic policymaking does not occur in an institutional vacuum but via arrangements, such as the court system, established and maintained by political principals. As third party intermediaries, individuals and organizations play a crucial role in determining the degree to which principals are well equipped to address issues of adverse selection and moral hazard and ultimately to mitigate the agency loss associated with the delegation of authority.

Principal-agent theory, however, does not directly speak to the desire and capacity of clients to take on the roles specified by executives, legislatures, and judiciaries. This is where the interest group mobilization framework comes in, pointing our attention to the benefits and costs associated with particular policy areas and choices. By offering a conditional perspective on client activism and influence, this framework recognizes citizens and interest groups as potentially powerful, and at times unwilling, participants in the hierarchical structures and processes of bureaucratic policymaking.

Importantly, agencies operate not only as agents on the receiving end of delegated authority but also as partners in **networks** that span agencies and governments as well as the public and private sectors. During his tenure as attorney general, Dick Thornburgh convened a body called the Financial Crimes Task Force. In the words of the attorney general, this organization "brought together on an interagency basis all the people who would be pursuing wrongdoing in that area," including agents from the Federal Bureau of Investigation. The task force, in other words, offered the possibility of coordination across a host of bureaucracies, all of which operated as agents to their own principals. The complexity of this arrangement, which is not at all uncommon, undoubtedly had implications for the mobilization of, and the influence exercised by, the intended beneficiaries and targets of executive branch activity in the area of financial crimes. These implications will become clearer after government networks are considered from a theoretical point of view in the following chapter.

Client Participation: Three Lessons and Beyond

At first glance the bureaucracy often appears insular and impervious to outside intervention. Complaints about red tape and out-of-control agencies abound, and at times these complaints have merit. This chapter, however, has demonstrated that the bureaucracy is a surprisingly open and accessible set of institutions and organizations. Three lessons, in particular, seem appropriate to draw regarding the bureaucracy and its clients.

Who Participates Varies

Both economic and environmental interests placed enormous pressure on the Forest Service during the debate over the revitalization of Bitterroot National Forest. This two-sided mobilization occurred even though the benefits of timber removal were to accrue narrowly to logging and other local interests, while the costs were to be borne by environmentalists all over the country. Although it might be tempting to conclude that agencies always hear from all relevant stakeholders, such a conclusion would ignore the variation in client participation that occurs over time and across policy areas. As noted above, in recent decades some iron triangles have been transformed into sloppy hexagons, making participation more fluid and uncertain than previously. Within these hexagons the activism of particular clients varies across issues as benefits and costs take on unique distributions. Although business organizations will undoubtedly continue to participate extensively in bureaucratic proceedings, given their direct material stake in agency actions, the extent to which this participation will be met by other interests is best assessed on a case-by-case basis.

Venues Vary

Just as the identities of client participants are remarkably diverse, so, too, are the venues through which these participants make their views known. When the Forest Service waived the public appeals process in its decision regarding logging in Bitterroot, environmentalists raised their grievances in the court system. In general, clients can communicate with agency officials through both direct and indirect channels. Direct channels, such as the advisory committee system, bring clients themselves before agencies. Indirect channels, in contrast, task legislatures and courts with addressing agencies on behalf of specific constituencies or parties. Importantly, venues are distinct in the resources clients must possess to take advantage of opportunities for participation. Clients seeking to comment on agency proposals must often exercise significant legal acumen, given the complexity of many contemporary rulemakings. When the goal is to entice legislators to intervene in bureaucratic decisions, clients are most capable when they can mobilize large numbers of constituents or help fill the campaign coffers of their prospective benefactors.

Influence Varies

Both sides got some of what they wanted when the Forest Service finally resolved the debate over Bitterroot's recovery. Many thousands of acres of burned trees were harvested, while the most pristine areas of the forest were left untouched. In other instances, however, influence accrues disproportionately to one interest or set of interests. When revising the way in which the Medicare program pays for physician services, the Health Care Financing Administration proved more responsive to comments submitted by high-income specialists than to comments submitted by family practitioners and other relatively low-income providers. These differences in influence were important because the agency had been charged by Congress with redistributing payments away from the specialists.[68] The influence patterns, at least as witnessed via the notice and comment process, may have made it more difficult for such an outcome to emerge from the rulemaking.

Issues of client influence raise a pair of broader, more normative questions: *Does client participation make policymaking in the bureaucracy more democratic? Does this participation enhance the ability of agencies to make high-quality, defensible decisions?* Although these questions do not have simple answers, this chapter has provided a framework for thinking about such concerns. Due in part to client participation, policymaking in the bureaucracy is a political process as well as an exercise in administration. Assessments of accountability and performance must be made with both aspects of bureaucracy in mind.

In the case of Bitterroot, the Forest Service's charge to foster multiple uses of the land under its domain would seem to make it difficult for the agency to act as an effective steward for any particular set of users, let alone all affected parties. The sustained activism of both environmentalists and local economic interests would seem to make the agency's task that much more difficult. Such client participation, however, can have exactly the opposite effect. In the words of former agriculture secretary Dan Glickman, "equality of engagement" among stakeholders can foster "genuine debate" and ultimately give rise to a policy community that is healthy and anchored by an agency that serves both its clients and the nation with distinction.

Key Terms

Advisory committee, 94

Client, 83

Client politics, 85

Concentrated benefits and costs, 84

Diffuse benefits and costs, 84

Digital divide, 100

Entrepreneurial politics, 86

Federal Advisory
    Committee Act, 94

Interest group politics, 86

Iron triangle, 88

Issue network, 90

Major rule, 93

Majoritarian politics, 86

Negotiated rulemaking, 95

Network, 109

Notice and comment process, 92

Policy image, 89

Professional association, 106

Public hearing, 95

Public interest group, 89

Public meeting, 95

Revolving door, 102

Rulemaking, 92

Sloppy hexagon, 90

5 | Networks

As THE POPULATION OF THE United States ages dramatically, the number of persons who could spend some portion of their lives in a nursing home increases. At its best, a nursing home provides high-quality medical care, plus tender loving care to make residents feel secure. At its worst, a nursing home is a smelly, noisy, scary place where frail and sick senior citizens suffer from indifference and neglect.

Government agencies run only about 5 percent of nursing homes. For-profit firms run the overwhelming majority of them; nonprofit organizations most of the rest.[1] Although government agencies seldom run nursing homes themselves, they are intimately involved in funding and monitoring them. The federal government funds nursing homes that care for Medicaid or Medicare clients. State human services agencies license all nursing homes, with additional oversight by the Centers for Medicare and Medicaid Services (CMS), the agency formerly known as the Health Care Financing Administration. State and federal laws require regular site visits by state officials, intermittent visits by federal officials.

All these organizations—federal and state agencies, for-profit firms, and nonprofit organizations—belong, in effect, to a **network**, albeit one that has no official name and is sometimes hard to detect. Other members of the network include state ombudsman offices representing nursing home clients, trade associations representing nursing homes, and citizens' groups representing clients, loved ones, or both.

These arrangements typify what H. Brinton Milward would call the "hollow state."[2] Instead of delivering social services, government bureaucracies frequently finance and scrutinize the delivery of such services by other organizations. This phenomenon, known as contracting out, originated in the "hard services" area (such as road repair and garbage pickup) but spread quickly to the social or human services (such as education and health). It is one element of a broader trend toward the privatization of public services.[3]

One way to view **contracting out** is through the lens of principal-agent theory. Just as CMS is the agent of Congress and the president, so, too, is the Manor Care nursing home in Bethesda, Maryland, an agent of the state of Maryland and the federal government. Contracts specify Manor Care's obligations to each of these government principals. The government entities have some leverage over their agent Manor Care (and other for-profit and nonprofit nursing homes) because of their ability to withhold funds or to accelerate regulatory enforcement. As predicted by principal-agent theory, however, monitoring is a constant challenge.

Yet principal-agent theory may not be the best way to think about nursing home politics. Consider, for example, the relationship between the federal and state agencies that regulate the homes. Under our federal system, that relationship is not truly hierarchical, as principal-agent theory implies. While the federal government can tell the state of Maryland how to spend federal Medicaid funds, it does not enjoy the same degree of leverage when federal funding is not involved. Even when it comes to Medicaid, the federal government often treats states with kid gloves for fear of stifling innovation or provoking a negative political reaction.

Furthermore, Manor Care is more than just an agent of Maryland and the federal government. As a for-profit firm, it has obligations to its shareholders and its customers that may not coincide with the views of government agencies. Complicating matters even more is the fact that Manor Care in Bethesda is part of a chain of nursing homes. This implies yet another set of obligations. Of course, one might simply treat this as a case involving multiple principals. But even this adjustment does not adequately account for relationships not easily portrayed in hierarchical terms.

Ultimately, it may be more useful to apply network theory or, more broadly, a network approach to nursing homes and the agencies that occupy so prominent a place in their functioning. The network approach has several advantages. First, it encompasses both hierarchical and nonhierarchical relationships. Second, it seeks to measure information flows, which need to be modeled and documented if complex relationships between organizations are to be understood. Third, it recognizes the extent of interorganizational bargaining not just over programmatic details but also, more fundamentally, over programmatic goals. Organizations that belong to a network have their own goals, which they can pursue and promote to a greater degree than agents can. Fourth, the network approach highlights problems of accountability that seem to be growing as we shift from hierarchical organizational forms to other, more fluid and more complex kinds of relationships.

In this chapter we focus on networks that include bureaucracies—how they work, how they are changing, and how they might be changed to work even better. The core questions we will explore:

- *HOW DO FEDERAL AGENCIES RELATE TO STATE AND LOCAL GOVERNMENT AGENCIES AND WITH WHAT RESULTS?* Health policy and environmental policy are strikingly intergovernmental in character. Even education policy, once regarded as the province of local governments, has become increasingly intergovernmental.

- *WHAT ARE THE ESSENTIAL FEATURES AND KEY CHALLENGES OF PUBLIC-PRIVATE PARTNERSHIPS, SUCH AS CONTRACTING OUT?* For years public-private partnerships have marked such fields as trash collection and economic development. Recently, such arrangements have arisen in social policy as well, sparking considerable controversy.

- *HOW DO BUREAUCRACIES COORDINATE WITH OTHER BUREAUCRACIES?* Interagency task forces and cabinet meetings are among the traditional mechanisms employed. In recent years presidents have appointed "czars" to manage such complex domains as energy policy, drug policy, and homeland security—with mixed results.

More broadly, we consider the challenges of accountability and whether networks alleviate or aggravate them. We also consider tools of government that may enhance the performance of networks comprising bureaucracies.

Network Theory

A network is an institution linking organizations or persons. Students of bureaucratic politics find **interorganizational networks** of particular interest.

Laurence O'Toole defines such networks as "structures of interdependence involving multiple organizations or parts thereof, where one unit is not merely the formal subordinate of the others in some larger hierarchical arrangement." [4] This definition, which we accept, is relatively broad. As long as two or more organizations are involved and their relationship is not strictly hierarchical, we posit that a network of organizations exists. The purpose of that relationship may be joint decision making or advocacy or information sharing or some combination of the above.

Whereas principal-agent theory originated in economics, network theory originated in sociology. For some sociologists it proved a useful concept for highlighting the surprising strength of weak ties between persons in social networks.[5] For others it proved a helpful tool in understanding how organizations share information.[6] More recently, students of public administration have seized upon the network as a vehicle for understanding how government agencies interact with other agencies and with private sector organizations.[7]

Unlike principal-agent theory, which treats the goals of principals as given and relatively fixed, network theory views goals as more fluid. Although each organization affiliated with a network undoubtedly has its own goals, the goals of the network itself evolve over time through a process of give-and-take.[8] This is probably a realistic perspective. Yet because a network's goals are more tentative and dynamic than those of an organization, and because a network's stakeholders are more numerous than those of a single organization, it is more difficult to evaluate a network's success.[9]

Students of networks, both social and organizational, have focused a good deal of attention on several key concepts, including centrality, density, size, complexity, multiplexity, and differentiation. **Centrality** refers to the degree to which information flows through a single individual or organization, strategically situated to serve as a clearinghouse or traffic cop. **Density** is defined as the number of actual connections among individuals or organizations divided by the number of potential connections among individuals or organizations.[10] **Size** is the number of persons or organizations that participate in the work of the system. **Complexity** means the number of different service or product sectors represented by the members or member organizations.[11] **Multiplexity** refers to the number of separate relationships between two parties (for example, two mental health agencies might be linked through referrals, service contracts, and information sharing).[12] And **differentiation** refers to the degree to which there is functional and service specialization among the members or member organizations.[13] Together these

Figure 5.1 Networks with Different Characteristics

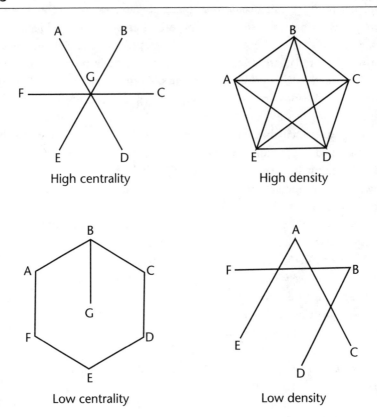

High centrality

High density

Low centrality

Low density

concepts help us understand the "structure" of a network or patterns of so-cial relations. It is sometimes useful, for example, to distinguish between a highly centralized and a highly decentralized network or between a high-density and a low-density network (see Figure 5-1).

At least one study has found that centrality and size are positively re-lated, which means that larger networks find it necessary or desirable to route communications through one organization or subunit. It also appears that larger networks are more complex and more differentiated but less dense.[14] Interestingly, centrality and density are inversely related. In other words, the presence of a dominant individual or organization (high central-ity) discourages connections with other individuals or organizations.

Network theory can be particularly useful in certain fields, such as law enforcement. For example, the relative centrality of different individuals in a crime network can help investigators determine whom to target first. Another useful concept is equivalence. As Malcolm Sparrow notes, "The disruptive effectiveness of removing one individual or a set of individuals from a network depends not only on their centrality, but also upon some notion of their uniqueness. The more unique, or unusual, their role the harder they will be to replace. The most valuable targets will be both central and difficult to replace." [15] The concept of weak ties can also be instructive in that it alerts investigators to the utility of focusing attention on communications channels that are seldom used but indispensable to the network's success.

In the wake of September 11, some scholars have sought to understand that most infamous of modern networks, al Qaeda. In attempting to trace connections among hijackers, Valdis Krebs found that the organization's cells were characterized by extraordinarily low density, with few communications links among the conspirators. He concluded that "covert networks trade efficiency for secrecy." [16] Noting the absence of "moment-to-moment top-down management" in al Qaeda, Richard Rothenberg argued that leadership is essential at the planning stages "but may not be critical for the maintenance of the terrorist activity." [17] He also noted the organization's formidable barriers to entry and exit—another technique for ensuring secrecy.

The Tools Approach

Although some political scientists have found network theory a fruitful source of insights into interorganizational behavior, a larger number of political scientists have found it more useful to import other ideas to understand networks and their consequences. One particularly promising line of inquiry is what is sometimes referred to as the **tools approach**. The essence of that approach is to understand that the choice of a particular policy tool typically implies the choice of a particular network or combination of organizations. Thus the effectiveness of a given network depends not only on the network's organizational characteristics but also on some of the distinctive characteristics of the underlying policy tool.

According to Lester Salamon, policy tools differ in several key respects, including coerciveness, directness, automaticity, and visibility. **Coerciveness** refers to the degree to which a tool compels a certain form of behavior, as opposed to merely encouraging it. **Directness** refers to the extent to which the organization authorizing, financing, or commencing an activity actually carries out that activity. **Automaticity** measures the extent to which a tool relies on existing structural arrangements as opposed to new ones. **Visibility** measures the degree to which resources devoted to a tool are featured prominently in normal budget and review processes.[18]

With these attributes in mind, it is possible to categorize a wide variety of policy tools, such as economic regulation, social regulation, grants, contracts, vouchers, direct loans, loan guarantees, labeling requirements, and information. For example, economic regulation tends to be high in coerciveness and directness, low in automaticity and visibility. In contrast, vouchers tend to be medium in coerciveness, low in directness, high in automaticity, and high in visibility.[19] When public officials choose vouchers rather than regulation, they inevitably advance one type of network rather than another. In the case of vouchers, the network will probably be decentralized and differentiated, with schools trying to establish a distinctive market niche. But the success or failure of vouchers will also depend on the distinctive characteristics of the vouchers themselves. Their high visibility, for example, helps to guarantee that they will be controversial. Their low directness fuels demands for systematic evaluations to demonstrate results.

The tools approach is closely linked to efforts to understand the phenomenon of **third-party government**.[20] Increasingly, public officials turn to third parties to deliver public services. These third parties include banks, day care centers, hospitals, nursing homes, schools, and other levels of government. To put it another way, the tools selected to deliver public services are more indirect than they used to be. This makes it all the more important to look at relationships between organizations—or the inner workings of networks. It also raises questions as to whether the network form enables us to hold service delivery organizations accountable for their results.

To return to our nursing home example, whom shall we blame if we discover numerous patients with bedsores and dirty linen at a particular nursing home facility? Is it the owner of the nursing home? If the home is part of a chain, is it the owner of the nursing home chain? Is it the state agency that failed to oversee the nursing home? Is it the federal agency that failed to oversee the state agency? Is it the ombudsman whose intervention was too little or too late? In a hierarchical situation, it is relatively easy to affix blame. In the immortal words of Harry S Truman, "The buck stops here!" Accountability is more elusive in a network characterized by public and private partners, federal and state officials.

As Paul Posner has noted, third-party government involves at least five different kinds of accountability challenges.[21] First, federal goals are sometimes diverted or compromised because state and local officials do not support them. Second, state and local governments often receive fiscal windfalls, with the federal government supporting programs that recipient governments would otherwise have funded themselves. Third, federal support, through insurance and loan guarantee programs, creates moral hazard problems, encouraging third parties to take risks they would not otherwise take. Fourth, third parties frequently lack fiscal incentives to avoid waste, fraud, and abuse; it's not their money and they do not benefit from the correction of the problem. Fifth, third-party subsidies can encourage opportunistic behavior by organizations that seek to enhance their profits or, in the case of nonprofit organizations, their customer base.

Despite these challenges, we must find ways to hold networks accountable because they are becoming increasingly important in some policy sectors. In health care, for example, networks of physicians, hospitals, and other health enterprises have grown dramatically since the rise of managed care.[22] In health care the network has become an attractive alternative to hierarchies (perceived as too rigid) and markets (perceived as unfair). More broadly, Laurence O'Toole believes that as policy problems grow more complex, the network becomes more attractive because of its flexibility and versatility.[23] You can, for example, create or dissolve a network much more easily than you can create or dissolve a government agency.

According to one careful study, 85 percent of significant new federal laws require the involvement of multiple actors at the implementation stage. Furthermore, the bureaucracy sometimes adopts rules requiring the involvement of additional actors, including state and local governments, private firms, and nonprofit organizations.[24] It is widely believed, though not firmly established, that network structures are growing in popularity and importance.[25]

At least three types of networks have been of interest to students of public administration: intergovernmental relationships, public-private partnerships, and interagency coordination. The first two involve third-party government and can be easily identified as networks. The third organizational form—interagency coordination—is often treated separately, as a useful coping mechanism employed by many hierarchical organizations, such as the federal government. Yet interagency coordination comprises "structures of interdependence involving multiple organizations or parts thereof, where one unit is not merely the formal subordinate of the others in some larger hierarchical arrangement." [26] From this vantage point it clearly qualifies as a network, albeit one with a more limited scope than those of the other two.

Although it is possible to use other theoretical frameworks to understand these phenomena (policy implementation theory for intergovernmental relations, principal-agent theory for public-private contracts, and public administration theory for interagency coordination), network theory and the tools approach are directly applicable to all three of them. In the sections that follow, we examine each type of network, its accountability challenges, and ultimately its performance.

Intergovernmental Relations

Because the United States is a federal system and because intergovernmental relations have become much more complex in recent years, the intergovernmental network is a particularly important type of network. Many public policies involve some sort of shared decision making by federal, state, and local governments. There are at least three possibilities. First, the Congress assigns responsibility for a program to a federal agency, which in turn delegates responsibility to run that program to a state or local government, subject to certain conditions. This phenomenon, known as **devolution,** increased during the 1980s and the 1990s. Second, Congress explicitly **mandates** states to implement a program or to perform certain tasks. Third, Congress appropriates **grants-in-aid** that may be used to entice states to participate in certain programs.[27]

Environmental Protection

Following the passage of significant federal environmental laws in the 1970s, the Environmental Protection Agency (EPA) discovered it to be increasingly difficult to implement several important statutes on its own. Furthermore, many state governments pleaded for more flexibility, arguing that they could implement federal laws more successfully than the federal government because of their greater familiarity with the unique geographic, topological, economic, and political circumstances of their states. During the early 1980s, coinciding with President Reagan's first term, the EPA devolved considerable authority to run federal environmental programs to the states. In network theory terms, intergovernmental networks became less centralized. By the dawn of the twenty-first century, an average of two-thirds of the states were in charge of those programs that could in principle be delegated to them (see Table 5.1).

Clearly, the flow of information from the federal government to the states and vice versa is particularly important when programs have been delegated to the states. The federal government must specify its expectations clearly, distinguishing between federal minimum standards that must be upheld and other domains in which states are more or less free to do as they please. As for the states, they must furnish information on their policy outputs and policy outcomes to the federal government. Otherwise, the federal agency cannot know whether delegation has been successful, and accountability breaks down.

To improve the quality of information transmitted through the environmental policy network, the EPA established a new institution in 1995 known as the performance partnership agreement, or PPA. Under this arrangement, any state can negotiate a PPA with the EPA regional office responsible for that state. The EPA grants the state greater flexibility in the administration of federal environmental programs and relaxes certain reporting requirements; in return, the state agrees to improve its environmental performance and to document those improvements better. Though voluntary, PPAs have been negotiated by thirty-three states.[28]

Part of a broader Clinton administration initiative known as the National Environmental Performance Partnership System (NEPPS), the PPA has received somewhat mixed reviews from outside observers.[29] Clearly, environmental performance measures at the state level are more widely used and more sophisticated than they used to be. NEPPS deserves some credit for this. Still most states continue to rely more on "output" measures (such as the number of inspections conducted) rather than "outcome" measures (such as changes in air or water quality), despite the latter's greater importance.

By definition the PPA is a dyadic relationship between the EPA and a state environmental agency. In contrast, some environmental networks are regional in nature. These include initiatives to improve the Chesapeake Bay and the Great Lakes Basin. According to Barry Rabe, both initiatives have been successful, thanks to a combination of grants, technical assistance, coordination, and collective efforts to achieve uniform standards throughout each region.[30] Note the absence of coercive tools in these regional networks. In intergovernmental relations, coercion, though tempting, can be counterproductive. That is particularly true when federal and state officials agree on certain basic goals or values.[31]

Table 5.1 The Number of States Authorized to Run Environmental Programs

	Yes	In Process	Partial	No	NA
Clean Air Act					
New Source Performance Standards	39	1	9	1	0
NESHAPS	38	2	10	0	0
Prevention of Significant Deterioration	45	0	4	1	0
Title V Operating Permit	21	29	0	0	0
New Source Review	46	1	1	0	2
Clean Water Act					
NPDES	37	0	4	8	1
Pretreatment/POTWs	29	1	0	19	1
State Revolving Fund	48	0	0	2	0
Sludge Management	9	3	0	37	1
Construction Grants	46	0	0	3	1
Wetlands	2	0	0	42	6
Resource Conservation and Recovery Act					
Subpart C, Base Program	47	1	0	2	0
Subpart C, Corrective Action	31	3	0	16	0
Subpart C, Mixed Waste	39	1	0	10	0
Subpart C, BIF	19	4	0	27	0
Toxicity Characteristics Revisions	34	3	0	13	0
LDR California Wastes	37	2	0	10	1
LDR 1/3 Wastes	36	3	0	11	0
LDR 2/3 Wastes	21	3	0	26	0
LDR 3/3 Wastes	27	6	0	17	0
Subpart D, Solid Waste	29	1	8	3	9
Underground Storage Tanks	28	2	0	20	0

Health Policy

In dealing with the health care needs of the poor, the federal government has long relied on networks. The Medicaid program, established in 1965, sets up shared responsibility for funding the health care needs of the poor, with the federal government providing at least half of the funding and state governments providing the rest, under a fixed formula that favors states with lower per capita incomes. Under this program, state Medicaid agencies determine eligibility standards and benefits, subject to federal rules and regulations. A

Table 5.1 *Continued*

	Yes	In Process	Partial	No	NA
Safe Drinking Water Act					
Public Water System Supervision	48	0	0	2	0
Wellhead Protection Program	36	1	0	4	9
Underground Injection Control 1422	34	0	0	16	0
Underground Injection Control 1425	35	0	1	9	5
Federal Insecticide, Fungicide, and Rodenticide Act					
23(a) State Cooperation, Aid, and Training	44	1	1	0	4
23(b) State Cooperation, Aid, and Training	44	1	1	0	4
Endangered Species	24	5	0	9	12
Worker Protection	48	1	1	0	0
Groundwater Protection	29	11	0	4	6

Source: National Academy of Public Administration *Environment.gov* (Washington, D.C.: NAPA, November 2000), 137–138.

Note:

NA = not ascertained

NESHAPS = National Emission Standards for Hazardous Air Pollutants

NPDES = National Pollutant Discharge Elimination System

POTWs = Publicly Owned Treatment Works

BIF = Regulation of Burning of Hazardous Wastes in Boilers and Industrial Furnaces

LDR = Land Disposal Restrictions

typical network includes federal and state agencies as payers and hospitals, nursing homes, and physicians as payees.

Beginning during the Nixon administration, the federal government expressed interest in developing **managed care** as an alternative to the traditional **fee-for-service** health insurance system, where insurance companies automatically pick up the full cost of health care. Although managed care takes many different forms, a common denominator is that health care providers have financial incentives to reduce unnecessary medical expenditures and procedures. Managed care originated on the commercial, or private, side of health care but eventually extended to the governmental, or public, side.

During the first Bush administration, the federal Health Care Financing Administration, then responsible for overseeing Medicaid, was authorized to grant waivers to state governments that wished to extend managed care to Medicaid clients. Available waivers included 1915b waivers, which allowed states to enroll some Medicaid clients in managed care plans, and 1115 waivers, which allowed states even broader discretion as part of a research-and-demonstration effort. Such waivers, relatively few at first, escalated sharply during the Clinton administration. When President Clinton took office in 1993, fifty 1915b waivers were in effect; when he left office, a hundred such waivers were in effect. When President Clinton took office, only one state (Arizona) had an 1115 waiver; when he left office, eighteen states had such waivers.[32]

The trend toward Medicaid managed care ensured that health care networks would become more important and more complex. Because health care payments are no longer automatic, the standard operating procedures of health care service delivery organizations and government overseers become more important. Because health care maintenance organizations (HMOs) limit access to physicians included in an HMO's "network," new norms have developed, with contractual arrangements that impose constraints on patients, physicians, and HMOs themselves.

To make matters even more interesting, Congress decided in 1997 to establish a new program, known as the Children's Health Insurance Program (CHIP). Modeled somewhat after Medicaid, CHIP nevertheless differed from it, having a somewhat more affluent clientele, somewhat more generous federal contributions, and somewhat more flexible rules. In implementing CHIP some states established a brand new program, others expanded Medicaid, and still others adopted a hybrid approach.

As implementation proceeded it soon became evident that better coordination was needed between the Medicaid network and the CHIP network. Some states, anxious to cash in on CHIP's more favorable matching rates and greater flexibility, enrolled children in CHIP who were in fact eligible for Medicaid. Such behavior exemplified poor coordination; it was also illegal. Eventually, thanks to federal pressure, states got better at assigning clients to the right program.

But additional problems remain, such as "churning" between the Medicaid and CHIP programs. Due to changes in parental employment, income, and related factors, children eligible for CHIP may suddenly become eligible for Medicaid or vice versa.[33] This phenomenon makes it all the more important that the Medicaid network and the CHIP network work closely together. If the networks do so, children may enjoy a smooth transition from one program to another; if they do not, health care services may be interrupted, with harmful consequences for children's health.

Other continuing problems involve perverse financial incentives and the attraction of opportunistic partners, discussed earlier. Under the Medicaid program, for example, some states have charged the federal government for expenses they never truly incurred. By inducing hospitals and nursing homes to demand payment under higher Medicare rates, as opposed to lower Medicaid rates, states have extracted higher matching payments from the federal government. After the transfers occurred, the hospitals and nursing homes returned most of the money to the state government, thus resulting in federal matching dollars for fictional expenditures.[34]

Although federal health care funding is much more likely to be channeled through the states than through local governments, the latter are also important, particularly with respect to public health. In response to terrorist attacks, the visibility of our nation's public health network has increased sharply. The anthrax mailings of October 2001 exposed some of the weaknesses of our public health system. When the anthrax attacks commenced, many local health agencies floundered. Because half of all local public health departments do not have access to the Internet and because communications with the Centers for Disease Control (CDC) were often weak, many of them relied on the mass media for guidance.[35] At least one CDC official has acknowledged coordination problems. Dr. Julie Gerberding, acting deputy director of the CDC's Center for Infectious Diseases, told the *New York Times*: "In retrospect, we were certainly not prepared for layers and levels of collaboration among a vast array of government agencies and professional organizations that would be required to be efficient and successful in the anthrax outbreak." [36]

A recent positive development is the emergence of a "health alert network" that permits the federal Department of Health and Human Services (HHS) and its CDC to communicate quickly with local governments. In April 2002 HHS secretary Tommy Thompson announced that such a network currently enjoys a connection to 68 percent of U.S. counties.[37]

Public-Private Partnerships

As is evident from some of the above examples, many networks involving government bureaucracies spill over into the private sector. Such networks may or may not include interagency or intergovernmental relationships. In some instances, they involve a direct contract between a government agency and a for-profit firm or nonprofit organization; in other instances, they involve a looser relationship where cooperative behavior emerges without an explicit contractual obligation.

Contracting Out

The most common public-private partnership in the United States is contracting out, in which a government agency establishes a contractual arrangement with a for-profit firm or a nonprofit organization to deliver some service. Principal-agent theory can be applied to such relationships.[38] A contract, though, is a voluntary relationship between two independent organizations.[39] To the extent that a relationship between organizations involves bargaining rather than commands, network theory may be more suitable.

Contracting out appeals to government officials because it offers the promise—and sometimes the reality—of saving money. The privatization of garbage pickups, for example, seems to have resulted in cost savings, with no apparent diminution in the quality of services provided.[40]

But contracting out presents government officials with real challenges. Monitoring and controlling service delivery is difficult enough when those delivering the services are fellow government officials. When service deliverers are employees of some other organization, oversight becomes even more difficult. Without corrective steps, accountability becomes an elusive goal.

Accountability suffers if government officials lack sufficient information to distinguish between good and bad contractors. Accountability suffers if little or no competition exists. Accountability suffers if the government has poorly defined the contractor's responsibilities. Accountability suffers if government officials adopt a laissez-faire position after the contract has been awarded.

Another concern is that contracting out may ultimately transform nonprofit organizations that receive the contracts and not for the better.[41] As nonprofit organizations become more dependent on government for funding, they may find it advantageous to adjust their priorities, habits, strategies, and norms to secure additional funding. While this is not necessarily perverse, it can result in nonprofit organizations that come to behave a lot like for-profit firms.

Energy Policy

The Department of Energy (DOE) relies more than most federal agencies on contracts with private firms. For every DOE employee, there are thirty-five contractor employees.[42] This has led Donald Kettl to describe DOE as "little more than an administrative shell over a vast empire of contractors."[43] Because there are so many contracts and the tasks being performed are so technical, DOE employees find it very difficult to monitor performance.

In 1989 government investigators uncovered serious problems at a nuclear weapons production facility in Rocky Flats, Colorado, run by Rockwell International. Investigators discovered numerous health and safety problems inside the plant, illegal dumping of hazardous wastes outside the plant, and gross insensitivity to environmental concerns. The severity of the problems, which ultimately led to an FBI raid on the plant, a temporary shutdown, and a new contractor, contrasted sharply with DOE's prior ratings of the plant, which had been quite positive.[44] Later it became evident that DOE's top managers had not been receiving accurate information. Without such information, it is impossible to hold an errant contractor accountable.

Part of the problem, one suspects, was a clash of organizational goals. For DOE, the production of nuclear weapons was a primary goal; environmental considerations were secondary but somewhat important. For Rockwell International, making a profit was the primary goal; environmental concerns mattered even less than for DOE. Under such circumstances, DOE managers had difficulty conveying the need to dispose of nuclear waste safely, securely, and legally.

Mental Health Policy

As noted earlier, networks have been especially conspicuous in health policy. In particular, managed care has ushered in a new series of arrangements in which nonprofit organizations or for-profit firms under contract to state Medicaid agencies provide vital health care services. This is true of both health policy generally and mental health policy in particular.

By using key concepts from network theory, some scholars have assessed the impact of managed care on the degree of system integration, which is generally regarded in positive terms. Following the introduction of managed care for the mental health system in Pima County, Arizona, both density and centrality increased for funding contract networks and also for referral networks.[45] This finding is especially noteworthy given prior research suggesting an inverse relationship between centrality and density.

Welfare Policy

Traditionally, welfare policy has been the province of federal, state, and local governments. As public discontent with welfare policy heightened during the 1990s, however, a number of state governments opted for public-private partnerships as part of broader welfare reform efforts. Wisconsin, widely considered the leader in state welfare reform initiatives, also became prominent in carving out a stronger role for the private sector in delivering welfare services. Under the state's Wisconsin Works (or W-2) program, county governments lost the exclusive right to run their welfare program. Approximately 70 percent of Wisconsin's welfare caseload is now managed by for-profit firms and nonprofit organizations.[46] In Milwaukee County the local government no longer administers W-2 at all; instead, such organizations as the YMCA, Goodwill Industries, and Maximus Inc. do.

The privatization of welfare service delivery is part of a broader phenomenon, which Mark Rom describes as a shift from "the welfare state" to

"Opportunity, Inc." Other examples of this phenomenon include child support enforcement, employment and training, and even child welfare. At least twenty states use private firms or nonprofit organizations to assist in some aspect of child support collection, such as identifying parents or maintaining the payment system. In at least three states— Kansas, Michigan, and Texas— the child welfare systems are substantially privatized.[47] In each of these instances, public and private organizations belong to a network responsible for delivering social services to clients.

Corrections

An equally startling development has occurred in law enforcement, where a number of state governments have turned over the administration of some of their prisons to for-profit firms. In 1997 approximately 8.5 percent of all U.S. prisoners were in private facilities. This phenomenon has been most striking in the South. Tennessee, home of the firm then known as the Corrections Corporation of America, was an early supporter of private prisons. Texas, another early supporter, now has nineteen private prisons.[48]

There is considerable debate about whether private prisons are more efficient than public prisons. Although private prisons sometimes cost less to run than their public counterparts, their lower wages have resulted in higher turnover, with attendant quality problems. One study found more assaults by inmates on both staff and other inmates in private prisons than in public ones. Another study found less reliable methods of classifying prisoners for security purposes in private prisons.[49]

Whatever the merits of private prisons, they do present accountability challenges. For instance, after securing approval to run a prison in Youngstown, Ohio, the Corrections Corporation of America seems to have misinformed state and local officials about security risks there. When five convicted murderers escaped from the prison in July 1998, company officials tried to cover up the escape. Ohio tried to terminate its contract with CCA but failed. Eventually, CCA agreed to move out of the Youngstown facility inmates unsuitable for a medium-security prison.[50] Of course, cover-ups are not unique to the private sector. Still, certain features of the public sector, including a relatively secure civil service, strong prodisclosure laws, and opportunities for judicial review, tend to discourage cover-ups.

Partnerships without Contracts

Despite their enormous importance, contracts do not offer the only mechanisms for achieving collaboration between public and private organizations.

Environmental Protection

In southern California, public officials, developers, and environmental groups have been participating in a cooperative governance arrangement that seeks to avoid the gridlock sometimes associated with enforcement of the Endangered Species Act. State and county parks and wildlife officials meet regularly with developers and environmentalists in an effort to anticipate problems with sensitive species and prevent the triggering of lengthy legal disputes. Under this program, developers receive permits to build on part of their land; in return, they agree to set aside some land for wildlife habitat and to fund environmental restoration work. In addition to participating in these negotiations, environmental groups provide volunteers to assist in restoration activities.[51] More than 450 habitat conservation plans like this one are in operation or in development in the United States.[52]

In many respects this kind of creative collaboration represents a constructive alternative to debilitating conflict. It brings together organizations with divergent goals that might otherwise be clutching at each other's throat. A potential danger, however, is that environmental groups might become co-opted by developers. As Steven R. Smith and Helen Ingram put it: "Democratic accountability may be compromised as environmental groups receive funding for collaboration in restoration activities they are supposed to monitor." [53] Fortunately, the very diversity of the environmental community means that any hint of co-optation is likely to trigger an outcry by other, more adversarial groups.

Emergencies

When a natural disaster strikes, the last thing victims need is a bureaucracy long on promises and short on performance. For some time that is what they got in the Federal Emergency Management Agency (FEMA). But FEMA reinvented itself during the 1990s with the leadership of James Lee Witt.

Under Witt, FEMA took the concept of a partnership very seriously. The agency developed new, stronger ties with state and local governments and with private industry. It formed partnerships with the construction industry to design and build houses that would be more hurricane resistant.[54] FEMA worked closely with state and local officials to improve evacuation plans. In one dramatic instance, agency officials and state and community leaders together moved a town imperiled by floods—Pattonsburg, Missouri—to higher ground.[55]

Interagency Networks

The most fundamental of all networks in which bureaucracies participate is the interagency network. Within any given level of government (federal, state, or local), the executive branch seeks to coordinate its programs, activities, and public testimony. At the very least, coordination implies some information sharing; frequently, it also implies some effort to reach a consensus and to speak with one voice.

The Cabinet

A familiar network within the executive branch is the president's cabinet. Ever since George Washington, the heads of the major departments have met on a regular basis to offer advice to the president, to learn from one another, and to hear what the president wants them to do. Contemporary students of the American presidency have not been very impressed by the cabinet as a policymaking institution or as a coordinating body. We know from Lyndon Johnson's presidency that cabinet officials sometimes concealed their true views of the war in Vietnam to avoid antagonizing a president who demanded fierce loyalty from his top officials.[56] We know from Richard Nixon's presidency that at least one cabinet member (the attorney general, no less) sanctioned illegal acts, including the infamous Watergate burglary.[57]

In general, political scientists have concluded that the cabinet has failed to live up to its potential. Its lack of coherence and limited ability to coordinate policy and management make the cabinet a weak institution.[58] Another problem is the selection process.[59] The president often seeks to placate particular constituencies and to make symbolic appointments that satisfy objectives such as ideological congruence (Reagan) and ethnic diversity (Clinton). Having appointed individuals for all sorts of reasons other than their qualifications for the job, presidents, not surprisingly, often ignore their cabinet members' advice.

Yet cabinet meetings do facilitate exchanges between cabinet secretaries and their respective departments. The very knowledge that they will see one another again on a regular basis encourages cooperation.[60] Meetings involving two or three cabinet secretaries are likely to be even more productive, particularly when they focus on a relatively discrete issue area, such as national security.

The Office of Management and Budget

In recent years the Office of Management and Budget (OMB), explicitly charged with coordinating government agencies and programs, has come to rival the cabinet in importance. On the budget side, OMB trims funding requests from individual agencies and departments and integrates the streamlined requests into a coherent budget document. To ensure official unity, especially for congressional testimony, OMB insists that all testimony by agency heads be cleared in advance. This doctrine, known as **legislative clearance,** helps the executive branch to speak with one voice.

By all accounts OMB has been less attentive to the management side of the equation, the most notable exception being the role OMB plays in reviewing major rules proposed by departments and other agencies. Ever since Reagan federal agencies have been required to prepare a regulatory impact analysis for all proposed major rules. An agency submits the proposed rule and the impact analysis to OMB for its approval. OMB can approve the rule, ask for modifications, or sit on the rule indefinitely. A recent study demonstrates that OMB influences the content and ideological direction of rules promulgated by the EPA.[61] Interestingly, OMB speaks for both the president

Inside Bureaucracy with	Donna Shalala *Secretary of Health and Human Services* *(1993–2001)*

"The best way to coordinate across federal agencies is to build relationships over time, to make sure that the general counsels and inspectors general know each other. We convened groups from the Department of Justice and HHS and the Census Bureau on data issues, to make sure we knew what we were doing. For disease outbreaks, Agriculture and the EPA and HHS had to be coordinated.

"Coordination depends a lot on goodwill at the top and at the middle levels of the bureaucracy. On the Patients' Bill of Rights, Alexis Hermann from DOL and I convened everybody and said, 'Look, we've been friends for years. Don't try to play us against each other! Work together!'

"Federal agencies are very turf conscious. Our biggest problem was always the FBI and the Department of Justice. They protected information and didn't share. The FBI simply would not share. The CIA and the security agencies were much more cooperative. The FBI was awful! And they didn't know anything! It's no different today."

"Our task force on savings and loans, our whole international schemata with respect to drugs—those are all networks. They depended on the exchange of information. They depended on personal relationships between people on the front lines and on a constant review of intelligence capabilities in the broad sense. We were networking before it was called networking. Part of it involves what Tom Ridge is up against now. You need to break down barriers between people who have related responsibilities. That's always been something I've been interested in. You beat people up. You make it clear to them that there's a high price to pay if they don't cooperate. Sometimes you can't beat people up because they're in other agencies, but we spent an awful lot of time on this. We had monthly meetings of all the levels of law enforcement agencies outside the Department of Justice. On a couple of occasions, I had the president speak and lay down the law. It wasn't contentious, but it was to make clear that we were all on the same team. The notion that intelligence or information would be withheld from an agency because it was the province of another agency was just wrong. Other agencies included the IRS, the Customs Service, the Bureau of Alcohol, Tobacco, and Firearms, and the Secret Service. We had the military intelligence people at these meetings. There are law enforcement components in almost every executive branch agency. Our task was to make sure that nobody was off on a frolic on their own."

and itself. Depending on who is president, OMB will be harder or softer in its dealings with the EPA. Regardless of who is president, OMB will try to reduce the costs to be borne by regulated firms.

Interagency Coordination

Despite efforts to promote specialization and differentiation, many agencies have overlapping jurisdictions. This is especially true in foreign affairs, which tends to be characterized by "bureaucratic interconnectedness."[62] The State Department has strong incentives to worry about the design and operation of the Defense Department and vice versa; the CIA has good reason to fret about the norms and decisions of the National Security Council and vice versa. In contrast, domestic agencies tend to be somewhat less dependent on one another and less tightly connected.

For agencies with overlapping jurisdictions, the interagency task force is a frequently used coordinating technique. For example, in 1999 and 2000 a Task Force on Export Control Reform brought together representatives from the Defense Department, the Commerce Department, and the State Department in an effort to modernize and liberalize the U.S. export control regime. The task force focused on how long it took to process licenses, which technologies should be easier to export, and how the United States should treat different countries.

Interagency task forces have sometimes aroused skepticism, especially among academics. Harold Seidman, for example, wrote: "Interagency committees are the crab grass in the garden of government. Nobody wants them, but everyone has them. Committees seem to thrive on scorn and ridicule, and multiply so rapidly that attempts to weed them out appear futile." [63] Nevertheless, interagency task forces abound because they serve a useful function. Despite their difficulties, they help individual agencies share information and look beyond their own narrowly defined missions.

Czars

Another approach has been to create a "czar" to coordinate agencies and programs when a crisis suddenly erupts. President Nixon tried this approach in 1973 with the first energy crisis. The job of energy czar proved so challenging and frustrating that five individuals held the job within a memorable twelve-

Inside Bureaucracy with	Donna Shalala *Secretary of Health and Human Services* *(1993–2001)*

"Bureaucrats solve problems by talking to each other a lot, particularly as a way of minimizing risk. They ask whether the problem to be solved will result in reward or punishment. The reward could be either financial or someone saying that was a good thing you did."

month period. The experience of former Colorado governor John Love was perhaps typical: despite a fancy title, he felt that he lacked both the staff and the authority to cope effectively with his duties.[64]

Since 1988 we have had a drug czar, who has the official title of director of the Office of National Drug Control Policy. That office, located within the Executive Office of the President, has been criticized by many observers as weak and ineffectual. Though it eventually received statutory authority, it has suffered from a lack of resources and authority. A key part of the problem is that responsibility for drug policymaking and enforcement is scattered across the federal bureaucracy, in more than sixty agencies.[65] Many of these agencies have different missions and cultures, making coordination extremely difficult.

Prior to the creation of the Department of Homeland Security in November 2002, the White House had tapped Tom Ridge, former governor of Pennsylvania, to serve as director of the Office of Homeland Security. When President Bush first announced Ridge's appointment as homeland security czar on September 21, 2001, the announcement provoked two strong reactions: praise for Ridge's leadership ability and skepticism that Ridge or anyone else would be able to function effectively without adequate authority.[66] Although some observers asserted that Ridge was the right man for the job, many experts believed he was being asked to perform an impossible mission.

The mission of the Office of Homeland Security was to "lead, oversee and coordinate a comprehensive national strategy to secure the United States from terrorist threats or attacks." [67] The executive order that had created the agency granted Ridge, as director, cabinet status. Ridge enjoyed an office in the West Wing of the White House, in close proximity to the president. In October 2001 Ridge emerged as the administration's leading spokesman on terrorism, holding press conferences two to three times a week.[68]

Despite these symbolic steps, the Office of Homeland Security and its director were severely handicapped. Their ultimate goal was to coordinate the forty or fifty federal agencies that shared responsibility for the nation's homeland defense. Unfortunately, however, the office had no direct line authority over any agency with significant staff or program responsibility. As of late 2001 Ridge directed only a skeleton staff of thirty.[69] Nor did Ridge possess any authority over other agencies' budgets. The fact that his very limited mandate was rooted in an executive order, not a statute, further weakened his legitimacy. The fundamental problem, though, lay in the executive order's lack of teeth.[70]

In a scathing editorial the *New York Times* put it bluntly: "Washington seems to have swallowed up Tom Ridge since he arrived in time last fall to take charge of domestic security. Instead of forcefully coordinating the work of a host of federal agencies, Mr. Ridge has bumped from one humiliation to another as various cabinet departments have openly flouted his advice and failed to address security problems identified by their own inspector general." [71]

Frustrated by these problems, President Bush reversed course and proposed the creation of a cabinet-level Department of Homeland Security. The new department, approved by Congress in November 2002, began operating in March 2003, with Ridge as the first secretary. Among other agencies, the department comprises the Coast Guard, the Customs Service, the Immigration and Naturalization Service, the Border Patrol, the Secret Service, the Federal Emergency Management Agency, and the newly created Transportation Security Administration.[72] Because the new department includes former employees from twenty-two other federal agencies, it faces a considerable integrative challenge. But Secretary Ridge has broader authority to hire, fire, and reassign employees than most cabinet secretaries, which should make it easier to achieve integration (see Table 5.2).

Table 5.2. Agencies Shifted to Create the Department of Homeland Security

Agency	Moved from	Employees
Transportation Security Administration	Transportation	44,000
Coast Guard	Transportation	43,639
Immigration and Naturalization Service	Justice	39,459
Customs Service	Treasury	21,743
Secret Service	Treasury	6,111
Federal Emergency Management Agency	Independent	5,135
Animal and Plant Health Inspection Service	Agriculture	2,000
Federal Protective Services	General Services Administration	1,408
National Infrastructure Protection Center	FBI	795
Lawrence Livermore National Laboratory	Energy	324
Civilian Biodefense Research Programs	Health and Human Services	150
Chemical, Biological, Radiological and Nuclear Response	Health and Human Services	150
Plum Island Animal Disease Center	Agriculture	124
National Communications System	Defense	91
Critical Infrastructure Assurance Office	Commerce	65
Federal Computer Incident Response Center	General Services Administration	23
National Domestic Preparedness Office	FBI	15
National Infrastructure Simulation and Analysis Center	Energy	2

Source: John Mintz, "Homeland Agency Launched," *Washington Post,* November 26, 2002, Sec. A. ©2002 the Washington Post. Reprinted with permission.

Note: Excludes agencies for which there is no information on employee transfers.

Networks' Effectiveness

When are networks more effective? Some empirical research has been devoted to this subject. In a study of fifteen social service networks in upstate New York, Catherine Alter and Jerald Hage identified several factors that helped to predict a "performance gap" between the status quo and an idealized standard, based on the perceptions of caseworkers and administrators. As they expected, Alter and Hage found that vertical dependency was negatively related to performance and that network autonomy was positively related to performance.[73] From this finding, they inferred support for resource dependency theory, which says that a lack of control over resources weakens an organization or a cluster of organizations (a network). They also found that network complexity undermined performance but that a larger number of communication channels enhanced performance.

In a study that compared mental health networks in four cities, Keith Provan and H. Brinton Milward reached rather different conclusions.[74] Defining network effectiveness as case managers' perceptions of the overall well-being of severely mentally ill clients, Provan and Milward concluded that direct external control had a positive effect on network effectiveness. They also found that network integration, system stability, and substantial resources enhanced network performance.

In contrast to Alter and Hage, who focused on networks in a particular state, and Provan and Milward, who focused on networks in a particular policy sector, Eugene Bardach studied nineteen interagency collaboratives encompassing diverse geographic sites and diverse policy sectors.[75] He also used a qualitative research methodology, while the other scholars used a quantitative approach. Bardach concluded that four factors were most likely to produce effective networks: a technically clear mission, external demands to perform better, vigorous leadership, and a culture of pragmatism. More broadly, he concluded that network managers need to work hard to create and sustain an atmosphere of mutual trust. Edward Jennings, who examined state and local government efforts to coordinate employment and training programs, too, found leadership to be particularly important as a predictor of success. He also found it important to recognize that different programs have their own goals and that the various agencies should be treated with respect.[76]

Together these studies highlight the importance of network leadership and mutual respect, while raising questions about the desirability of external control. Because they reach somewhat different conclusions, the studies also suggest that the kind of network appropriate for one setting may be less appropriate for another. As Robert Axelrod and Michael Cohen have noted, the Linux computer software system proved itself an enormously successful network despite its being neither tightly controlled nor well funded.[77] Other observers have noted that "loosely coupled systems" can be quite effective under certain circumstances. For example, public transit in the Bay Area relies heavily on informal structures to achieve "coordination without hierarchy." [78] More ominously, al Qaeda, which wreaked havoc on the United States on September 11, offers a classic example of a loosely coupled system that has successfully pursued some of its goals.[79]

The most familiar and most celebrated of all networks is, of course, the Internet. Originally developed by the Advanced Research Projects Agency of the Defense Department as a tool for standardizing and integrating federal data, it quickly spread beyond the federal bureaucracy to academia, business, and ultimately wider society.[80] In recent years, Internet traffic has increased dramatically, by 100 percent per year.[81] By any reckoning, the Internet has been an extraordinarily successful network and, increasingly, a useful way for citizens to connect with government officials. In 2001, 55 percent of Americans who used the Internet went online to interact with the government.[82]

Tools' Effectiveness

Public officials have many tools at their disposal. As we have seen, these tools differ in their characteristics. Which tools are effective and when? In our discussion below, we focus on three of the most essential tools: grants-in-aid, regulation, and information. Each of these tools is widely used by bureaucrats, though grants-in-aid must first be authorized by politicians.

Grants-in-Aid

In intergovernmental relations, the federal government uses grants-in-aid to encourage state and local governments to spend more money on certain policy problems. Such grants-in-aid take different forms. **Categorical grants** must be used for a relatively narrow, specific program category. The Head Start program, which disburses money to local communities for the purpose of improving the school readiness of disadvantaged preschoolers, is a good example of a categorical grant. In contrast, **block grants** may be used for a variety of purposes, within a broad program area. The Child Care and Development Block Grant is a good illustration. These funds may be used to pay for child care for low-income families, to improve the availability of child care facilities, or to improve the quality of child care for all families.

Although grants-in-aid have many specific purposes, a key thrust of federal grants-in-aid has been to promote **redistributive spending** by state and local governments.[83] In general, state and local governments are less willing to allocate resources to disadvantaged residents for fear that poor citizens might migrate across political boundaries and take advantage of a specific locale's more generous social benefits. In the context of welfare policy, this phenomenon has sometimes been called the **welfare magnet effect** because states with higher welfare payments are thought to exert a magnetic pull on disadvantaged citizens.[84]

Some grants-in-aid programs have produced relatively clear and relatively positive results. The interstate highway program, inaugurated during the Eisenhower administration, within two decades produced a remarkable latticework of highways that facilitates interstate commerce and tourism. The Medicaid program, initiated during the Lyndon Johnson administration, has enabled millions of poor persons, especially children and senior citizens, to receive timely medical care. The Head Start program, another Johnson-era initiative, has also generated generally favorable reviews, though doubts remain as to the persistence of its effects on cognitive development.

Yet some federal grants-in-aid programs essentially substitute federal dollars for expenditures that state and local governments would have undertaken in any event. Students of fiscal federalism posited this phenomenon, known as the **crowd out hypothesis,** years ago, and it has recently found empirical support.[85] The extent of crowd out, however, seems to depend on tool design: the generosity of the federal match, whether there is ceiling, or "cap," on matching funds, and related factors.[86] Through better tool design, public officials may be able to mitigate the phenomenon of state and local governments' substituting federal dollars for their own dollars.

Other problems have proved even more vexing. Whatever economic theories or theories of justice might suggest, political factors play a major role in determining how grants-in-aid will be distributed. As a result, the federal government allocates grants not just to the neediest of states and communities but to less needy governments as well. Another concern is that grants undermine accountability by creating a disjunction between the level of government that raises the money and the level of government that spends the money. If an intergovernmental program becomes embroiled in controversy, as the Medicaid program sometimes does, then who should be blamed? The federal government that failed to prevent abuse, or the state government that perpetrated the abuse?

After weighing the evidence, two careful students of grants-in-aid, David Beam and Timothy Conlan, have concluded that "grants merit an overall moderate rating in terms of effectiveness." [87] When properly administered, grants-in-aid enable federal officials to promote redistributive goals and to compensate for externalities that spill across state boundaries (for example, water pollution, air pollution). More broadly, grants-in-aid represent a **hortatory control** that can be extremely useful as an alternative to more coercive mechanisms that often produce dysfunctional results.[88]

Regulation

If grants are carrots, regulations are sticks. By definition, regulation is a coercive policy instrument, though the degree of coercion varies considerably. A regulation requiring a coal-burning utility to use low-sulfur coal is far more coercive than a regulation requiring that same utility to open its doors to periodic inspections. A regulation requiring a day care center to maintain child-staff ratios of seven to one for preschool children is far more restrictive than a regulation requiring that center to arrange for periodic in-service training experiences for its professional staff.

Regulations can make a difference in policy outcomes. A careful study of state air pollution standards found that states with stronger regulatory standards experienced sharper reductions in sulfur dioxide and nitrogen dioxide.[89] A study of day care centers in four states found the poorest quality in the state with the weakest standards.[90] Regulatory enforcement can also make a difference. The imposition of monetary penalties by Occupational Safety and Health Administration inspectors improved the safety records of penalized firms.[91] Reduced surveillance of day care centers with reasonably good track records led to a higher number of code violations at the neglected centers.[92]

Critics argue that regulation is less efficient than reliance on markets or marketlike incentives. Certainly, under favorable circumstances marketlike approaches can produce good results. For example, the Clean Air Act authorizes **emissions trading** in an effort to encourage plants to agree to sharper than average emissions reductions in return for cash payments if they can make such reductions more cheaply than other plants. The early returns suggest that emissions trading has been a success.[93]

The case for or against regulation depends in part on the type of regulation involved. Consider, for example, **economic regulation,** which seeks to improve the functioning of certain markets through entry and exit restrictions or price controls. Such regulation is necessary when an industry is characterized by **natural monopolies,** in which the presence of competitive firms would be inefficient and inadvisable. For years analysts considered telephone companies and electric companies to be natural monopolies. With technological advances, however, it has become possible to achieve even greater efficiency through the introduction of competition or limited competition. Under such circumstances, **deregulation** makes sense. It can, however, backfire if pursued too zealously, as when California deregulated its electric utilities without providing for adequate safeguards.[94] As a result of hasty deregulation, California's electric utilities experienced dramatic increases in wholesale electricity prices. When utility companies could not pay their bills, some suppliers balked at selling electricity to them, resulting in intermittent blackouts throughout the state.

In contrast, **social regulation** seeks to curb or restrict behavior by individuals or firms that interferes with public health or safety. The case for social regulation is particularly strong when liability and tort systems prove cumbersome as mechanisms for correcting market failures.[95] But much depends on the willingness of individuals and firms to comply with regulatory requirements. Sometimes compliance is slow at first but picks up over time. When the federal government first required the use of seatbelts, many citizens balked at what seemed like a silly requirement. In time seatbelt use has become common enough to save thousands of lives, which in turn has encouraged even higher levels of seatbelt use.[96]

Information

A central aim of interagency coordination is the sharing of information. Such information sharing may help agencies to specialize in different tasks, to share wisdom concerning best practices, or to move in tandem toward mutual goals. Information sharing is also important in intergovernmental relations and in public-private partnerships. Feedback on performance is one vital form of information sharing; clarification of goals and procedural rules another.

In recent years bureaucracies have devoted more resources to sharing information with the general public. The Federal Trade Commission has required cigarette manufacturers to place warning labels on their products, and the Food and Drug Administration has required companies to prepare nutritional labels to clarify the contents of foods and vitamins. The empirical literature on labeling suggests that it can have an impact. For example, one study found a decline in drinking during pregnancy beginning in 1990, eight months after the implementation of alcohol warning labels.[97]

Bureaucracies have also launched information campaigns aimed at discouraging drug use and promiscuous sexual behavior and at recruiting young people for military careers. Such campaigns have succeeded in some instances, though not in others. Energy conservation messages from the New York Public Service Commission proved more effective than identical messages from a private utility company.[98] Energy conservation messages from the Department of Energy proved more effective when less technical and less complex.[99]

Increasingly, bureaucracies have promoted the use of **organizational report cards,** which compare the performance of two or more organizations. Studies show that such report cards can affect both public and organizational behavior. Following the introduction of a hospital report card in New York state, deaths resulting from botched heart surgery declined more rapidly in New York than in other states.[100] Following the introduction of a public school report card in North Carolina, schools whose students had performed poorly on standardized tests did better the next time around.[101]

When is information a useful policy tool? Janet Weiss, a careful student of the subject, argues that information is most useful under the following circumstances:

- when the problem is caused by information asymmetry or information that is difficult to obtain;
- when the targets of public policy are very broadly dispersed but not organized;
- when the interests of policymakers and those of targeted individuals or groups are closely aligned so that voluntary compliance is likely to occur;
- when there is broad agreement about desired outcomes; and
- when no legal or politically acceptable alternative tools are available or when policy outcomes occur in partnerships or coalitions in which command-and-control approaches are impermissible.[102]

We would add to these excellent observations that information is an especially potent tool when combined with other tools, such as financial incentives or the threat of government regulation.

Networks: Some Conclusions

Although bureaucracies might prefer to act independently, much of what they do is done in concert with other bureaucracies, other levels of government, nonprofit organizations, and for-profit firms. In short, bureaucracies work through interorganizational networks. A key characteristic of such networks is that each organization has its own distinctive goals. Furthermore, organizations that belong to a network often differ in their political and economic resources. Another key characteristic is that the relationship between organizations is not purely hierarchical: one network member cannot simply tell another network member what to do.

For some networks to be effective, much is required. In many intergovernmental networks and in many public-private partnerships, some modus vivendi must be achieved between organizations with different missions and goals. Without this, organizations will be pulling in different directions and performance will suffer. In addition, some consensus must be reached on which organization is responsible for the success or failure of a particular task. Without this, citizens and politicians will be unable to hold networks accountable.

For other networks to be effective, less is required. Interagency coordination, for example, is sometimes a matter of information sharing. When one organization is not being asked to implement another organization's policies, it may be sufficient for organizations to share timely information about activities and initiatives so that agencies with overlapping jurisdictions can avoid conflict or duplication. One can easily underestimate the difficulty of information sharing across agencies. Still, it is, in principle, more feasible than changing another agency's point of view.

In thinking about networks, we have borrowed from two theoretical traditions. The first, from sociology, is often called network theory. It emphasizes such concepts as centrality and density and seeks to map network structures. Some progress has been made in identifying key network characteristics and in linking such characteristics to network performance. On balance, however, the empirical literature is relatively sparse, especially when it comes to outcomes. The second tradition, from political science and public administration, is sometimes called the tools approach. While this literature is more scattered and diffuse, it is also more extensive. Its theoretical propositions are less cohesive, and its empirical applications often confined to a single type of network, such as public-private partnerships or intergovernmental relations. But the tools literature, unlike the network theory literature, almost always seeks to explain variations in performance rather than studying communication for its own sake.

From the network theory literature we may conclude that networks function better if they possess ample resources and strong leadership. The role of external control is less clear. Although some research celebrates the advantages of network autonomy, other research finds that external control enhances performance, perhaps because it strengthens accountability.

From the tools literature we may conclude that the effectiveness of particular tools is highly contextual. Grants-in-aid can be useful tools for federal policymaking if designed to promote goals that state and local governments would not otherwise pursue (for example, redistribution) and to inhibit state and local governments from substituting federal dollars for their own resources. Contracts can be useful tools for officials at all levels of government if contractors are selected not just to reduce costs but also with the quality of services in mind. Regulations can be useful tools for officials at all levels of government, provided that the economics of a given industry (air transportation, child care, occupational safety and health) is carefully understood by government regulators.

As for information, it is the one indispensable tool that makes the other tools work. Without good information, federal policymakers cannot know how state and local officials are using federal tax dollars. Without good information, bureaucracies cannot be sure that contractors are accomplishing designated goals. Without good information, government regulators cannot correct for unexpected consequences that have the potential to undermine government policies. In this respect the network theory literature is right on target—communication between organizations that share responsibility for service delivery is essential. However, as the tools literature reminds us, what matters is not just who communicates with whom and how often but also what they say to one another and how much leverage the various parties have over one another.

Key Terms

6 | Bringing the Theoretical Frameworks Together—Four Bureaucracies in Action

As THE PRECEDING CHAPTERS HAVE demonstrated, the bureaucracy is an amalgam of individuals and organizations that makes fundamentally important policy decisions in areas ranging from aircraft repair and maintenance to zinc chloride contamination of drinking water. The bureaucracy's scope and complexity are evident in the processes agency officials use to formulate rules, in the instruments of agency design and oversight employed by legislators and other political principals, in the activities and influence exercised by the beneficiaries and targets of agency actions, and in the networks and tools that connect agencies to one another and to the outside world.

Despite this scope and complexity, we have found it fruitful to conduct a systematic inquiry of the executive branch by applying four social scientific theories to various aspects of bureaucratic accountability and performance. Our approach has been to explicate these frameworks one at a time and then to assess the insights provided by each in a specific domain in which that framework has proven to be particularly useful. For example, through its emphasis on delegation, the management of delegated authority, and the inevitability of agency loss, principal-agent theory has much to say about the relationship between agencies and their supervisors. Along the way we have emphasized that the frameworks have broad applications, well beyond those explored in the heart of the analysis. In the case of principal-agent theory, the role occupied by clients takes on a unique cast, as citizens and organized interests come across as potentially powerful third parties in the political-bureaucratic hierarchy.

In this chapter, we seek to broaden the application of the theoretical frameworks even further. Specifically, we bring the theories together by applying them jointly to four case studies of bureaucracies in action. Two concern federal agencies—the Federal Trade Commission and the Centers for Medicare and Medicaid Services—while the other two concern state bureaucracies—the Florida Department of Environmental Protection and the Maryland Department of Health and Mental Hygiene.

These joint applications have two main advantages. First, in a single institutional context the theoretical frameworks can be viewed and assessed side by side. To this point we have observed the theories at work in lots of different agencies and decisional settings. By holding such factors constant, the relative merits of the frameworks can be judged from a different vantage point. Second, important interactions between the predictions of the theoretical frameworks can be seen, interactions that cannot be discerned in isolation. To take one example, the utility of standard operating procedures as problem solving devices depends in part on the prevalence of interorganizational networks and the degree of centrality, density, multiplexity, and differentiation found in these networks. Connections such as this highlight the importance of bringing the theories together, a task made easier by the fact that the frameworks are, by this point in the analysis, well understood in all of their individual nuances.

In the sections that follow, we focus on three core questions:

- *DOES EACH THEORY LEND ITSELF TO PREDICTIONS AND APPLICATIONS?* A good theory has some predictive utility.

- *DO THE THEORIES COMPLEMENT ONE ANOTHER AND ENHANCE OUR UNDERSTANDING OF HOW THE BUREAUCRACY ACTUALLY WORKS?* Each theory highlights a different set of relationships and different aspects of bureaucratic behavior. We expect the theories together to be more illuminating than any single theory.

- *UNDER WHAT CIRCUMSTANCES IS ONE THEORY MORE USEFUL THAN THE OTHERS?* It is entirely possible, for example, that one theory is more relevant to more salient issues, that another theory is more relevant to less salient issues.

The Federal Trade Commission: An Agency Out of Control?

The Federal Trade Commission (FTC) is an independent agency of the executive branch, outside the jurisdiction of the fifteen cabinet departments. As documented in chapter 1, the FTC shares this status with about sixty other organizations, including the Environmental Protection Agency (EPA), the National Science Foundation, and the Equal Employment Opportunity Commission. Relatively small, with a staff of fewer than 1,000, the FTC is led by five **commissioners,** each appointed by the president and confirmed by the Senate for a seven-year term. One commissioner is designated as chair. The agency is charged with enforcing a variety of federal antitrust and consumer protection laws. Specifically, its mission is to ensure that the nation's markets are competitive and that consumers are free to exercise informed choices within these markets.[1]

The four theories highlighted in the book can help us understand the FTC's internal operation as well as its interactions with political institutions and societal forces. In some cases the frameworks lead to conclusions that fly in the face of conventional accounts of the agency and its environment. For a long time, observers considered the FTC a poster child for runaway bureaucracy, a reputation developed in the late 1970s, when Congress publicly took the agency to task and placed curbs on its regulatory authority. These actions were widely seen as a response to a burst of activism prior to, and during, the Carter administration in which the FTC stoked controversy by, among other things, aggressively pursuing antitrust lawsuits against oil producers and cereal manufacturers. Congress, so the argument went, took drastic steps to bring back into line an agency long out of control.[2]

An application of principal-agent theory, however, suggests that the FTC may have been broadly responding to congressional wishes all along. One of the main lessons of principal-agent theory is that a lack of active, visible oversight may be an indication that institutional design and the threat of sanctions are effective in compelling agencies to make decisions basically consistent with the desires of their political bosses. In other words, well-designed institutions and monitoring devices minimize the amount of agency shirking or sabotage that accompanies delegation to the bureaucracy.

A look at the Senate subcommittee with jurisdiction over the FTC provides some support for this account. For years liberal consumer activists who backed and encouraged an expansive FTC mission dominated the Subcommittee on Consumer Affairs. The 1976 elections radically altered the subcommittee's membership, bringing to power a much more conservative majority. This new group of legislators used the subcommittee's authority to curb and redirect the agency's activities. When viewed in this way, the FTC has always been reasonably accountable to Congress, and the abrupt confrontation of the late 1970s reflected changes within Congress rather than long-standing agency intransigence.

The dispute between Congress and the FTC raises an interesting question: How does the agency decide what types of actions to pursue? Consistent with the bounded rationality perspective, economists and lawyers at the FTC rely on standard operating procedures rooted in professional norms.[3] For economists, trained to be skeptical of government solutions to social and economic problems, these norms dictate pursuing a small number of cases. More often than not, these cases entail complex structural matters that, when resolved, deliver significant benefits to consumers. In contrast, lawyers favor an expansive caseload, with a special focus on matters that can be brought to trial quickly, a preference derived from the prosecutorial nature of the legal profession. In addition, many FTC lawyers have their eyes on lucrative careers outside of government, and trial experience is a prerequisite for making the leap to the private sector. For both economists and lawyers, then, professional norms provide valuable shortcuts for dealing with the complex process of case selection. In the end such shortcuts result in outcomes that are, from the perspective of these decision makers, if not ideal, then certainly satisfactory. As we have seen, however, these outcomes may not be pleasing to the outside political world.

Generally speaking, the actions the FTC takes and the policies it implements entail the imposition on industry of concentrated costs and the delivery to the public of diffuse benefits. With this in mind, the interest group mobilization framework predicts that the politics of antitrust regulation and consumer protection will more often than not be driven by policy entrepreneurs—advocates from both inside and outside government who take on organized interests in the name of the citizenry. The long history of the politics of cigarette labeling bears out this prediction.

Since the 1960s public health experts have sought to draw ever-greater attention to the hazards of cigarette smoking. One of their initial policy prescriptions was the placement of warning labels on cigarette packs and cartons. For many years the tobacco industry fended off this effort by politically out-muscling advocacy organizations such as the American Cancer Society. Not until the emergence of several entrepreneurs did the tide turn and labeling become a reality. Perhaps the most important entrepreneur was Matt Myers, the chief lobbyist for the Coalition on Smoking or Health, an amalgam of public health organizations. Displaying extraordinary persistence and skill, Myers managed to drum up support for labeling not only among sympathetic northeastern liberal Democrats but also among legislators from tobacco states, including a young Tennessee representative named Al Gore. In the end it was the actions of policy entrepreneurs that shattered the aura of invincibility that had long surrounded the tobacco industry, paving the way for a series of significant policy changes implemented by the FTC and still in effect today.[4]

The FTC is not the only agency that deals with antitrust and consumer protection issues. Since 1948 the FTC has shared responsibility for investigating proposed corporate mergers with the Antitrust Division of the Department of Justice (DOJ). On both sides the practice has long been not to begin an investigation until the other agency has issued a "clearance." **Clearance agreements** lay out which of the two agencies will take the lead in investigating particular mergers. Through this arrangement, the FTC and the DOJ avoid duplicating each other's efforts and take best advantage of their collective expertise. For example, since the FTC has experience in dealing with automobile manufacturers, it normally investigates mergers in that industry. Similarly, the DOJ typically takes the lead when it comes to investigating steel mergers.

Up until recent years the clearance system worked well. The blurring of traditional industrial boundaries, however, has led to a sharp rise in conflict between the FTC and the DOJ. One investigation was delayed by more than a year because neither agency would clear it to the other. It was in this context that, in 2002, the agencies negotiated a new clearance agreement that recognized the overlapping nature of the contemporary economy and brought greater speed and transparency to the process.[5]

Although the new agreement had wide support, it faced opposition from Sen. Fritz Hollings, D-S.C., the chair of the Senate Commerce Committee, as well as from some consumer groups. Primarily, these parties objected to the fact that the agreement gave the DOJ jurisdiction over media mergers. In the critics' view, DOJ investigations would be subject to greater political pressure than those conducted by an independent regulatory commission. Opponents worried that under Republican administrations, such pressure could produce merger decisions with a decidedly pro-industry bent. In light of complaints such as these, and Senator Hollings's threat to suspend funding for the salaries of the FTC's commissioners and senior staff, the agreement was scuttled only months after its announcement.[6]

As the theoretical frameworks have demonstrated, the FTC is hardly an agency impervious to outside influence and control. Members of Congress, through threats and sanctions, have significantly shaped the agency's behavior, in terms of both its general stance on antitrust and consumer protection and its decision making in particular cases. Similarly, the FTC's interactions with other agencies, including the DOJ, have fundamentally affected its jurisdiction, performance, and accountability. Forces outside of government shape the FTC's environment as well, as entrepreneurial politics have played a recurring role in the agency's history. Finally, the FTC is far from united internally. Ongoing conflicts, such as the one between economists and lawyers over case selection, make it difficult to speak of the FTC as a monolithic organization.

The Centers for Medicare and Medicaid Services: To Waive or Not to Waive?

In June 2001 the name of the agency that administers many of the nation's largest health care programs was changed from the Health Care Financing Administration to the Centers for Medicare and Medicaid Services (CMS). In announcing this new identity, Tommy Thompson, the secretary of Health and Human Services, emphasized, "We're making quality service the Number One priority." This service orientation was to be witnessed in a number of ways, such as the expansion of a 1-800 telephone line to answer questions about Medicare and a $35 million public relations campaign to alert the elderly to their health insurance options.[7]

CMS runs some of the programs under its jurisdiction, such as Medicaid and the Children's Health Insurance Program, in partnership with state governments, thus making service to the states an important component of the agency's ongoing mission. One way in which CMS provides such service is by granting states **waivers** from the legal requirements of its programs. In 1994 Tennessee received a waiver that enabled it to create TennCare, a landmark program that shifted its Medicaid population to managed care providers such as health maintenance organizations. For Tennessee the waiver offered the promise of providing health care to a greater number of needy citizens without the imposition of new taxes. From the agency's perspective, programs such as TennCare act as policy experiments. Successful waivers can be imitated by other states or even required for adoption by the federal government, while waivers that fall short of expectations can be abandoned before their reach extends beyond their initial boundaries.

With such high stakes, CMS subjects waiver requests to a process of critical consideration. Consistent with the notion of bounded rationality, the agency relies heavily on standard operating procedures when deciding whether to grant a waiver. To secure one, a state must show that access to quality care will not be "substantially impaired." [8] A state must also demonstrate budget neutrality. To simplify the waiver application and approval process, CMS has developed model waiver documents, which are made available to the states. The agency has also prepared a checklist summarizing the key requirements of the process. These procedures help CMS zero in on the substantive and political issues that really matter to its decision makers, generally making the waiver process much more manageable for all parties.

Like other federal agencies, CMS is accountable to a number of political principals, including Congress and the president. Because the agency is located within the Department of Health and Human Services, the chain of command flows from these principals through the department's secretary and then down to CMS. Following a waiver request, the agency often hears from elected officials and their surrogates, including members of Congress, congressional aides, and White House staff.

During the Clinton administration, the White House was generally supportive of waiver requests. According to Tim Westmoreland, who served as the head of CMS's Center for Medicaid and State Operations, "President Clinton, as a former governor, was sympathetic to letting states try different ideas." [9] Occasionally, the White House applied pressure on the agency to approve a waiver. For example, Ned McWherter, Democratic governor of Tennessee and an old friend of Bill Clinton's, enjoyed considerable political capital within the White House. When he proposed the establishment of TennCare, CMS approved the waiver despite significant reservations within the agency. Indeed, as it turned out, the transition to managed care was rocky and controversial for reasons ranging from bad planning to insufficient funding to poor administration. [10]

Organized interests routinely get involved in the waiver process, either on their own initiative or at the behest of government officials. During the Clinton administration, CMS sometimes required states to conduct public hearings as part of their applications. At a series of such hearings in New

York, officials heard from advocacy groups and representatives of medical providers. As a result of the input of these interests, clauses were included in the waiver agreement that improved access for persons with limited English proficiency and that strengthened the fair hearing and grievance process for individuals denied services.

Although the norm is for organized interests to shape the content of waiver agreements, groups occasionally influence the more basic decision of whether a waiver will be granted. When New Mexico requested reauthorization of a managed care waiver, known as a 1915b waiver, the Bazelon Center for Mental Health Law opposed the request, arguing that serious deficiencies marred the state's managed care services in the area of mental health. In opposing the waiver, the Bazelon Center worked closely with New Mexico's Human Needs Coordinating Council, a coalition of 600 health and human services clients and organizations. The center also aligned itself with members of the state's congressional delegation from both political parties.[11] From the perspective of the interest group mobilization framework, the effort to terminate the waiver involved concentrated costs (to mental health service providers) and concentrated benefits (to mental health clients). In this instance, interest group lobbying, supported by legislative pressure, helped to convince CMS to end the waiver. The Bazelon Center's victory, however, proved short-lived. When the Bush administration came to office in 2001, CMS promptly reinstated the waiver.

By the tenets of network theory, the flow of communication within and across organizations helps to determine the content of the decisions emanating from them. If the White House insists on being consulted before managed care waivers are approved or denied, as was the case in the Clinton administration, the president's preferences stand a better chance of being reflected in CMS decisions. This reality illustrates the importance of centrality in networks.

Within CMS itself, structural arrangements magnified or diminished the influence of particular officials. Prior to 1997 the Office of Research and Demonstrations processed certain types of waivers, while the Medicaid Bureau handled others. Following a reorganization, requests of all sorts were funneled through the director of the Center for Medicaid and State Operations.[12] This redirection undoubtedly enhanced the director's influence over the waiver process and its outcomes.

The general inclination of CMS to be favorably disposed toward waivers is indicated in Table 6.1. Nineteen state governments and the District of

Table 6.1 State Experiences with Section 1115 Medicaid Waivers

Approved Waivers	Proposals Withdrawn	Waiver Terminated	Waiver Expired
Arizona	Florida	Alabama	Illinois
Arkansas	Kansas		Ohio
California	Texas		Tennessee
Delaware			
District of Columbia			
Hawaii			
Kentucky			
Maryland			
Massachusetts			
Minnesota			
Missouri			
New Jersey			
New York			
Oklahoma			
Oregon			
Rhode Island			
Tennessee			
Utah			
Vermont			
Wisconsin			

Source: Centers for Medicare and Medicaid Services, http://www.cms.gov/medicaid/1115/default.asp, March 31, 2003.

Note: Tennessee has operated its TennCare program under two waivers. The first waiver was approved in 1993 and expired in 2002. The second waiver, which redesigned TennCare, has been in operation since the initial waiver ended.

Columbia currently operate their Medicaid programs under Section 1115 health care reform demonstrations, a broad designation that allows states to test a wide variety of managed care and other new policy ideas. By contrast, only three states have withdrawn their waiver proposals, only three waivers have expired, and only one waiver has been terminated. Furthermore, well less than a year typically elapses between the submission of a proposal by a state and CMS approval of the proposal. From this perspective, CMS has been effectively serving state governments, one of the agency's vital clients and partners, for many years.

The Florida Department of Environmental Protection: Accountability through Performance Reports

In the late 1990s the Florida Department of Environmental Protection (DEP) committed itself to a new approach to addressing environmental problems. The essence of this approach was to define problems with precision, prioritize these problems, gather good information to guide agency officials, explore possible solutions, develop policy prescriptions, and follow up to make sure the problems had abated.[13] A key operational decision was the inauguration of quarterly performance reports, which were to be filled with lots of indicators aimed at measuring progress toward established goals. Another important decision was for the DEP's secretary to use these reports to designate certain problems as "watch" areas (the rough equivalent of a tornado watch) and other, more urgent problems as "focus" areas (the rough equivalent of a tornado warning).

In several respects, the DEP's strategy epitomized bounded rational decision making. It explicitly recognized that the agency's resources are limited and acknowledged that tasks need to be decomposed into manageable parts. It explicitly appreciated the need to socialize agency officials to accept norms that promote forward progress. And it explicitly utilized attention as a device for ensuring that some pressing problems get placed at the head of the queue.

The origin of the DEP's strategy can be traced to several key individuals, including Mike Phillips, then chief of staff to Secretary Virginia Wetherell, and Malcolm Sparrow, a Harvard University lecturer and agency consultant. The strategy reflected the DEP's growing level of comfort with the federal government's Environmental Protection Agency, in particular the agency's regional office in Atlanta. A barbecue held in Tallahassee in fall 1996 for DEP and EPA staff proved a key event as it provided them with an excellent opportunity to initiate and cement informal relationships. As relations between the DEP and its federal counterpart grew friendlier, the two organizations agreed on the rough outlines of a **performance partnership agreement.** Adopted in 1997, the agreement offered Florida greater flexibility in its reporting and offered the federal government assurances of more rapid progress toward environmental goals. Slowly but surely, the DEP was becoming part of a wider intergovernmental network. A new partnership had begun, rooted in hortatory controls rather than mandates.

Ultimately, however, civil servants are constrained by politicians and their appointees. When a new governor, Jeb Bush, took office in 1999, he appointed David Struhs to replace Wetherell as secretary of the DEP. Although Struhs expressed initial support for the quarterly reports and **focus/watch designations** inaugurated by his predecessor, he eventually suspended the designations and converted the reports into electronic updates. In addition, Struhs's deputy, Kirby Greene, made it clear that the DEP would not automatically accept a series of core performance measures approved by the EPA and the Environmental Council of the States. As he put it, "We question the applicability [of core performance measures] across all states. We're not going to report for the sake of reporting." [14] In effect, Florida was saying that it rejected the premise of a principal-agent relationship between the EPA and the DEP. Beyond that, Florida was also saying that understandings reached under previous governors were not binding on the new administration, which came to office with its own set of political and policy convictions.

Somewhat surprisingly, environmental groups never really got involved in the development of the new problem-solving strategy or the drafting of environmental performance reports. Instead they focused their attention on more substantive policy problems, such as the safety of the public water supply and underground injection systems. [15] In theory, an action-oriented performance measurement system should be enticing to environmental advocates because it offers widely distributed benefits to the general public. In practice, however, it is hard to convince public interest groups that managerial reform warrants their attention.

In contrast, industry groups did get involved, particularly when the focus/watch system singled out a specific industry. For example, when the DEP designated shellfish processing as a focus area, representatives of the shellfish industry played a significant consultation role. Ultimately, the DEP institutionalized several new management practices, such as voluntary in-plant training, that were acceptable to shellfish processors. [16]

The DEP's experiences highlight the fact that accountability and performance often cannot be treated separately. Put differently, the agency's movement toward quarterly reports and focus/watch designations did not occur in a political vacuum. Rather, these reforms occurred with the blessing of the agency's appointed leadership and were undone when the electoral tides turned. As will be discussed in chapter 7, accountability in all of its forms has significant implications for agencies and their ability to deliver well-received performances.

The Maryland Department of Health and Mental Hygiene: The Promise and Limitations of Leadership

In the summer of 2000 Debbie Chang found herself in an unenviable position. As director of the Medicaid program in Maryland, Chang was responsible for ensuring that the state's low-income families had access to health care services. This mission was jeopardized when CareFirst BlueCross BlueShield, a health maintenance organization with more than 100,000 Medicaid clients, announced its intention to pull out of the program.[17] CareFirst's executives complained that state reimbursement rates were woefully inadequate, causing the company to lose millions of dollars. On the one hand, if Medicaid payments were not dramatically raised, poor families would be at best inconvenienced by CareFirst's departure and at worst find it prohibitively difficult to secure essential services. On the other hand, increasing Medicaid spending was not fiscally and politically viable at a time when the economic boom of the 1990s was ending and the state's budget was tightening. What could Chang do?

Almost immediately Chang and other key decision makers in the Department of Health and Mental Hygiene ruled out a variety of plausible options.[18] For example, the agency never seriously entertained the idea of discontinuing its managed care program, dubbed HealthChoice, in the urban areas where many of CareFirst's clients resided. A return to fee-for-service medicine, the traditional way of paying for Medicaid and other forms of health care, was out of the question because of the significant spending increases such a move would have precipitated.

In some respects Chang initiated a decision-making process consistent with the tenets of bounded rationality. She quickly focused attention on identifying a way to cover CareFirst's clients through managed care plans already serving the state's Medicaid population. In other respects, however, this case demonstrates the limits of bounded rationality as a way of understanding bureaucratic behavior. Shortcuts such as memory and habit, given great currency in bounded rationality, were not very useful to Chang as CareFirst's pullout was unprecedented and unique in its economic and political implications.

In place of such shortcuts the department initiated a brainstorming effort that produced a novel solution to the CareFirst crisis.[19] Another health maintenance organization—Maryland Physicians Care (MPC)—agreed to take over the beneficiaries dropped by CareFirst. In return the agency agreed to assume the financial risk of these beneficiaries for the rest of the year. Under this arrangement the agency would compensate MPC if the costs of delivering care to the beneficiaries exceeded Medicaid reimbursements. If, however, costs turned out to be lower than reimbursements, then MPC would return excess payments to the agency.

Although this solution came largely from within the department, Chang and other agency leaders have historically maintained close connections with their counterparts in other states. One forum for such networks is the National Association of State Medicaid Directors. Through this association Medicaid directors act jointly in a variety of capacities, such as offering comments on federal regulations, holding conferences and publishing reports, and conducting research on specific policy problems and their prospective solutions.[20]

The myriad informal interactions that occur continually among Medicaid directors augment this network. For example, other directors who face difficulties or uncertainties in their Children's Health Insurance Program (CHIP) regularly sought Chang's assistance because, prior to becoming Maryland's Medicaid director, she served in the Clinton administration as a specialist on CHIP and its implementation.

Department officials interact not only with policymakers from other states but also with organized interests operating inside of Maryland's borders. Many of these groups represent constituencies, such as managed care organizations, physicians, and other providers, that reap significant financial benefits from the HealthChoice program. These organizations include the Maryland State Medical Society and the six health plans that enroll Medicaid beneficiaries.[21]

Most of the time these constituencies communicate with the department on an individual basis. Occasionally, however, the agency utilizes the Maryland Medicaid Advisory Committee, a collaborative body charged with offering advice on the implementation, operation, and evaluation of the HealthChoice program.[22] Chang also solicited the participation of Medicaid families themselves by periodically convening beneficiary focus groups. Although time consuming, these sessions allow the agency to receive feedback directly from clients. Importantly, this feedback often varies significantly from the positions articulated by organized interests, even those that advocate on behalf of Medicaid beneficiaries.

All in all, Maryland's Medicaid program, with its emphasis on managed care, usually operates within the context of client politics. The costs of the program are widely distributed across taxpayers at both the federal and state levels. The program's financial benefits accrue to a much smaller set of interests, most notably the half-dozen health plans participating in HealthChoice and the physicians and other providers delivering managed care to Medicaid recipients. The prospect of reaping significant material rewards clearly mobilizes these interests.

In contrast, Medicaid clients often loom as latent participants in Health-Choice, even though they hold a vital stake in the program. It is only when advocacy groups or department officials actively solicit client involvement that this constituency's voices are loudly heard. In these instances the politics of Medicaid managed care become increasingly majoritarian, with broad, ideological considerations brought into discussions of HealthChoice's role in serving the state's neediest residents.

The department is an agent to principals at both the state and federal levels. The HealthChoice program is highly salient to Maryland's Senate and General Assembly, and legislators in both chambers are in constant contact with Chang and other key officials. The agency also works closely with the Centers for Medicare and Medicaid Services, particularly in developing and implementing innovative approaches to health care financing, organization, and delivery. In 2002 the agency received a waiver for a novel pharmacy discount program.

The waiver system vividly illustrates the importance of the identity of an agency's principals. The Clinton and second Bush administrations strongly advocated state experimentation and innovation, a similarity not at all surprising given that both presidents had previously served as governors. The nature of the waivers favored by each administration differed markedly, however. Under Bill Clinton great emphasis was placed on experiments designed to expand Medicaid coverage to new adult populations. Under George W. Bush the emphasis shifted to innovations that significantly reduce the costs of the Medicaid program. In the end political directives such as these set the broad parameters within which the department must work. Although very real, these constraints nevertheless leave room for significant discretion on the part of agency decision makers. In the case of the CareFirst pullout, Chang used this discretion to craft a solution that ultimately proved satisfactory not only to politicians but also to Medicaid officials, the managed care industry, and the beneficiaries of the Health-Choice program.

In general, the experiences of the Department of Health and Mental Hygiene highlight the importance of agency leaders as well as the difficulties faced by even the most capable executives. From the perspective of federal officials, policymakers in other states, and program constituencies within Maryland, Chang's expertise and professional background made her a standout among Medicaid directors. The political context, however, placed limits on what Chang could accomplish by establishing the broad agenda for the Medicaid program and setting specific policy priorities. When the 2002 election of Republican governor Bob Ehrlich ended decades of Democratic hegemony in Maryland's executive branch, Chang's tenure as Medicaid director came to an end as well.

Lessons and Limitations

What lessons can be learned from bringing together the theoretical frameworks via the case studies explored in this chapter? First, the theories provide insights into agency behavior that might otherwise be obscured. The emphasis of principal-agent theory on institutional design draws our attention to the political underpinnings of agency structures and processes. The Federal Trade Commission's zigs and zags may seem arbitrary and capricious at first but are in fact roughly consistent with the changing policy preferences of the agency's congressional overseers. Shirking may occur but is far less likely when principals send strong, consistent signals on issues of concern.

Second, there are important interactions between the insights provided by the frameworks. All four agencies exhibited behaviors compatible with the tenets of bounded rationality. The specifics of the satisficing approaches that were adopted, however, owed much to the political environment within which the agencies' decision makers operated. For example, the standard operating procedures developed by CMS served to facilitate, rather than impede, the consideration and approval of waiver requests. Such facilitation was clearly in line with the expressed preferences of Presidents Clinton and Bush, both former governors and staunch advocates of state-level policy experimentation.

As with any case study or set of case studies, there are limitations to what can be learned from the experiences of the agencies at hand. In sitting out the fight over the Florida Department of Environmental Protection's performance reforms, environmental advocates failed to provide the entrepreneur-ship expected by the interest group mobilization framework. This observation raises the question of whether similar dynamics have occurred in other states, a question that can only be answered through additional analysis. Even in highlighting such uncertainties the case studies have illustrated the utility of the theoretical frameworks in sharpening our understanding of accountability and performance in the executive branch.

Key Terms

7 | Why Are Some Bureaucracies Better Than Others?

As the theoretical frameworks and case studies throughout the book have demonstrated, executive branch bureaucracies are policymaking organizations that operate as institutions of American democracy. As one observer has put it, agencies "shape decisions that influence the quality of the air you breathe, how safe your car is, which immigrants will enter and stay in this country, how airports will be protected from terrorism, what you can expect from your employer in terms of working conditions and pension, and how safe that hamburger is that you just put in your mouth." [1] In terms of affecting our lives on a day-to-day basis, the bureaucracy has no peer among government institutions.

Although this influence is exercised by organizations not directly connected to the elections that form the backbone of U.S. democracy, it is inaccurate to portray the bureaucracy as being aloof from citizens and their elected representatives. From oversight by powerful congressional committees to testimony by the most common of folk, agencies stay in constant contact with their political supervisors and those in society upon whom their actions bestow benefits and impose costs. In the context of these interactions, two standards have become paramount in judging agencies as public policymakers: accountability and performance. Accountability has been a concern since the bureaucracy emerged as a policymaking force early in the twentieth century. More recently, strength in performance has come to rival clear accountability as a desirable, even necessary, trait in public bureaucracies.

As we have seen, success in measuring up to accountability and performance standards varies from one agency to another. Such variation can also be seen within an agency, as the organization moves from issue to issue and from one policy area to another. Many of the reasons for these variations have been highlighted in the preceding chapters. We now bring these insights together and amplify them in important ways by taking on two final questions:

- *WHICH AGENCIES ARE THE HIGHEST, AND LOWEST, PERFORMING ORGANIZATIONS IN THE EXECUTIVE BRANCH?*

- *WHAT FACTORS, INCLUDING ACCOUNTABILITY, HELP TO EXPLAIN DIFFERENCES IN BUREAUCRATIC BEHAVIOR AND OUTCOMES?*

Rating the Performance of Agencies

Several years ago, a team of researchers set out to document differences in the performance of federal agencies. To account for the fact that performance is a multifaceted concept, these researchers developed a rating scheme that evaluated agencies on thirty-four criteria in five crosscutting areas—financial management, capital management, human resources, information technology, and managing for results. After conducting hundreds of interviews with individuals from the legislative and executive branches, think tanks, the press, interest groups, academic institutions, and many other organizations, the researchers deliberated and reached conclusions about the performance of fifteen agencies.[2]

In 1999 the researchers published these performance ratings in *Government Executive* magazine,[3] with grades ranging from A (the Social Security Administration) to C- (the Immigration and Naturalization Service). Since then twelve more agencies have been evaluated, including the Postal Service and the Army Corps of Engineers. The researchers have also rated six agencies again in an effort to track changes in performance over time. In 2002 the Internal Revenue Service received a B-, a modest improvement over the C it had received in 1999.

These report cards confirm that some agencies perform better than others. On occasion, as in the case of the Social Security Administration (SSA) and Immigration and Naturalization Service (INS), these differences are dramatic. More often than not, however, they are much subtler. According to the researchers, the Federal Emergency Management Agency (FEMA) performs higher than the Environmental Protection Agency (EPA) but only by a small

Figure 7.1 Report Cards for Selected Federal Agencies

1999	Immigration and Naturalization Service	Customs Service	Health Care Financing Administration	Environmental Protection Agency	Social Security Administration
	C–	C	C	B–	A

2000	National Park Service	Occupational Safety and Health Administration	Veteran Benefits Administration	Army Corps of Engineers	Coast Guard
	C	C	B–	B	A

2001	Bureau of Indian Affairs	Bureau of Consular Affairs	National Aeronautics and Space Administration	Postal Service	National Weather Service
	D	C	B	A–	A

2002	Immigration and Naturalization Service	Centers for Medicare and Medicaid Services	Internal Revenue Service	Federal Aviation Administration	Social Security Administration
	D	C–	B–	B	B

Source: Government Executive, February 1999, March 2000, April 2001, May 2002 Consolidated table prepared by the authors.

Note: In 2001 the Health Care Financing Administration was renamed the Center for Medicare and Medicaid Services.

margin (FEMA received a B, while the EPA received a B-). Figure 7.1 presents grades for some of the agencies that have been evaluated over the years.

Explaining Variations in Performance

To what extent are these variations in performance systematic, as opposed to reflections of idiosyncrasies in agencies and their evaluators? To answer this question, we examine the insights generated by the theoretical frameworks and case studies. We believe three factors are particularly relevant in distinguishing agencies on the basis of their performance: **tasks, political support,** and **leadership.** Some agencies confront relatively clear, easy, and manageable tasks; others have more imposing responsibilities. Some agencies benefit from sustained accountability to diverse sovereigns and clients as well as solid political support. Some agencies enjoy competent, sensitive, and creative leadership; others suffer from leadership that fails in fundamental respects. From these key premises flow ten more specific propositions about the performance of public bureaucracies, specified below.

Tasks

We begin with a proposition that follows from a distinction made back in chapter 1. At times agencies engage in policymaking, while at others they implement decisions made elsewhere in the political system. Although implementation can pose significant difficulties, policymaking is, generally speaking, a more foreboding responsibility. For this reason agencies that primarily engage in routine implementation tasks are likely to perform better than those whose central mission is resolving complex and contentious policy problems. This holds especially for implementation tasks viewed favorably by the agency's clients.

> • *PROPOSITION 1: AGENCIES WHOSE PRIMARY TASK IS TO DISTRIB-*
> *UTE MONEY TO INDIVIDUALS TEND TO PERFORM WELL.*

The SSA, which received an A in 1999 and a B in 2002, exemplifies this proposition. Much of what the agency does is write checks to retirees and disabled individuals. Once eligibility has been determined, the rest is really quite straightforward. The criteria for retirement payments are crystal clear, and agency officials have extensive documentation of individual work histories at their fingertips. Determining eligibility for disability payments is somewhat trickier, but even here statutory criteria exist and are supplemented by more specific administrative rules and judicial decisions.

By way of contrast, consider the Centers for Medicare and Medicaid Services (CMS)—known as the Health Care Financing Administration until 2001—the lead agency in delivering health care services to the elderly, poor, and other segments of the population. In carrying out the Medicaid portion of this task, CMS relies on state governments to decide who is eligible for the program and who is authorized to provide the program's services. In turn state governments rely on hospitals, managed care plans, and other health care organizations to hire, deploy, and compensate personnel. Finally, health care organizations rely on physicians, nurses, and other medical professionals to deliver services in accordance with program rules. With such a long chain of responsible parties, performance difficulties are bound to arise.[4] Not surprisingly, then, CMS received a C in 1999 and a C- in 2002.

Not all implementation tasks are created equal, however, or viewed with favor. At times agencies must engage in routine behaviors that stakeholders do not find at all endearing—such as collecting money. Whereas agencies distributing money are likely to be blessed, agencies extracting money are likely to be cursed.

- ### *PROPOSITION 2: AGENCIES WHOSE PRIMARY TASK IS TO COLLECT MONEY TEND TO PERFORM POORLY.*

The Internal Revenue Service (IRS), which has never received a grade higher than a B-, epitomizes this proposition. It goes without saying that hardly anyone likes the IRS and many people fear it. Despite that fear a number of taxpayers cheat, banking on the fact that the agency audits only a relatively small portion of tax returns. In the late 1990s revelations that some IRS officials were overzealous in their tax collection efforts made it even more difficult for the agency to perform its auditing duties. In a series of highly publicized hearings and the subsequent Internal Revenue Service Restructuring and Reform Act, Congress made it clear that it wants the IRS to be relatively benign in its enforcement efforts. Congress also undoubtedly wants the IRS to offer better services, such as timely and accurate advice to taxpayers, but legislators have not provided the funding necessary to bring about such performance enhancements. Yet even if Congress increases funding levels for these improvements, the IRS, by the very nature of its task, would likely continue to suffer from a negative image.

The Office of Student Financial Assistance is an interesting agency to consider because it both distributes money and collects it. Like the SSA, it writes checks, in its case mainly to students of relatively modest means who wish to attend college. These payments, however, are primarily loans that must eventually be repaid. Like the IRS, then, the Office of Student Financial Assistance is also a revenue collection operation. Its task is particularly difficult because recent college graduates, if saddled with substantial debt, may lack the resources necessary to make rent payments, car payments, and student loan payments at the same time. In 1999–2000, 64 percent of college students graduated with student loan debt, a debt that exceeded, on average, $16,000,[5] and although the default rate on student loans has declined significantly since 1990, it is still a not-so-trivial 6 percent.[6] Not surprisingly, the Office of Student Financial Assistance earned no better than a C in 2000.

Throughout the preceding chapters we have highlighted the missions bestowed upon agencies by political principals. These missions reflect the fact that public problems are often hard to solve, especially without running afoul of powerful constituencies. The Forest Service's delicate balancing act between the conservation of natural resources and the fostering of rural economic development offers just one example of such a mission. In general, ambiguity and conflict in missions make it difficult for agencies to satisfy the desires and needs of their stakeholders and political supervisors.

- *PROPOSITION 3: AGENCIES WITH AMBIGUOUS OR CONFLICTING MISSIONS TEND TO PERFORM POORLY.*

The Immigration and Naturalization Service is an example of a bureaucracy bedeviled by competing goals. The agency is expected to "keep out illegal immigrants but let in necessary agricultural workers" and to "carefully screen foreigners seeking to enter the country, but facilitate the entry of foreign tourists."[7] It is extremely difficult, and perhaps impossible, to reconcile these goals. A looser touch allows agricultural workers and foreign tourists in but unintentionally whisks in illegal immigrants and individuals seeking to harm the United States. The stakes of getting this trade-off right were never so apparent as on September 11, 2001. In 2002, several months after the terrorist attacks, the agency received a D, even lower than the grade it received in 1999, a C-.

By contrast, the National Weather Service, which suffers no existential angst as it contemplates its raison d'étre, received an A in 2001. Everyone inside and outside the agency knows that the National Weather Service is responsible for predicting the weather as accurately as possible. Nothing cloudy about that mission! Fully aware of its mission, and equipped with the personnel and technology to do it, the National Weather Service tracks hurricanes and other disturbances in the atmosphere with considerable finesse and precision. An agency with such a clear mission is likely to perform well, especially when that mission enjoys wide support. No one doubts the need for good weather forecasts to anticipate emergencies and to enhance the quality of our lives.

At the outset we introduced the distinction between outputs—the activities of agencies—and outcomes—the results of these activities. Importantly, the observability of these facets of bureaucratic behavior varies across policy areas and agencies.[8] In other words, the difficulty of the moral hazard problem facing political principals and their constituents is anything but constant.

In dealing with the SSA, one question the agency's supervisors and clients ask is, *How quick and accurate are Social Security payments?* Fortunately, for all concerned parties, the information necessary to gauge these outputs and outcomes is readily available. Similarly, it is relatively easy for those inside and outside the Postal Service to keep tabs on the agency's activities and results. No great mystery exists about how long it takes a letter carrier to deliver the mail or a first class letter to reach its destination.

Agencies such as the SSA and the Postal Service are known as **production organizations.** In such organizations, clarity in outputs and outcomes makes it relatively easy for agency leaders to see what is being done and what is being accomplished. This clarity also helps interested parties outside the organization; agency mistakes, for example, are relatively transparent to bosses and clients. For these reasons production organizations, in most cases, perform with considerable strength and precision.

- *PROPOSITION 4: AGENCIES WHOSE OUTPUTS AND OUTCOMES ARE BOTH OBSERVABLE TEND TO PERFORM WELL.*

The National Aeronautics and Space Administration (NASA), which received a B in 2001, would seem to qualify as a production agency. Although the long-term implications of space exploration are difficult to assess, the short-term consequences of NASA's exertions—landing a man on the moon, taking pictures from outer space—are easy to spot. Furthermore, whereas its 1999 effort to probe the surface of Mars proved a dramatic failure, two years later it produced remarkably precise photographs of the comet Borrelly.[9] Whether NASA employees and contractors meet the agency's deadlines for a launch is also easy to document. With this in mind, and despite the tragedy of the Space Shuttle *Columbia*'s final mission, many of NASA's recent ventures appear to have been rather successful.

What about agencies whose outputs and outcomes are difficult to observe? Such agencies, known as **coping organizations,** find it difficult to perform well.[10] Leading examples of coping organizations include public schools and police departments. Diplomacy—the State Department's stock in trade—is also emblematic of this state of affairs. Perhaps not surprisingly, then, the State Department's Bureau of Consular Affairs received a C in 2001. The bureau takes care of American citizens overseas—reissuing lost passports, for example—and gives visas to foreigners who wish to visit the United States, important tasks. But because the bureau's consulates are scattered throughout the world and because its information technology is antiquated, it is problematic for agency leaders to manage the organization's tasks and for members of Congress to keep tabs on what the organization is doing.[11]

The Interior Department's Bureau of Indian Affairs, which received a D in 2001, also possesses some coping organization characteristics. The agency's activities, such as supporting education on tribal reservations, are difficult to measure and monitor. Although test scores offer some indication of how much students have learned, it is exceedingly tough to disentangle the effects of teacher intervention from those of student initiative and home environment. In short, the agency's management lapses arise in part from the complexity of the tasks it is charged with carrying out. Like the Bureau of Consular Affairs, the agency also suffers from woefully outdated technology.[12]

The much-maligned INS suffers from multiple problems, including the difficulty of discerning its outputs and outcomes. To cite the clearest one, illegal immigration is extremely hard to document because those who enter the country on the sly have compelling incentives to remain hidden from government authorities. Although it is possible to gather statistics on the number of individuals apprehended at U.S. borders, the ratio of successful to unsuccessful illegal border crossings is for all intents and purposes unknowable.

Political Support

As has been emphasized throughout, accountability and performance are the two main standards by which public bureaucracies are judged. Though distinct in some respects, these standards are inextricably linked in others. For decades, one of the central ways in which chief executives, legislatures, and judiciaries have sought to foster bureaucratic accountability has been by influencing the processes through which agencies go about producing outputs. The Administrative Procedure Act, with its dictates regarding public notices and comments, is perhaps the classic example of this fundamental connection.

But what about the linkage in the reverse direction? In what ways does accountability facilitate performance? Are there forms of accountability, and political support more generally, that hinder the ability of agencies to perform their most crucial tasks?

In iron triangles political support comes from narrow constituencies that stand to benefit greatly from bureaucratic decision making. Opposing interests do not typically mobilize against these constituencies. Such a pattern can lead to difficulties in both processes and results. For decades the Interstate Commerce Commission had the authority to regulate the rates charged by railroads and motor carriers. Working closely with these interests, the agency developed what has been called "congenital schizophrenia." [13] In other words, taking care of the rail and trucking industries' needs case by case took precedence over consistent application of particular standards or rationalizations, to the detriment of other interested parties, including consumers and members of Congress.

- **PROPOSITION 5: AGENCIES THAT ARE PRESSURED BY DIVERSE SETS OF CONSTITUENCIES TEND TO PERFORM WELL.**

In general, support from diffuse constituencies is a way to avoid the kinds of problems that eventually contributed to the demise, in 1995, of the Interstate Commerce Commission. The EPA is perhaps the leading example of an agency that, from its inception, has been exposed to diverse points of view, including business interests, environmental advocates, and state and local regulators charged with carrying out federal policies. At times this exposure has proved frustrating for agency officials, who must negotiate political minefields when making decisions. Such negotiations have to be undertaken with great care and deliberation, and as a result the agency seldom sets records for the speed of its policymaking. Nevertheless, the EPA's diverse constituency helps guarantee that it will pay at least some attention to both economic efficiency and ecological concerns whenever it makes a decision. As a case in point, reductions in air and water pollution over the past three decades owe a great deal to the persistent efforts of environmentalists, while technological advances and the enhanced importance of economic incentives reflect the input of regulated industries. Although the agency's grades have not been perfect (a B- in 1999 and a B in 2002), they almost certainly would have been worse had the agency been dominated by either business firms or environmental activists.

In contrast, the Customs Service suffered from lopsided external pressure prior to the terrorist attacks of September 11, 2001. Shipping interests, anxious to speed the flow of goods and therefore to increase their profits, lobbied the agency to expedite checks at the nation's borders. Security interests were poorly represented in this lobbying process. In the aftermath of the attacks, investigations revealed that every year the agency had been allowing millions of containers to enter the country with minimal scrutiny to guard against a bomb or a biological attack. In retrospect, the C received by the agency in 1999 accurately captured an organization poorly prepared to prevent terrorists from gaining a toehold inside the United States.

- *PROPOSITION 6: AGENCIES WHOSE PROGRAMS AND POLICIES ENJOY DIFFUSE SUPPORT TEND TO PERFORM WELL.*

A closely related covariate of performance is the level of support enjoyed by the programs and policies under an agency's jurisdiction. Consider, at one end of the spectrum, the Social Security Administration, the Postal Service, and the National Weather Service, agencies that have received very good or excellent ratings. Social Security is probably the most popular income support program in the United States. Senior citizens anxiously wait to receive their monthly check in the mail, and most working Americans probably feel a little more secure knowing that when they retire they, too, will receive a minimum pension from the federal government. Mail delivery, which dates back to the nation's earliest days, also enjoys widespread public support, despite periodic increases in the price of stamps. Even with a growing number of alternatives to traditional mail delivery, such as faxes, e-mails, and Federal Express and similar private services, Americans continue to rely heavily upon the Postal Service for personal and professional communications. Though not as old as the Postal Service, the National Weather Service is just as familiar and highly regarded. Weather reports are particularly useful for farmers and travelers. The work of the agency's forecasters is also of critical importance for those who find themselves in the path of blizzards, hurricanes, tornados, and other natural disasters. As each one of us can undoubtedly attest, this work helps to enhance the quality of our daily lives, as when we choose to picnic on Saturday rather than Sunday because the weather looks more promising.

At the other end of the spectrum, the Bureau of Indian Affairs is an agency whose programs and policies enjoy specific support from some Native Americans but not diffuse support from the general American public. One reason is that in an effort to build consensus, the agency has deliberately disaggregated issues, thus conveying the impression that its actions will probably promote nothing more than local benefits.[14] Another reason is the succession of highly conflictive issues the agency has had to deal with in recent years, including various disputes over Native American treaty rights. Because such controversies tend to pit Native Americans against other Americans, these issues are unlikely to generate diffuse support for an agency badly in need of performance enhancements.[15]

Support, or a lack thereof, for agencies and their jurisdictions comes not only from societal clients but from political supervisors as well. These supervisors seek to foster accountability through several different techniques of control.

A **catalytic control** places on an agency's agenda an issue requiring some kind of response but allows the agency considerable discretion in how it does so. A **hortatory control** offers incentives, such as financial rewards, to encourage an agency to take specific actions. Finally, a **coercive control** compels an agency to behave in a certain way, regardless of the preferences of the agency's leaders, managers, and operations staff. As a general rule, coercive controls inhibit creative problem solving and produce unintended, negative side effects. Although coercion is sometimes necessary, as when civil rights or civil liberties are threatened, it is usually a suboptimal technique for controlling the bureaucracy.[16]

- *PROPOSITION 7: AGENCIES SUBJECT TO CATALYTIC CONTROLS OR HORTATORY CONTROLS TEND TO PERFORM BETTER THAN THOSE SUBJECT TO COERCIVE CONTROLS.*

Congress's intervention in the area of ergonomics policy offers a good example of a coercive control. Rather than relying on legislative appropriations and oversight hearings to encourage an ergonomics rule that reflected its priorities, Congress waited for the Occupational Safety and Health Administration to adopt a rule and then, with the help of the newly inaugurated Bush administration, promptly overturned it. Repudiated by Congress, and consistent with the aims of its new leadership, the agency declined to revise and reissue the regulation. As a result, the status of millions of American workers with repetitive stress injuries remained unchanged, an unpleasing outcome on many fronts.

By way of contrast, Congress has historically given the Postal Service considerable discretion and autonomy. Under an arrangement dating back to 1970, an independent Postal Rate Commission makes recommendations on rate increases to an independent board of governors, which then makes the final decisions. A requirement that its members be appointed to nine-year terms and can be removed only under the rarest of circumstances insulates the board from political pressure. Such noncoercive controls free the Postal Service to take actions that raise very little political ire, even when they entail rate hikes that are inevitably unpopular with consumers.

As this example illustrates, political support is not an all or nothing proposition. Agencies that most clearly recognize the opportunities and constraints presented by different types of accountability put themselves in a position to generate the political capital necessary to perform their tasks effectively. This awareness often comes from the top, with skillful, visionary leaders.

Leadership

Although it is commonly acknowledged that leadership matters in public bureaucracies, much less agreement exists regarding the specific ingredients that make for an effective leader. This lack of agreement should not be viewed as surprising, as the qualities that make for strong leadership at some agencies may not be those that facilitate appropriate leadership at others. For example, a moribund agency with programs escalating in economic, social, and political importance may benefit from a bold leader willing to rock the boat, even if this rocking causes some inside and outside the agency to feel queasy. In contrast, an embattled agency with programs constantly being challenged may benefit from a coalition-builder who can effectively reach out to influential constituencies prior to making crucial decisions. Still, despite these complexities and subtleties, several general propositions about bureaucratic leadership can be advanced.

Agency heads are appointed for a variety of reasons—their qualifications, their demographic characteristics, their long-standing friendship with the president, their support from influential backers or constituencies, and so forth. Of these factors, effective leadership derives primarily from professional expertise and prior work experience. Without these qualities, agency heads will probably flounder, no matter how much support key bosses and clients provide. With these qualities, success is much more likely, even for agency heads who are not the president's personal friends or closely aligned with powerful societal interests.

Carole Browner, who led the EPA during the Clinton administration, had headed Florida's Department of Environmental Protection prior to serving in the federal government. Browner had also worked on Capitol Hill, assisting Sen. Al Gore, D-Tenn., on environmental issues. Importantly, Browner made good use of the substantive knowledge and political connections she had accumulated prior to her EPA stint. During her tenure the agency launched a number of major initiatives, including Project XL, which allows businesses and state and local governments to experiment with innovative, cost-effective approaches for achieving environmental goals.[17]

Consider as well the background of James Lee Witt, who headed FEMA for much of the 1990s. Before taking the reins there Witt had served as director of the Arkansas Office of Emergency Services. While in Arkansas he witnessed firsthand the management problems that would lead Sen. Fritz Hollings, D-S.C., to characterize FEMA as "the sorriest bunch of bureaucratic jackasses I have ever encountered in my life." [18] Witt's emergency management background, which his predecessors had lacked, as well as several other factors, enabled him to transform the agency, virtually overnight, into one of the federal government's highest-performing organizations.

Leaders can also enhance bureaucratic performance by taking actions that advance their agencies' long-term interests, even if such actions undermine their personal interests in the short run. By making such **credible commitments,** leaders foster a sense of cooperation and esprit de corps among agency managers and operators, which in turn boosts the prospects that the organization will take major strides toward achieving its most fundamental goals.[19]

Credible commitments can be made and demonstrated in a variety of ways. For example, Greg Woods was brought in to lead the Office of Student Financial Assistance at a time when the agency had just received a C rating. Rather than take steps to immediately endear himself to the organization's bosses and clients, Woods set about giving the agency a complete makeover. Symbolically, he restated its mission in human terms: "We help put America through school." In terms of service, he reorganized the agency around its three central clientele groups—students, schools, and financial institutions. Facing perhaps his most daunting challenge, he took steps to streamline and integrate the organization's computer systems, which had been created haphazardly over a period of many years.[20]

The initial assessments of Woods's leadership were somewhat mixed. He received praise for his energy and enthusiasm as well as for assembling a strong management team. But he received criticism for, among other things, placing too much emphasis on Access America for Students, a new initiative that would allow students to manage their financial-aid accounts over the Internet. At one level, the complaints were about the supposed diversion of Woods's attention from his most pressing task of revamping the agency's computer systems. At another level, the complaints were about politics, as the initiative was a pet project of presidential candidate Al Gore.[21]

Despite these controversies, Woods was eventually credited with pointing the Office of Student Financial Assistance in the right direction. Even former critics rushed to his defense when Secretary of Education Rod Paige tried to rein in Woods's authority. Emotions ran high in May 2002 when Woods stepped down from his post to devote his full energy to a life-threatening battle with pancreatic cancer. In the end many in the financial aid community agreed with this assessment of Woods's tenure: "The investments that have been made in modernization are beginning to return dividends to us. We cannot afford to start at square one again, because if we do, it'll be years before we get back to the point where we're making significant progress." [22]

At times agencies need not leaders who shake up internal operations but ones adept at attracting external support. Leaders who are savvy in this respect find it relatively easy to capture the attention and enthusiasm of not only the democratic public but agency bosses and clients as well. Generating favorable coverage in the mass media has become an essential component of this leadership skill. As we discovered earlier, through the Forest Service's success with Smokey Bear, positive reputations can enhance performance by making it easier, for example, for the organization to attract valuable resources and political capital.

- *PROPOSITION 10: AGENCIES WITH LEADERS WHO HAVE A FLAIR FOR PUBLICITY TEND TO PERFORM WELL.*

Jane Garvey, who led the Federal Aviation Administration from 1997 to 2002, attracted nationwide attention by vowing to be airborne when midnight struck on January 1, 2000. Her promise, which she kept with great fanfare, was broadcast on nightly news programs and reported in morning papers all across the country. Garvey's publicity stunt was substantively important because it helped reassure the public that the safety of air travel would be not be compromised by the year 2000 (Y2K) computer bug.[23] Overall, the agency's performance improved markedly during Garvey's tenure, as indicated by its jump from a C in 1999 to a B in 2002.

James Lee Witt was also a master of public relations. On his first morning as FEMA director, Witt personally greeted his employees as they arrived at agency headquarters. Even more important, he became a ubiquitous presence at disaster scenes, drinking coffee with cleanup crews, chatting up local officials, and reassuring victims that the agency was there to aid them. All of this helped the agency build an image as an organization committed to customer service.[24] In 1999, under Witt's leadership, the agency received a B, a solid grade that would have been unthinkable merely a decade earlier.

Witt's successful tenure demonstrates that leaders hold in their hands one of the keys to effective performance in executive branch bureaucracies. They cannot, however, unlock the door to praiseworthy outputs and outcomes on their own. Leadership does not operate in a vacuum but in a context colored by the tasks assigned to agencies and the level of political support provided by agency bosses and clients.

What this implies is that agencies favorably situated on multiple dimensions are especially well equipped to perform at a high level. The Social Security Administration embodies such an organization. The agency's primary task is to distribute money, a popular mission easily observable in terms of both outputs and outcomes. The diffuse support the agency receives provides the resources and political capital necessary to perform well across presidential administrations and changes in the Social Security program. So long as the agency's leadership does not get in the way, the SSA is likely to continue its record of success in the years and decades ahead.

Bureaucracy in the Twenty-First Century

As seen from the outset, public bureaucracies are institutions of democratic policymaking that are constantly evolving and being transformed. Consider the prominent, and by now particularly familiar, example of education reform.

Figure 7.2 Mean Reading Scores: Success for All Schools v. Control Schools

Reading scores

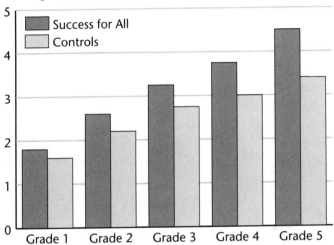

Source: Robert Slavin and Nancy Madden, "'Success for All' and African American and Latino Student Achievement," in *Bridging the Achievement Gap,* ed. John Chubb and Tom Loveless (Washington, D.C.: Brookings Institution Press, 2002), 80.

Many education reforms have been tried in recent years, ranging from smaller classrooms to stronger testing requirements to school voucher programs enabling disadvantaged children to use public dollars to attend private schools. One innovation that has attracted considerable interest is Success for All, a comprehensive reform model for elementary schools initiated in Baltimore in 1987 and now utilized in approximately 1,600 U.S. schools.

Success for All, which focuses primarily on reading, seeks to ensure that virtually every student will reach the third grade on schedule with adequate basic skills and will build on those skills throughout elementary school. Its elements include a schoolwide curriculum, specially trained tutors, preschool and kindergarten programs, eight-week assessments of elementary school students, a family support team to work with parents, and a facilitator to help teachers implement the program.

A systematic comparison of Success for All schools and a comparable group of schools suggests that the program works. For each grade, from grade 1 through grade 5, Success for All students perform better on standardized reading tests than other students with similar socioeconomic backgrounds (see Figure 7.2). The program is especially noteworthy for its ability to improve the educational performance of African American and Latino students.[25]

The broader lesson is that bureaucratic innovations can make a difference. This is particularly encouraging in an area as challenging as elementary and secondary education. With ample opportunities for experimentation at the state and local levels, we should be able to determine which innovations work generally and which innovations are particularly advantageous for disadvantaged populations.

When thinking about bureaucratic policymaking in general, several broad trends encapsulate the changes that have been occurring and that will likely continue to occur in the years and decades ahead. First, the emergence of performance as a standard of evaluation has brought concepts from the private sector to bear on organizations at all levels of government. These concepts are articulated in actions such as the Government Performance and Results Act, which places great emphasis on strategic plans and the measurement and reporting of agency outputs and outcomes. There are, however, aspects of the movement toward performance that reflect the fact that bureaucracies are distinctly public institutions. For example, equity is an inescapable manifestation of performance for organizations charged with distributing and redistributing societal resources and with regulating the behavior of individuals, business firms, and other private actors.

Second, the authority vested in executive branch bureaucracies continues to increase, despite some appearances to the contrary. In his 1996 State of the Union Address President Clinton declared, to much bipartisan applause, that "the era of big government is over." By only one measure is this claim sustainable. From 1968 to 1996 the number of full-time permanent civilian federal workers dropped from 2.3 million to 1.9 million.[26] Once, however, the activities of institutions such as the **shadow government**—the nongovernmental positions created by public sector grants and contracts—are factored in, the size of the federal workforce actually approaches 17 million. Add to this number the ever-burgeoning workforces at the state and local levels, and the extraordinary scope of the contemporary American bureaucracy becomes even more readily apparent. Policymaking in the United States simply cannot be understood without paying close attention to executive branch organizations and their partners.

Third, as the bureaucracy continues to expand in scope and responsibility, the resulting organizational apparatus increasingly reflects a combination of hierarchical and network arrangements. Such a combination is certainly present in the newest federal agency, the Department of Homeland Security. The agency's leadership possesses stronger than normal authority to hire, fire, and reassign subordinate personnel. This authority provides principals inside and outside the department with an unusually robust way of dealing with adverse selection and moral hazard difficulties. At the same time defending the nation's homeland inevitably entails public-private partnerships, such as those embodied in contracting-out relationships. Firms such as InVision Technologies and L-3 Communications play a fundamental role in the area of transportation security by manufacturing the explosives detection devices that have been installed in airports in the aftermath of the September 11 terrorist attacks.

Fourth, public involvement in bureaucratic proceedings continues to evolve. Over the past four decades, the portfolio of organized interests playing an active role in policymaking has diversified greatly. On the heels of this diversification has come a veritable revolution in the venues of public participation. The application of principles of bargaining and negotiation to the rulemaking process has been a significant addition in an area long governed by the notice and comment requirements of the Administrative Procedures Act. The Internet appears to be on the verge of forever changing the way in which agencies interact with the beneficiaries and targets of their activities.

In the face of all these changes, a set of analytical tools that transcend the particulars of agencies and policy areas will be necessary to foster an ongoing understanding of the bureaucracy and its place in American democracy. The four social scientific frameworks presented here—bounded rationality, principal-agent theory, interest group mobilization, and network theory—offer just such an array of overarching perspectives. As the problems that agencies address, and the constellation of agencies themselves, evolve, these theoretical orientations toward the bureaucracy's people, bosses, clients, and networks will remain fruitful sources of guidance for students puzzling over policymaking inside the executive branch.

Key Terms

Catalytic control, 174

Coercive control, 174

Coping organization, 170

Credible commitment, 176

APPENDIX | Web Resources

Agency Web Sites

These are Web sites of particularly important agencies, as well as agency sites that have useful information.

Federal

CENTERS FOR MEDICARE AND MEDICAID SERVICES (cms.hhs.gov): This Web site contains a list of answers to frequently asked questions about Medicare, Medicaid, and the State Children's Health Insurance Program. It also describes the waiver and demonstration process, from the stage where states apply for relief from program requirements to the stage where flexibility is granted and implemented.

DEPARTMENT OF AGRICULTURE (www.usda.gov): This Web site includes links to all of the agencies, services, and programs that operate within the department. From these links, information can be retrieved about farm loans, child nutrition programs, forest fires, and many more areas of department responsibility.

DEPARTMENT OF HOMELAND SECURITY (www.dhs.gov/dhspublic): This Web site provides information about the color-coded terrorist threat levels. It also covers topics such as immigration and borders and lays out how citizens, private industry, trade organizations, and all levels of government can partner with the department.

DEPARTMENT OF TRANSPORTATION'S DOCKET MANAGEMENT SYSTEM (dms.dot.gov): Dockets are official public records of agency decision-making processes and actions. This Web site is where the Department of Transportation stores information about proposed and final regulations, copies of public comments on proposed rules, and many other useful documents. The documents can be searched by keywords or by the identification numbers that the department assigns to particular actions.

ENVIRONMENTAL PROTECTION AGENCY (www.epa.gov): This Web site provides quick links to key topics like ecosystems, pollution prevention, and compliance and enforcement. It also can be used to access the agency's docket system (EDOCKET) and to view current environmental legislation before Congress.

FEDERAL COMMUNICATIONS COMMISSION (www.fcc.gov): This Web site provides information about the commissioners who are charged with regulating interstate and international communications by radio, television, wire, satellite, and cable. It also lists upcoming commissioner meetings and the auctions that the commission holds to distribute licenses for the electromagnetic spectrum.

FEDERAL EMERGENCY MANAGEMENT AGENCY (www.fema.gov): This Web site provides information about topics such as storm preparation, urban search and rescue, and disaster help. It also contains a searchable map of counties that are currently designated for disaster and emergency assistance.

FEDERAL RESERVE SYSTEM (www.federalreserve.gov): This Web site provides access to the congressional testimony and public speeches of Federal Reserve officials, as well as information about monetary policy, banking regulation, and economic data and research.

OFFICE OF MANAGEMENT AND BUDGET (www.whitehouse.gov/omb): This Web site contains documents related to the president's budget and the management of agency regulatory activities, including letters that prompt agencies to initiate rulemakings and letters that return proposed rules to agencies for further consideration.

U.S. EXECUTIVE BRANCH WEB SITES (lcweb.loc.gov/global/executive/fed.html): This Web site presents an official list of executive branch Web sites. Organizations covered include cabinet departments, independent agencies, and regulatory commissions.

State

CALIFORNIA STATE GOVERNMENT (www.ca.gov/state/portal/myca_homepage.jsp): This site features links to the governor's Web site, the online appointment system of the Department of Motor Vehicles, and to state organizations and policies in areas ranging from business to health and safety.

FLORIDA DEPARTMENT OF ENVIRONMENTAL PROTECTION (www.dep.state.fl.us): This Web site provides information about breaking ecological news, the state's Clean Marina program, and opportunities for green lodging in Florida.

MARYLAND DEPARTMENT OF HEALTH AND MENTAL HYGIENE (www. dhmh.state.md.us): This Web site covers hot issues like bioterrorism, as well as traditional concerns like substance abuse, food stamps, and the Medicaid program.

NORTH CAROLINA STATE GOVERNMENT (www.ncgov.com): This Web site provides a directory of all state agencies and departments, as well as links to these organizations' home pages. It also offers online access to a wide range of services for citizens, businesses, and state employees.

Research Web Sites

These are Web sites that are not specific to particular agencies, but contain information that is useful across many policy domains.

AEI-BROOKINGS JOINT CENTER FOR REGULATORY STUDIES (www.aei. brookings.org): This center, a joint effort on the part of the American Enterprise Institute and the Brookings Institution, provides analyses of existing regulatory programs and new regulatory proposals. The center's focal points include developing an agenda for regulatory reform, analyzing the benefits and costs of regulations, and improving accountability in the regulatory system.

FEDERAL ADVISORY COMMITTEE ACT DATABASE (www.fido.gov/ facadatabase): This Web site contains information about the meetings, reports, and other activities of the nearly 1,000 advisory committees that operate in the executive branch.

FEDERAL PERFORMANCE PROJECT (www.govexec.com/fpp/index.htm): The Federal Performance Project rates the management abilities of federal agencies. This Web site contains the grades that have been handed out to agencies since 1999, as well as articles that highlight particular success stories or examples of agencies that fail to measure up.

FEDERAL REGISTER (www.gpoaccess.gov/fr/index.html): The *Federal Register* is the official daily publication for rules, proposed rules, and notices of federal agencies and organizations, as well as executive orders and other presidential documents. Every document published in the *Federal Register* since 1994 can be accessed via this Web site.

GENERAL ACCOUNTING OFFICE (www.gao.gov): The General Accounting Office is the audit, evaluation, and investigative arm of Congress. This Web site includes a list of reports on a plethora of topics that is updated daily, as well as assessments of all major rules issued by federal agencies.

GOVERNMENT PERFORMANCE PROJECT (www.maxwell.syr.edu/gpp): The Government Performance Project has assessed the management capacity of all the states, the nation's 35 largest cities, and 40 large counties. A series of grade reports can be accessed via this Web site.

LIBRARY OF CONGRESS (thomas.loc.gov): The Library of Congress's Web site has information about legislative affairs, much of which pertains to the executive branch, including presidential nominations, appropriations bills, and delegations of authority from Congress to agencies.

MERCATUS CENTER (www.mercatus.org): The Mercatus Center is an education, research, and outreach organization based at George Mason University that advances the idea of market-based solutions to public problems. Links to research papers on a wide range of topics can be found at this Web site.

REGULATIONS.GOV (www.regulations.gov): Launched in 2003, this Web site is a central clearinghouse for information about the regulatory activities of federal agencies. Regulations can be searched by agency and by topic, and comments can be electronically submitted on any pending agency action.

| NOTES

Chapter 1

1. William Gormley Jr. and David Weimer, *Organizational Report Cards* (Cambridge: Harvard University Press, 1999).

2. Charles Clotfelter and Helen Ladd, "Recognizing and Rewarding Success in Public Schools," in *Holding Schools Accountable: Performance-Based Reform in Education,* ed. Helen Ladd (Washington, D.C.: Brookings Institution Press, 1996).

3. Kathy Christie, "State Leadership: Is the New ESEA the Chicken or the Egg?" *Phi Delta Kappan* 83 (April 2002): 571.

4. Valerie Strauss, "GAO Faults States on School Funds," *Washington Post,* April 5, 2002, 21.

5. Linda McNeil, *Contradictions of School Reform: Educational Costs of Standardized Testing* (New York: Routledge, 2000).

6. Ibid., 245.

7. Rod Paige, "An Overview of America's Education Agenda," *Phi Delta Kappan* 83 (April 2002): 711.

8. Robert Behn, *Rethinking Democratic Accountability* (Washington, D.C., Brookings Institution Press, 2001).

9. Cornelius M. Kerwin, *Rulemaking: How Government Agencies Write Law and Make Policy,* 2d ed. (Washington, D.C.: CQ Press, 1999).

10. Barbara Romzek and Melvin Dubnick, "Accountability in the Public Sector: Lessons from the Challenger Tragedy," *Public Administration Review* 47 (May/June 1987): 229.

11. Ibid., 230.

12. William Gormley Jr., *Taming the Bureaucracy: Muscles, Prayers, and Other Strategies* (Princeton: Princeton University Press, 1989).

13. Steven J. Balla, "Administrative Procedures and Political Control of the Bureaucracy," *American Political Science Review* 92 (September 1998): 663–673.

14. John Brehm and Scott Gates, *Working, Shirking, and Sabotage* (Ann Arbor: University of Michigan Press, 1997).

15. Romzek and Dubnick, "Accountability in the Public Sector."

16. Joel D. Aberbach, *Keeping a Watchful Eye: The Politics of Congressional Oversight* (Washington, D.C.: Brookings Institution Press, 1990.

17. William Gormley Jr., "The Representation Revolution: Reforming State Government through Public Representation," *Administration and Society* 18 (August 1986): 179–196.

18. Paul C. Light, *The Tides of Reform: Making Government Work, 1945–1995* (New Haven: Yale University Press, 1997).

19. Gormley, "Representation Revolution"; Kathleen Bawn, "Political Control Versus Expertise: Congressional Choices about Administrative Procedures," *American Political Science Review* 89 (March 1995): 62–73; David Epstein and Sharyn O'Halloran, "Administrative

Procedures, Information, and Agency Discretion," *American Journal of Political Science* 38 (August 1994): 697–722.

20. Bob Woodward, *Maestro: Greenspan's Fed and the American Boom* (New York: Touchstone Books, 2001).

21. John M. Berry, "Nervous Eyes on Greenspan's Big Shoes," *Washington Post*, August 7, 2002.

22. Anne M. Khademian, *The SEC and Capital Market Regulation: The Politics of Expertise* (Pittsburgh: University of Pittsburgh Press, 1997).

23. Terry M. Moe, "The Politics of Structural Choice: Toward a Theory of Public Bureaucracy," in *Organization Theory: From Chester Barnard to the Present and Beyond*, ed. Oliver E. Williamson (New York: Oxford University Press, 1990).

24. Charles Goodsell, *The Case for Bureaucracy*, 3d ed. (Chatham, N.J.: Chatham House, 1994).

25. Justin Blum, "Anthrax Cited in 2 D.C. Postal Deaths," *Washington Post*, October 23, 2001, Sec. A.

26. Ben White, "Postmaster General Lauded Despite Mixed Performance," *Washington Post*, October 25, 2001, Sec. A.

27. U.S. Office of Management and Budget, *Draft Report to Congress on the Cost and Benefits of Regulation* (Washington, D.C.: OMB, March 28, 2002).

28. Richard Nathan, introduction to *Quicker Better Cheaper? Managing Performance in American Government*, ed. Dall Forsythe (Albany, N.Y.: Rockefeller Institute Press, 2001).

29. U.S. General Accounting Office, *The Government Performance and Results Act: 1997 Governmentwide Implementation Will Be Uneven* (Washington, D.C.: GAO, 1997), 9.

30. U.S. General Accounting Office, *Managing for Results: Opportunities for Continued Improvements in Agencies' Performance Plans* (Washington, D.C.: GAO, 1999), 3.

31. U.S. Office of Management and Budget and National Science Foundation, *Improving the Measurement of Program Effectiveness* (paper presented at OMB/NSF workshop on Strengthening Program Effectiveness Measurement of Federal Programs, Arlington, Va., May 21, 2002).

32. Princeton Survey Research Associates (for the Pew Charitable Trusts), *Customers Judge the Performance of Federal Agencies*, Report (Washington, D.C.: April 2000).

33. Senate Governmental Affairs Committee, *Reports on the Study of Federal Regulation* (Washington, D.C.: GPO, January/February 1997).

34. Bloomberg News, "Spitzer Criticizes SEC, Pitt," *Newsday*, July 26, 2002, 56.

35. Kathleen Day, "Harvey Pitt Raises a Promotion Commotion," *Washington Post*, July 25, 2002, Sec. E.

36. Daniel P. Carpenter, *The Forging of Bureaucratic Autonomy: Reputations, Networks, and Policy Innovation in Executive Agencies, 1862–1928* (Princeton: Princeton University Press, 2001).

37. Ibid.

38. Eugene Lewis. *Public Entrepreneurship: Toward a Theory of Bureaucratic Practice* (Bloomington: Indiana University Press, 1980), 109.

39. Carpenter, *Forging of Bureaucratic Autonomy*.

Chapter 2

1. William Gormley Jr., "Regulatory Enforcement Styles," *Political Research Quarterly* 51 (June 1998): 363–383.

2. Bryan Jones, Saadia Greenberg, Clifford Kaufman, and Joseph Drew, "Service Delivery Rules and the Distribution of Local Government Services: Three Detroit Bureaucracies," *Journal of Politics* 40 (May 1978): 332–368.

3. Michael Powell, "N.Y. Rescuers Disorganized in 9/11 Attack," *Washington Post,* August 20, 2002, Sec. A.

4. Bryan Jones, *Politics and the Architecture of Choice: Bounded Rationality and Governance* (Chicago: University of Chicago Press, 2001).

5. Herbert Simon, *Administrative Behavior,* 4th ed. (New York: Free Press, 1997).

6. George Akerlof, "The Market for Lemons," *Quarterly Journal of Economics* 84 (August 1970): 488–500; Burton Weisbrod, *The Nonprofit Economy* (Cambridge: Harvard University Press, 1988).

7. Simon, *Administrative Behavior,* 119.

8. Jonathan Bendor, *Parallel Systems: Redundancy in Government* (Berkeley: University of California Press, 1985), 85–118, 209–215.

9. Malcolm Sparrow, *The Regulatory Craft* (Washington, D.C.: Brookings Institution Press, 2000), 127.

10. Clarence Davies and Jan Mazurek, *Pollution Control in the United States* (Washington, D.C.: Resources for the Future, 1998), 59–63.

11. Simon, *Administrative Behavior,* 89.

12. Michael Lipsky, *Street-Level Bureaucracy* (New York: Russell Sage Foundation, 1980).

13. Robert Axelrod, *The Evolution of Cooperation* (New York: Basic Books, 1984), 73–87.

14. William Gormley Jr., *Everybody's Children: Child Care as a Public Problem* (Washington, D.C.: Brookings Institution Press, 1995), 113–117.

15. Jane Waldfogel, *The Future of Child Protection: How to Break the Cycle of Abuse and Neglect* (Cambridge: Harvard University Press, 1998), 148–151.

16. Sparrow, *Regulatory Craft,* 86–87.

17. Simon, *Administrative Behavior,* 105.

18. Charles Perrow, *Normal Accidents: Living with High-Risk Technologies* (Princeton: Princeton University Press, 1999), 403.

19. Deborah Stone, *Policy Paradox: The Art of Political Decision Making* (New York: W. W. Norton, 2002), 256. It should be noted that Stone is describing, not endorsing, the rational choice model.

20. Simon, *Administrative Behavior,* 94.

21. Stone, *Policy Paradox,* 375.

22. Greenspan, quoted in Stone, *Policy Paradox,* 244.

23. Martha Feldman, *Order without Design: Information Production and Policy Making* (Stanford: Stanford University Press, 1989), 81, 106–114.

24. Jane Mansbridge, "The Rise and Fall of Self-Interest in the Explanation of Political Life," in *Beyond Self-Interest,* ed. Jane Mansbridge (Chicago: University of Chicago Press, 1990), 3–22.

25. Peter Clark and James Q. Wilson, "Incentive Systems: A Theory of Organizations," *Administrative Science Quarterly* 6 (September 1961): 129–166.

26. Anthony Downs, *Inside Bureaucracy* (Boston: Little, Brown, 1967), 88.

27. Amartya Sen, "Rational Fools: A Critique of the Behavioral Foundations of Economic Theory," in Mansbridge, *Beyond Self-Interest,* 33.

28. Marissa Golden, *What Motivates Bureaucrats? Politics and Administration during the Reagan Years* (New York: Columbia University Press, 2000), 154–168.

29. Barry Rubin, *Secrets of State: The State Department and the Struggle over U.S. Foreign Policy* (New York: Oxford University Press, 1985), 124–129, 127.

30. Ibid., 127.

31. Joel Aberbach, Robert Putnam, and Bert Rockman, *Bureaucrats and Politicians in Western Democracies* (Cambridge: Harvard University Press, 1981), 84–112.

32. Amos Tversky and Daniel Kahneman, "Availability: A Heuristic for Judging Frequency and Probability," *Cognitive Psychology* 5 (1973): 207–232.

33. Perrow, *Normal Accidents*, 321.

34. Herbert Simon, "Why Public Administration?" *Journal of Public Administration Research and Theory* 8 (January 1998): 10.

35. Albert Hirschman, *Exit, Voice, and Loyalty* (Cambridge: Harvard University Press, 1970).

36. Herbert Kaufman, *The Forest Ranger* (Baltimore: Johns Hopkins University Press, 1960), 214–215.

37. Robert Katzmann, *Regulatory Bureaucracy: The Federal Trade Commission and Antitrust Policy* (Cambridge: MIT Press, 1980).

38. Simon, *Administrative Behavior*, 111.

39. Bendor, *Parallel Systems*, 117.

40. Anne Lamott, *Bird by Bird: Some Instructions on Writing and Life* (New York: Anchor Books, 1994), 18–19.

41. See Barry Rabe, "Power to the States: The Promise and Pitfalls of Decentralization," in *Environmental Policy in the 1990s*, 3d ed., ed. Norman J. Vig and Michael E. Kraft (Washington, D.C.: CQ Press, 1997), 35–36; see also Barry Rabe, "Permitting, Prevention, and Integration: Lessons from the States," in *Environmental Governance*, ed. Donald Kettl (Washington, D.C.: Brookings Institution Press, 2002), 14–57.

42. Sparrow, *Regulatory Craft*, 123–124.

43. A. Myrick Freeman III, "Economic Incentives and Environmental Regulation," in Vig and Kraft, *Environmental Policy*, 193.

44. Ibid., 191.

45. Eugene Bardach and Robert Kagan, *Going By the Book: The Problem of Regulatory Unreasonableness* (Philadelphia: Temple University Press, 1982).

46. Martha Feldman, *Order without Design*.

47. Perrow, *Normal Accidents*, 170–231.

48. C. Edward Lindblom, "The Science of 'Muddling Through,' " *Public Administration Review* 29 (spring 1959): 79–88.

49. John Kingdon, *Agendas, Alternatives, and Public Policies*, 2d ed. (Boston: Little, Brown, 1995); Bryan Jones, Frank Baumgartner, and James True, "Policy Punctuations: U.S. Budget Authority, 1947–1995," *Journal of Politics* 60 (February 1998): 1–33.

Chapter 3

1. Cindy Skrzycki, "Aiming Rusty Legislative Artillery," *Washington Post*, March 6, 2001, Sec. E; Helen Dewar and Cindy Skrzycki, "Workplace Health Initiative Rejected," *Washington Post*, March 7, 2001, Sec. A; Helen Dewar and Cindy Skrzycki, "House Scraps Ergonomics Regulation," *Washington Post*, March 8, 2001, Sec. A.

2. Ellen Nakashima and Greg Schneider, "U.S. Likely to Miss Goal on Screening," *Washington Post*, November 28, 2001, Sec. A.

3. David Epstein and Sharyn O'Halloran, *Delegating Powers: A Transaction Cost Politics Approach to Policy Making under Separate Powers* (New York: Cambridge University Press, 1999).

4. Terry M. Moe, "The New Economics of Organization," *American Journal of Political Science* 28 (November 1984): 739–777; John D. Huber and Charles R. Shipan, "The Costs of Control: Legislators, Agencies, and Transaction Costs," *Legislative Studies Quarterly* 25 (February 2000): 25–52.

5. D. Roderick Kiewiet and Mathew D. McCubbins, *The Logic of Delegation: Congressional Parties and the Appropriations Process* (Chicago: University of Chicago Press, 1991).

6. Morris P. Fiorina, *Congress: Keystone of the Washington Establishment,* 2d ed. (New Haven: Yale University Press, 1989).

7. R. Douglas Arnold, *The Logic of Congressional Action* (New Haven: Yale University Press, 1990).

8. William Gormley Jr., "Regulatory Issue Networks in a Federal System," *Polity* 18 (summer 1986): 595–620.

9. Ibid.

10. Lucy Drotning and Larry Rothenberg, "Predicting Bureaucratic Control: Evidence from the 1990 Clean Air Act Amendments," *Law and Policy Quarterly* 21 (January 1999): 1–20.

11. Ibid., 12.

12. Epstein and O'Halloran, *Delegating Powers.*

13. Morris P. Fiorina, "Congressional Control of the Bureaucracy: A Mismatch of Incentives and Capabilities," in *Congress Reconsidered,* 2d ed., ed. Lawrence C. Dodd and Bruce I. Oppenheimer (Washington, D.C.: CQ Press, 1981).

14. Richard E. Neustadt, *Presidential Power and the Modern Presidents: The Politics of Leadership from Roosevelt to Reagan* (New York: Free Press, 1990).

15. Fiorina, "Congressional Control of the Bureaucracy."

16. Terry M. Moe, "The Presidency and the Bureaucracy: The Presidential Advantage," in *The Presidency and the Political System,* 4th ed., ed. Michael Nelson (Washington, D.C.: CQ Press, 1995); Terry M. Moe and William G. Howell, "The Presidential Power of Unilateral Action," *Journal of Law, Economics, and Organization* 15 (March 1999): 132–179. For a much earlier, yet similar argument, see Edward S. Corwin and Louis W. Koenig, *The Presidency Today* (New York: New York University Press, 1956).

17. James Pfiffner, *The Modern Presidency* (New York: St. Martin's Press, 1994).

18. B. Dan Wood and Richard W. Waterman, "The Dynamics of Political Control of the Bureaucracy," *American Political Science Review* 85 (September 1991): 828.

19. Ronald N. Johnson and Gary D. Libecap, *The Federal Civil Service System and the Problem of Bureaucracy: The Economics and Politics of Institutional Change* (Chicago: University of Chicago Press, 1994).

20. Paul C. Light, *The True Size of Government* (Washington, D.C.: Brookings Institution Press, 1999).

21. Joel D. Aberbach and Bert A. Rockman, *In the Web of Politics: Three Decades of the U.S. Federal Executive* (Washington, D.C.: Brookings Institution Press, 2000).

22. "Division on Homeland Security Department: Labor Rights Issue Still a Stumbling Block," 2002, http://www.cnn.com/2002/ALLPOLITICS/11/11/homeland.security," November 11, 2002.

23. William Gormley Jr. "Counterbureaucracies in Theory and Practice," *Administration and Society* 28 (November 1986): 275–298.

24. Cornelius Kerwin, *Rulemaking,* 2d ed. (Washington, D.C.: CQ Press, 1999).

25. Ibid.

26. Helen Boutrous, "Presidential Influence and Regulatory Review" (Ph.D. diss., Georgetown University, 2002).

27. Mathew D. McCubbins, Roger G. Noll, and Barry R. Weingast, "Administrative Procedures as Instruments of Political Control," *Journal of Law, Economics, and Organization* 3 (fall 1987): 243–277.

28. Fiorina, "Congressional Control of the Bureaucracy."

29. Terry M. Moe, "The Politics of Bureaucratic Structure," in *Can the Government Govern?* ed. John E. Chubb and Paul E. Peterson (Washington, D.C.: Brookings Institution Press, 1989.)

30. Terry M. Moe, "The Politics of Structural Choice: Toward a Theory of Public Bureaucracy," in *Organization Theory: From Chester Barnard to the Present and Beyond,* ed. Oliver E. Williamson (New York: Oxford University Press, 1990).

31. Ibid., 125.

32. Ibid., 326.

33. Kerwin, *Rulemaking.*

34. Mark H. Tessler, Federal Railroad Administration, interview by author, March 11, 2002.

35. Mathew D. McCubbins, Roger G. Noll, and Barry R. Weingast, "Structure and Process, Politics and Policy: Administrative Arrangements and the Political Control of Agencies," *Virginia Law Review* 75 (March 1989): 431–482.

36. Steven J. Balla and John R. Wright, "Interest Groups, Advisory Committees, and Congressional Control of the Bureaucracy," *American Journal of Political Science* 45 (October 2001): 799–812.

37. McCubbins, Noll, and Weingast, "Administrative Procedures."

38. Ibid.

39. David B. Spence, "Agency Policy Making and Political Control: Modeling Away the Delegation Problem," *Journal of Public Administration Research and Theory* 7 (April 1997): 199–219.

40. Morris S. Ogul and Bert A. Rockman, "Overseeing Oversight: New Departures and Old Problems," *Legislative Studies Quarterly* 15 (February 1990): 5–24.

41. John F. Bibby, "Oversight and the Need for Congressional Reform," in *Republican Papers,* ed. Melvin R. Laird (Garden City, N.Y.: Anchor Books, 1968).

42. Joel D. Aberbach, *Keeping a Watchful Eye: The Politics of Legislative Oversight* (Washington, D.C.: Brookings Institution Press, 1990).

43. Mathew D. McCubbins and Thomas Schwartz, "Congressional Oversight Overlooked: Police Patrols versus Fire Alarms," *American Journal of Political Science* 28 (February 1984): 165–179.

44. Steven J. Balla and Christopher J. Deering, "Police Patrols and Fire Alarms: An Examination of the Legislative Preference for Oversight" (unpublished manuscript).

45. Terry M. Moe, "An Assessment of the Positive Theory of 'Congressional Dominance,' " *Legislative Studies Quarterly* 12 (November 1987): 475–520.

46. James F. Spriggs II, "The Supreme Court and Federal Administrative Agencies: A Resource-Based Theory and Analysis of Judicial Impact," *American Journal of Political Science* 40 (November 1996): 1122–1151.

47. Christopher Banks, *Judicial Politics in the D.C. Circuit Court* (Baltimore: Johns Hopkins University Press, 1999).

48. Ibid., 42.

49. Ibid., 45, 82.

50. *Greater Boston Television Corp. v. FCC,* 444 F. 2d 841 (D.C. Cir. 1970).

51. *International Harvester Co. v. Ruckelshaus,* 478 F. 2d 615 (D.C. Cir. 1973).

52. Banks, *Judicial Politics,* 44.

53. *Vermont Yankee Nuclear Power Corp. v. Natural Resources Defense Council, Inc.,* 435 U.S. 519 (1978).

54. See, for example, *Motor Vehicle Manufacturers Association of the U.S. v. State Farm Mutual Automobile Insurance Co. et al.,* 463 U.S. 29 (1983).

55. See, for example, *Chevron U.S.A., Inc. v. Natural Resources Defense Council, Inc.,* 467 U.S. 837 (1984).

56. Charles Lane, "Clean-Air Authority of EPA Is Upheld," *Washington Post,* February 28, 2001, Sec. A; *EPA v. American Trucking Associations, Inc., et al.,* 531 U.S. 457 (2001).

57. Reginald Sheehan, "Administrative Agencies and the Court: A Reexamination of the Impact of Agency Type on Decisional Outcomes," *Western Political Quarterly* 43 (December 1990): 875–885.

58. John R. Wright, *Interest Groups and Congress: Lobbying, Contributions, and Influence* (Boston: Allyn and Bacon, 1996).

59. Helen Dewar, "Senate Passes Homeland Security Bill: Bush Calls Step 'Historic and Bold,' " *Washington Post,* November 20, 2002, Sec. A.

60. James T. Hamilton and Christopher H. Schroeder, "Strategic Regulators and the Choice of Rulemaking Procedures: The Selection of Formal vs. Informal Rules in Regulating Hazardous Waste," *Law and Contemporary Problems* 57 (spring 1994): 111–160.

61. John Brehm and Scott Gates, *Working, Shirking, and Sabotage: Bureaucratic Response to a Democratic Public* (Ann Arbor: University of Michigan Press, 1997).

Chapter 4

1. Scott Baldauf, "Fires Force US to Stretch for Crews," *Christian Science Monitor,* August 21, 2000, 1; Andrew Gumbel, "Singed Bear Cub Survives Forest Wildfires," *The Independent,* August 22, 2000, 10.

2. Jim Robbins, "Logging Plan for West's Burned Forests Incites a Debate," *New York Times,* July 22, 2001, Sec. A; Todd Wilkinson, "Move to Log Fire-Damaged Trees Ignites Controversy," *Christian Science Monitor,* December 17, 2001, 2.

3. "Forest Service Mission, Vision, and Guiding Principles," http://www.fs.fed.us/intro/mvgp.html, November 11, 2002.

4. Katharine Q. Seelye, "U.S. Approves Timber Sale, Prompting Court Challenge," *New York Times,* December 18, 2001, Sec. A; Bill McAllister, "Forest Service Sued over Logging," *Denver Post,* December 19, 2001, Sec. A; Elizabeth Shogren, "Timber Sale Stalled to Allow Appeal," *Los Angeles,* December 20, 2001, Sec. A.

5. Eric Pianin, "Settlement Is Reached in Sale of Charred Trees," *Washington Post,* February 8, 2002, Sec. A; Jim Robbins, "Forest Service and Environmentalists Settle Logging Dispute," *New York Times,* February 8, 2002, Sec. A.

6. James Q. Wilson, "The Politics of Regulation," in *The Politics of Regulation,* ed. James Q. Wilson (New York: Basic Books, 1980); James Q. Wilson, *Bureaucracy: What Government Agencies Do and Why They Do It* (New York: Basic Books, 1989).

7. Frank R. Baumgartner and Bryan D. Jones, *Agendas and Instability in American Politics* (Chicago: University of Chicago Press, 1993).

8. Lawrence S. Rothenberg, *Regulation, Organizations, and Politics: Motor Freight Policy at the Interstate Commerce Commission* (Ann Arbor: University of Michigan Press, 1994).

9. Wilson, "Politics of Regulation"; Wilson, *Bureaucracy.*

10. Ibid.

11. Kathleen Day and James V. Grimaldi, "Lay's Lobbying Reached the Top of Treasury; Enron Chief Leaned Hard as Company Sought to Avoid U.S. Oversight of Derivatives Deals," *Washington Post,* February 21, 2002, Sec. E.

12. Samuel P. Huntington, "The Marasmus of the ICC: The Commission, the Railroads, and the Public Interest," *Yale Law Journal* 62 (April 1952): 467–509; Grant McConnell, *Private Power and American Democracy* (New York: Knopf, 1966).

13. Kay Lehman Schlozman and John T. Tierney, *Organized Interests and American Democracy* (New York: Harper and Row, 1986).

14. Baumgartner and Jones, *Agendas and Instability in American Politics.*

15. Dan Morgan, "Restarting Reactor Could Boost Nuclear Power Industry: TVA Board to Vote on $1.7 Billion Proposal to Switch on Mothballed Unit in Alabama," *Washington Post,* May 16, 2002, Sec. A.

16. Charles O. Jones, "American Politics and the Organization of Energy Decision Making," in *Annual Review of Energy,* ed. Jack M. Hollander, Melvin K. Simmons, and David O. Wood (Palo Alto, Calif.: Annual Reviews, 1979).

17. Hugh Heclo, "Issue Networks in the Executive Establishment," in *The New American Political System,* ed. Anthony King (Washington, D.C.: American Enterprise Institute, 1978).

18. Elaine B. Sharp, "The Dynamics of Issue Expansion: Cases from Disability Rights and Fetal Research Controversy," *Journal of Politics* 56 (November 1994): 919–939.

19. Cornelius M. Kerwin, *Rulemaking: How Government Agencies Write Law and Make Policy,* 2d ed. (Washington, D.C.: CQ Press, 1999).

20. Each of the fifty states and the District of Columbia have their own administrative procedure acts, which govern rulemaking within their jurisdictions. For more information see http://www.law.fsu.edu/library/admin/admins3.html, October 17, 2002.

21. Major rules are cataloged by the General Accounting Office at http://www.gao.gov, October 16, 2002.

22. U.S. General Accounting Office, *Congressional Review Act* (Washington, D.C.: GAO, 1997).

23. U.S. General Accounting Office, *Food and Drug Administration: Regulation of Tobacco Products* (Washington, D.C.: GAO, 1997).

24. Philip J. Harter, "Negotiated Rulemaking: A Cure for Malaise," *Georgetown Law Journal* 71 (December 1982): 1–113.

25. Neil Eisner, "Regulatory Negotiation: A Real World Experience." *Federal Bar News and Journal* 31 (November 1984): 371–376.

26. Department of Transportation, Federal Aviation Administration, "Notice of Establishment of Advisory Committee for Regulatory Negotiation and Notice of First Meeting," *Federal Register,* June 28, 1983, 29771.

27. The Committee Management Secretariat of the General Services Administration maintains an online database pertaining to advisory committees at http://www.fido.gov/facadatabase, October 16, 2002.

28. Mark P. Petracca. "Federal Advisory Committees, Interest Groups, and the Administrative State," *Congress and the Presidency* 13 (spring 1986): 83–114.

29. Harter, "Negotiated Rulemaking."

30. Cary Coglianese, "Assessing Consensus: The Promise and Performance of Negotiated Rulemaking," *Duke Law Journal* 46 (April 1997): 1255–1349.

31. Department of Transportation, Federal Railroad Administration, "Use of Locomotive Horns at Highway-Rail Grade Crossings," *Federal Register,* March 22, 2000, 15298; Mark H. Tessler, Federal Railroad Administration, interview by Balla, March 11, 2002.

32. Http://dmses.dot.gov/docimages/pdf42/70969_web.pdf, March 3, 2003.

33. Michael Grunwald, "Growing Pains in Southwest Florida," *Washington Post,* June 25, 2002, Sec. A.

34. Ibid. See also http://www.fgcu.edu/info/HistoricalPerspective.asp, October 23, 2002.

35. Roger Faith, Donald Leavens, and Robert Tollison, "Antitrust Pork Barrel," *Journal of Law and Economics* 25 (October 1982): 329–342.

36. John Scholz and Feng Heng Wei, "Regulatory Enforcement in a Federalist System," *American Political Science Review* 80 (December 1986): 1249–1270.

37. Http://www.faa.gov/apa/pr/pr.cfm?id=1009, June 25, 2002. See also Department of Transportation, Federal Aviation Administration, "Small-Scale Rockets," notice of public meeting, *Federal Register*, December 30, 1999, 73597–73599.

38. Http://www.faa.gov/apa/pr/pr.cfm?id=1009, June 25, 2002.

39. U.S. General Accounting Office, "Federal Rulemaking: Agencies' Use of Information Technology to Facilitate Public Participation," June 30, 2000. Available at http://www.gao.gov, May 22, 2003.

40. The link is http://www.epa.gov/epahome/rules.html#proposed, March 3, 2003.

41. U.S. General Accounting Office, "Federal Rulemaking."

42. Ibid.

43. Http://www.usda.gov/news/releases/2000/12/0425.htm, June 26, 2002.

44. U.S. General Accounting Office, "Federal Rulemaking."

45. Jonathan Rauch, *Demosclerosis: The Silent Killer of American Government* (New York: Times Books, 1994).

46. Http://www.fortune.com/lists/power25/index.html, October 23, 2002.

47. Wilson, *Bureaucracy.*

48. Joel Aberbach and Bert Rockman, *In the Web of Politics: Three Decades of the U.S. Federal Executive* (Washington, D.C.: Brookings Institution Press, 2000).

49. C. Edward Lindblom, *Politics and Markets* (New York: Basic Books, 1977), 5.

50. William T. Gormley Jr., "A Test of the Revolving Door Hypothesis at the FCC," *American Journal of Political Science* 23 (November 1979): 665–683.

51. Judith Layzer, *The Environmental Case: Translating Values into Policy* (Washington, D.C.: CQ Press, 2002).

52. Ibid., 308.

53. Maureen Cropper, "The Determinants of Pesticide Regulation," *Journal of Political Economy* 100 (February 1992): 175–197.

54. William T. Gormley Jr., *The Politics of Public Utility Regulation* (Pittsburgh: University of Pittsburgh Press, 1983).

55. Evan Ringquist, *Environmental Protection at the State Level* (Armonk, N.Y.: M. E. Sharpe, 1993).

56. Finley Peter Dunne, as quoted in Bill Kovach and Tom Rosenstiel, "Are Watchdogs an Endangered Species?" *Columbia Journalism Review* 40 (May/June 2001): 50.

57. Layzer, *Environmental Case,* 107.

58. Paul Sabatier, John Loomis, and Catherine McCarthy, "Hierarchical Controls, Professional Norms, Local Constituencies, and Budget Maximization: An Analysis of U.S. Forest Service Planning Decisions," *American Journal of Political Science* 39 (February 1995): 204–242.

59. Sally Cohen, *Championing Child Care* (New York: Columbia University Press, 2001).

60. Ibid.

61. Anne Camissa, *Governments as Interest Groups: Intergovernmental Lobbying and the Federal System* (Westport, Conn.: Praeger, 1995).

62. Helen Boutrous, "Presidential Influence and Regulatory Review" (Ph.D. diss., Government Department, Georgetown University, 2002), 123.

63. William Gormley Jr., "An Evolutionary Approach to Federalism in the U.S." (paper presented at the annual meeting of the American Political Science Association, San Francisco, August 31, 2001).

64. Cathleen Willging, Rafael Semansky, and Howard Waitzkin, "New Mexico's Medicaid Managed Care Waiver: Organizing Input from Mental Health Consumers and Advocates," *Psychiatric Services* 54 (March 2003): 289–291.

65. E. E. Schattschneider, *The Semi-Sovereign People* (New York: Holt, Rinehart, and Winston, 1960).

66. Henry Eichel, "Appeals Court Bars Blockade of Plutonium," *Charlotte Observer,* August 7, 2002, 1.

67. David Firestone, "South Carolina Battles U.S. on Plutonium," *New York Times,* April 12, 2002, 22.

68. Steven J. Balla, "Administrative Procedures and Political Control of the Bureaucracy," *American Political Science Review* 92 (September 1998): 663–673.

Chapter 5

1. Lester Salamon, *America's Nonprofit Sector* (New York: Foundation Center, 1992), 65.

2. H. Brinton Milward, "Symposium on the Hollow State," *Journal of Public Administration Research and Theory* 6 (April 1996): 193–195.

3. E. S. Savas, *Privatization: The Key to Better Government* (Chatham, N.J.: Chatham House, 1987); William Gormley Jr., "The Privatization Controversy," in *Privatization and Its Alternatives,* ed. William Gormley Jr. (Madison: University of Wisconsin Press, 1991), 3–16; and Harvey Feigenbaum, Jeffrey Henig, and Chris Hamnett, *Shrinking the State: The Political Underpinnings of Privatization* (Cambridge: Cambridge University Press, 1998).

4. Laurence O'Toole, "Treating Networks Seriously: Practical and Research-Based Agendas in Public Administration," *Public Administration Review* 57 (January/February 1997): 45–52.

5. Mark Granovetter, "The Strength of Weak Ties," *American Journal of Sociology* 78 (May 1973): 1360–1380.

6. Edward O. Laumann and David Knoke, *The Organizational State: Social Choice in National Policy Domains* (Madison: University of Wisconsin Press, 1987), 206–225.

7. Keith Provan and H. Brinton Milward, "A Preliminary Theory of Interorganizational Network Effectiveness: A Comparative Study of Four Community Mental Health Systems," *Administrative Science Quarterly* 40 (March 1995): 1–33; O'Toole, "Treating Networks Seriously."

8. Walter J. M. Kickert, Erik-Hans Klijn, and Joop F. M. Koppenjan, "Introduction: A Management Perspective on Policy Networks," in *Managing Complex Networks: Strategies for the Public Sector,* ed. Walter J. M. Kickert, Erik-Hans Klijn, and Joop F. M. Koppenjan (London: Sage Publications, 1997), 7–11; Paul Posner, "Accountability Challenges of Third-Party Government," in *The Tools of Government: A Guide to the New Governance,* ed. Lester Salamon (New York: Oxford University Press, 2002), 546.

9. Keith Provan and H. Brinton Milward, "Do Networks Really Work? A Framework for Evaluating Public-Sector Organizational Networks," *Public Administration Review* 61 (July/August 2001): 416.

10. John Scott, *Social Network Analysis: A Handbook,* 2d ed. (Beverly Hills, Calif.: Sage Publications, 2001), 82, 71.

11. Catherine Alter and Jerald Hage, *Organizations Working Together* (Newbury Park, Calif.: Sage Publications, 1993), 155, 157.

12. We are indebted to Brint Milward for bringing this concept to our attention.

13. Alter and Hage, *Organizations Working Together,* 158.

14. Ibid., 163.

15. Malcolm Sparrow, "The Application of Network Analysis to Criminal Intelligence: An Assessment of the Prospects," *Social Networks* 13 (September 1991): 266.

16. Valdis Krebs, "Mapping Networks of Terrorist Cells," *Connections* 24 (winter 2001): 43–52, 46.

17. Richard Rothenberg, "From Whole Cloth: Making up the Terrorist Network," *Connections* 24 (winter 2001): 37.

18. Lester Salamon, "The New Governance and the Tools of Public Action: An Introduction," in Salamon, *Tools of Government*, 1–47.

19. Ibid., 24–37.

20. Ibid., 2.

21. Paul Posner, "Accountability Challenges of Third-Party Government," 528–532.

22. Walter Zelman and Robert Berenson, *The Managed Care Blues and How to Cure Them* (Washington, D.C.: Georgetown University Press, 1998), 142–145.

23. O'Toole, "Treating Networks Seriously."

24. Thad Hall and Laurence O'Toole Jr., "Shaping Formal Networks through the Regulatory Process" (paper presented at the annual meeting of the American Political Science Association, Boston, August 30, 2002), 5, 27.

25. H. George Frederickson, "The Repositioning of American Public Administration," *PS* 32 (December 1999): 705.

26. O'Toole, "Treating Networks Seriously," 45.

27. Denise Scheberle, *Federalism and Environmental Policy* (Washington, D.C.: Georgetown University Press, 1997), 13–14.

28. U.S. Environmental Protection Agency, *Reinventing Environmental Protection: 1998 Annual Report* (Washington, D.C.: EPA, March 1999), 26.

29. National Academy of Public Administration, *Environment.gov* (Washington, D.C.: NAPA, 2000), 135–153.

30. Barry Rabe, "Power to the States: The Promise and Pitfalls of Devolution," in *Environmental Policy: New Directions for the Twenty-First Century*, ed. Norman Vig and Michael Kraft (Washington, D.C.: CQ Press, 2000), 43.

31. William Gormley Jr., *Taming the Bureaucracy: Muscles, Prayers, and Other Strategies* (Princeton: Princeton University Press, 1989), 3–31, 173–193.

32. William Gormley Jr., "An Evolutionary Approach to Federalism in the U.S." (paper presented at the annual meeting of the American Political Science Association, San Francisco, August 31, 2001).

33. Centers for Medicare and Medicaid Services, *The State Children's Health Insurance Program: Annual Enrollment Reports* (Baltimore: CMS, February 6, 2002).

34. Dan Morgan, "States Given Breaks on Medicaid Funding Loophole," *Washington Post*, November 4, 2000, Sec. A.

35. Tara O'Toole, "Institutional Issues in Biodefense," in *Governance and Public Security*, ed. Alasdair Roberts (Syracuse, N.Y.: Campbell Public Affairs Institute, 2002), 98–110.

36. Lawrence K. Altman and Gina Kolata, "A Nation Challenged: Anthrax Missteps Offer Guide to Fight Next Bioterror Battle," *New York Times*, January 6, 2002, Sec. A.

37. U.S. Senate. Tommy Thompson, Secretary of Health and Human Services, testimony before the U.S. Senate Governmental Affairs Committee, Washington, D.C., April 18, 2002, Y4.G 74/9: S.HRG 107-507.

38. Steven Kelman, "Contracting," in Salamon, *Tools of Government*, 305.

39. Donald Kettl, "Managing Indirect Government," in Salamon, *Tools of Government*, 491.

40. Savas, *Privatization*, 124–131.

41. Stephen R. Smith and Michael Lipsky, *Nonprofits for Hire* (Cambridge: Harvard University Press, 1993).

42. Paul Light, cited in Kettl, "Managing Indirect Government," 490.

43. Donald Kettl, *Sharing Power: Public Governance and Private Markets* (Washington, D.C.: Brookings Institution Press, 1993), 131.

44. Ibid., 134–138.

45. Keith Provan, H. Brinton Milward, and Kimberley R. Isett, "Collaboration and Integration of Community-Based Health and Human Services in a Nonprofit Managed Care System," *Health Care Management Review* 27 (winter 2002): 26.

46. Mark Rom, "From Welfare State to Opportunity, Inc.: Public-Private Partnerships in Welfare Reform," in *Public-Private Policy Partnerships*, ed. Pauline Rosenau (Cambridge: MIT Press, 2000), 161–182.

47. Ibid., 161, 170.

48. Anne Schneider, "Public-Private Partnerships in the U.S. Prison System," in Rosenau, *Public-Private Policy Partnerships*, 203.

49. Judith Greene, "Bailing Out Private Jails," *The American Prospect*, September 10, 2001, 23–27.

50. Pauline V. Rosenau, "The Strengths and Weaknesses of Public-Private Policy Partnerships," in Rosenau, *Public-Private Policy Partnerships*, 227; Greg Jaffe and Rick Brooks, "Violence at Prison Run by Corrections Corp. Irks Youngstown, Ohio," *Wall Street Journal*, August 5, 1998, Sec. A.

51. Steven R. Smith and Helen Ingram, "Policy Tools and Democracy," in Salamon, *Tools of Government*, 565.

52. Charles Sabel, Archon Fung, and Bradley Karkkainen, *Beyond Backyard Environmentalism* (Boston: Beacon Press, 2000), 5.

53. Smith and Ingram, "Policy Tools and Democracy," 565.

54. Kettl, "Managing Indirect Government," 504.

55. James Lee Witt, *Stronger in the Broken Places* (New York: Times Books, 2002), 55–77.

56. David Halberstam, *The Best and the Brightest* (New York: Random House, 1972).

57. Carl Bernstein and Bob Woodward, *All the President's Men* (New York: Simon and Schuster, 1974).

58. Jeffrey Cohen, *The Politics of the U.S. Cabinet* (Pittsburgh: University of Pittsburgh Press, 1988), 33–42.

59. James Pfiffner, *The Modern Presidency* (New York: St. Martin's Press, 1994), 117–128.

60. For numerous examples of this general phenomenon, see Robert Axelrod, *The Evolution of Cooperation* (New York: Basic Books, 1984).

61. Helen Boutrous, "Presidential Influence and Regulatory Review" (Ph.D. diss., Government Department, Georgetown University, 2002).

62. Amy Zegart, *Flawed by Design: The Evolution of the CIA, JCS, and NSC* (Stanford: Stanford University Press, 1999), 52.

63. Harold Seidman, *Politics, Position and Power* (New York: Oxford University Press, 1970), 171.

64. David Howard Davis, *Energy Politics*, 2d ed. (New York: St. Martin's Press, 1978), 93.

65. Luis Payan, "Cops, Soldiers, and Diplomats" (Ph.D. diss., Government Department, Georgetown University, 2001), chap. 3, 41.

66. Edward Walsh, "Challenges Familiar to Bush Pick," *Washington Post*, September 22, 2001, Sec. A.

67. Michael Wermuth, "Mission Impossible? The White House Office of Homeland Security," in Roberts, *Governance and Public Security*, 31.

68. Mike Allen, "White House to Increase Ridge's Exposure," *Washington Post*, October 28, 2001, Sec. A.

69. Eric Pianin and David Broder, "Ridge Defends His Role as 'Coordinator,'" *Washington Post,* November 18, 2001, Sec. A.

70. For example, the executive order used the words *coordinate* and *coordinating* thirty-seven times but never used the words *direct* or *directing.* Michael Wermuth, "Mission Impossible?" 32.

71. Editorial, "Faltering on the Home Front," *New York Times,* May 12, 2002, Sec. 4.

72. Helen Dewar, "Senate Passes Homeland Security Bill," *Washington Post,* November 20, 2002, Sec. A.

73. Alter and Hage, *Organizations Working Together,* 210.

74. Provan and Milward, "Preliminary Theory of Interorganizational Network Effectiveness."

75. Eugene Bardach, *Getting Agencies to Work Together* (Washington, D.C.: Brookings Institution Press, 1998).

76. Edward Jennings, "Building Bridges in the Intergovernmental Arena: Coordinating Employment and Training Programs in the American States," *Public Administration Review* 54 (January/February 1994): 52–60.

77. Robert Axelrod and Michael Cohen, *Harnessing Complexity* (New York: Free Press, 1999), 52–58.

78. Donald Chisholm, *Coordination without Hierarchy* (Berkeley: University of California Press, 1989).

79. Charles Wise, "Organizing for Homeland Security," *Public Administration Review* 62 (March/April 2002): 132.

80. Jane Fountain, "Toward a Theory of Federal Bureaucracy for the 21st Century," in *Governance.com,* ed. Elaine Kamarck and Joseph Nye Jr. (Washington, D.C.: Brookings Institution Press, 2002), 120.

81. Joseph Nye Jr. "Information Technology and Democratic Governance," in Kamarck and Nye, *Governance.com,* 7.

82. Center for e-Service, University of Maryland, cited in OMB 2002, "Governing with Accountability," January 2002, 4.

83. Paul Peterson, Barry Rabe, and Kenneth Wong, *When Federalism Works* (Washington, D.C.: Brookings Institution Press, 1986).

84. At least one study has found evidence in support of the welfare magnet theory. See Paul Peterson and Mark Rom, *Welfare Magnets: A New Case for a National Standard* (Washington, D.C.: Brookings Institution Press, 1990). For contrary evidence, see Sanford Schram, Lawrence Nitz, and Gary Krueger, "Without Cause or Effect: Reconsidering Welfare Migration as a Policy Problem," *American Journal of Political Science* 42 (January 1998): 210–230.

85. For the original version of this hypothesis, see David Bradford and Wallace Oates, "Towards a Predictive Theory of Intergovernmental Grants," *American Economic Review* 61 (May 1971): 440–448. For the recent empirical work, see Brian Knight, "Endogenous Federal Grants and Crowd-Out of State Government Spending: Theory and Evidence from the Federal Highway Aid Program," *American Economic Review* 92 (March 2002): 71–92.

86. Knight, "Endogenous Federal Grants and Crowd-Out of State Government Spending," 88.

87. David Beam and Timothy Conlan, "Grants," in Salamon, *Tools of Government,* 371.

88. Gormley, *Taming the Bureaucracy,* 173–193.

89. Evan Ringquist, *Environmental Protection at the State Level* (Armonk, N.Y.: M. E. Sharpe, 1993), 126–154.

90. Suzanne Helburn, ed., *Cost, Quality, and Child Outcomes in Child Care Centers, Technical Report* (Denver: Economics Department, University of Colorado–Denver, January 1995).

91. Wayne Gray and John Scholz, "Does Regulatory Enforcement Work? A Panel Analysis of OSHA Enforcement," *Law and Society Review* 27 (1993): 177–213.

92. William Gormley Jr., *Everybody's Children: Child Care as a Public Problem* (Washington, D.C.: Brookings Institution Press, 1995), 113–117.

93. J. Clarence Davies and Jan Mazurek, *Pollution Control in the United States* (Washington, D.C.: Resources for the Future, 1998), 140–142.

94. Peter Schrag, "Blackout," *The American Prospect*, February 26, 2001, 29–33.

95. Peter May, "Social Regulation," in Salamon, *Tools of Government*, 171.

96. According to the National Highway Traffic Safety Administration, seatbelts have saved approximately 135,000 lives since 1975. See Rick Popely and Jim Mateja, "Life Savers," *Chicago Tribune*, April 21, 2002, 1.

97. James Hankin et al., cited in Janet Weiss, "Public Information," in Salamon, *Tools of Government*, 242.

98. C. S. Craig, cited in Weiss, "Public Information," 240.

99. B. Farquhar-Pilgrim, cited in Weiss, "Public Information," 240.

100. William Gormley Jr. and David Weimer, *Organizational Report Cards* (Cambridge: Harvard University Press, 1999), 141–142.

101. Charles Clotfelter and Helen Ladd, cited in Gormley and Weimer, *Organizational Report Cards,* 156.

102. Weiss, "Public Information," 233–234.

Chapter 6

1. Kenneth J. Meier, *Politics and the Bureaucracy: Policymaking in the Fourth Branch of Government,* 4th ed. (Fort Worth: Harcourt College Publishers, 2000). Additional source material: http://www.ftc.gov, July 31, 2002.

2. Barry R. Weingast and Mark J. Moran, "The Myth of Runaway Bureaucracy: The Case of the FTC," *Regulation* (May/June 1982), 33–36. For a contrasting viewpoint, see Terry M. Moe, "An Assessment of the Positive Theory of 'Congressional Dominance,' " *Legislative Studies Quarterly* 12 (November 1987): 475–520.

3. Robert A. Katzmann, *Regulatory Bureaucracy: The Federal Trade Commission and Antitrust Policy* (Cambridge: MIT Press, 1980).

4. Michael Pertschuk, *Giant Killers* (New York: W. W. Norton, 1986).

5. "Overview of the FTC/DOJ Clearance Agreement," online at http://www.ftc.gov/opa/2002/04/clearanceoverview.htm, August 2, 2002.

6. "FTC Gives Media Merger Review Power to DOJ," http://www.internetnews.com/bus-news/article.php/985721; "Senator Wants to 'Eliminate' FTC Chief: Ugly Feud Heats Up Further," http://www.ftc.gov/opa/2002/04/adagenews.pdf; "Statement of FTC Chairman Timothy J. Muris," http://www.ftc.gov/opa/2002/04/020415stmt.htm. All accessed on August 2, 2002. Alan E. Wiseman of the FTC also provided helpful information.

7. Robert Pear, "Medicare Agency Changes Name in an Effort to Emphasize Service," *New York Times,* June 15, 2001, Sec. A.

8. Michael Fiore, interview with Gormley, Baltimore, November 8, 2000.

9. Timothy Westmoreland, interview with Gormley, Washington, D.C., November 16, 2000.

10. George Anders, *Health against Wealth* (Boston: Houghton Mifflin, 1996), 190–209.

11. Bazelon Center for Mental Health Law, "Advocates Praise Unprecedented Removal of Federal Support for Mental Health in New Mexico Managed Care Program," press

release, Washington, D.C., October 20, 2000, http://www.bazelon.org/1020nmexicodata.html.

12. Fiore, interview.

13. Malcolm Sparrow, *The Regulatory Craft: Controlling Risks, Solving Problems, and Managing Compliance* (Washington, D.C.: Brookings Institution Press, 2000), 142.

14. Kirby Greene, interview with Gormley, Tallahassee, Florida, May 20, 1999.

15. Suzi Ruhl, executive director, Legal Environmental Assistance Foundation, interview with Gormley, Tallahassee, Florida, May 20, 1999.

16. William Gormley Jr., "Environmental Performance Measures in a Federal System," in *Environment.gov* (Washington, D.C.: National Academy of Public Administration, 2000), 13–53.

17. Bill Brubaker, "CareFirst May Drop Medicaid HMO in Md.," *Washington Post*, August 16, 2000, Sec. E.

18. Some of the material in this section is taken from Debbie Chang, telephone interview with Balla, September 3, 2002.

19. M. William Salganik, "HMO to Take Dropped Medicaid Members; MPC, State in Deal for Absorbing 40,000," *Baltimore Sun*, February 15, 2001, Sec. D.

20. http://medicaid.aphsa.org/default.htm, September 30, 2002.

21. http://www.dhmh.state.md.us/mma/healthchoice, October 1, 2002.

22. http://www.mdarchives.state.md.us/msa/mdmanual/16dhmh/html/16agen.html#medicaidadvisory, October 1, 2002.

Chapter 7

1. Cindy Skrzycki, *The Regulators: Anonymous Power Brokers in American Politics* (Lanham, Md.: Rowman and Littlefield, 2003), 4.

2. The Internet home page for the Federal Performance Project is http://www.govexec.com/fpp/index.htm, October 2, 2002. Researchers have also rated the performance of state and local governments. See the Internet home page for the Government Performance Project: http://www.maxwell.syr.edu/gpp, October 2, 2002.

3. *Government Executive* (February 1999).

4. Jeffrey Pressman and Aaron Wildavsky, *Implementation* (Berkeley: University of California Press, 1973).

5. PIRG, "The Burden of Borrowing: Executive Summary," online at http://www.pirg.org/highered/burdenofborrowing/html, August 27, 2002.

6. Http://www.ed.gov/offices/OSFAP/defaultmanagement/defaultrates.html, October 2, 2002.

7. James Q. Wilson, *Bureaucracy: What Government Agencies Do and Why They Do It* (New York: Basic Books, 1989), 158.

8. Ibid., 158–171.

9. Warren Leary, "Deep Space 1 Ends Mission, But Triumphs Are Clear," *New York Times*, December 19, 2001, 24.

10. Wilson, *Bureaucracy*, 168–171.

11. Susannah Figura, "Travel Advisory," *Government Executive*, April 1, 2001, 79.

12. Katherine Peters, "Trail of Trouble," *Government Executive*, April 1, 2001, 91.

13. Theodore J. Lowi, *The End of Liberalism: The Second Republic of the United States*, 2d ed. (New York: W. W. Norton, 1979), 109.

14. Cathy Johnson, *The Dynamics of Conflict between Bureaucrats and Legislators* (Armonk, N.Y.: M. E. Sharpe, 1992), 71–73.

15. Ibid., 78–80.

16. William Gormley Jr., *Taming the Bureaucracy: Muscles, Prayers and Other Strategies* (Princeton: Princeton University Press, 1989).

17. W. Anthony Rosenbaum, "Escaping the 'Battered Agency Syndrome': EPA's Gamble with Regulatory Reinvention," in *Environmental Policy*, 4th ed., ed. Norman Vig and Michael Kraft (Washington, D.C.: CQ Press, 2000), 176–181.

18. Mark Murray, "FEMA Administrator Wins Management Kudos," online at http://www.govexec.com/dailyfed/0101/011601/fema.htm, August 21, 2002.

19. Gary J. Miller, *Managerial Dilemmas: The Political Economy of Hierarchy* (New York: Cambridge University Press, 1992).

20. Kenneth J. Cooper, "Higher Ed: Department of Education; 'Customer' Service, the New Frontier," *Washington Post*, October 22, 1999, Sec. A.

21. Stephen Burd, "Top Aide to Gore Is Named to Revamp the Delivery of Federal Student Aid: Greg Woods Will Try to Replace Federal Bureaucracy with a 'Performance-Based Organization,'" *Chronicle of Higher Education*, December 11, 1998, Sec. A; Stephen Burd, "Federal Panel Lambastes Education Department's Plan on Computer Modernization," *Chronicle of Higher Education*, December 17, 1999, Sec. A.

22. Stephen Burd, "Rift Emerges over Independence of Federal Financial-Aid Office: College Officials Cry Foul as Education Dept. Seeks to Rein in 'Performance-Based' Agency," *Chronicle of Higher Education*, October 19, 2001, Sec. A; Stephen Burd, "Impending Departure of Education Department Official Worries Many Student-Aid Administrators," *Chronicle of Higher Education*, May 31, 2002, Sec. A.

23. Matthew Brelis, "Earning Her Wings: When Jane Garvey Took the Controls, the Federal Aviation Administration Was Having a Bumpy Flight. Can She Smooth It Out?" *Boston Globe Magazine*, September 6, 1998, 12; Michael Skapinker and Charles Batchelor, "Aviation Chief Puts Faith in Flight: FAA Head Jane Garvey Will Be Airborne When the Millennium Midnight Hour Strikes. But Not in a Third World Airliner," *Financial Times*, November 27, 1998, 8.

24. "Mastering Disaster," http://www.govexec.com/gpp/0299fema.htm, August 21, 2002; Murray, "FEMA Administrator Wins Management Kudos."

25. Robert Slavin and Nancy Madden, " 'Success for All' and African American and Latino Student Achievement," in *Bridging the Achievement Gap*, ed. John Chubb and Tom Loveless (Washington, D.C.: Brookings Institution Press, 2002), 74–90.

26. Paul C. Light, "The True Size of Government," *Government Executive*, January 1, 1999, 18; Paul C. Light, "The Total Federal Workforce," *Government Executive*, January 1, 1999, 12.

INDEX

INDEX

venues of participation, 92–100, 110
Climbers, 37–38
Clinton, Bill, 180
  cabinet, 131
  child care policy, 60–61, 105–106
  environmental protection, 121
  ergonomics rule, 51
  GPRA, 18
  health care policy, 124
  waivers, 107–108, 124, 154, 161
Clinton, Hillary, 106
Clotfelter, Charles, 187, 200
CMS (Centers for Medicare and Medicaid Services), 17, 93, 112–113, 153–156, 166, 167–168
Coalition on Smoking or Health, 152
Coast Guard, 166
Coercive control, 174–175
Coerciveness, 117, 121
Coglianese, Cary, 194
Cohen, Jeffrey, 198
Cohen, Michael, 140, 199
Cohen, Sally, 195
Collaboration, 94–96
Collective bargaining, 66
Columbia space shuttle, 170
Commissioners, 150
Committee hearings, 73
Commodity policy, 58, 88, 90
Communication, 27
Complexity, 58–59, 115–116
Compromise, political, 70–71
Concentrated benefits and costs, 84–85, 155
Congress
  administrative procedures, 71–72
  control of EPA, 58–59
  control of the bureaucracy, 68–74
  intergovernmental relations, 120
  judicial review, 74–78
  oversight, 72–74
  politics of bureaucratic structure, 69–71
Congressional Review Act, 51
Conlan, Timothy, 142, 199
Conservers, 38
Constituencies. *See* Clients
Constitution, U.S., 63–64, 74
Consumer Product Safety Commission, 69–70
Contracting out, 126–127
Coordinated control, 63
Coping organizations, 170–171
Corrections, 35, 129
Corrections Corporation of America, 129
Corwin, Edward S., 191
Cost-benefit analysis, 37, 46–47, 91–92

Costs
  concentrated, 84–85, 155
  diffuse, 84–85
  perceived, 91–92
  of public policy, 84–87
  sunk costs, 34–35, 49
Council of Economic Advisors, 65
Craig, C. S., 200
Credible commitments, 176–177
Crisis situations, 14–15, 27, 135
Cropper, Maureen, 195
Crowd out hypothesis, 141
Customs Service, 30, 92, 166, 172–173
Czars, 135–138

Daschle, Tom, 15
Davies, J. Clarence, 189, 200
Davis, David Howard, 198
Day care centers, 26, 142
D.C. Circuit, 76–78
Decision making, 26–49
  bounded rationality model, 28–30
  consequences of bounded rationality, 44–48
  implications for policy analysis, 36–44
  policy analysis and, 26–49
  problem solving, 30–35
Deering, Christopher J., 192
Delegation, 53–55
  congressional control of bureaucracy, 68–74
  judicial review, 74–78
  managing, 63–78
  presidential power and, 63–68
  variation in, 58–60
Democracy, 9–10, 164
Density, 115–116
Department of Agriculture (USDA), 88, 90, 99
Department of Education, 107
Department of Energy (DOE), 36–37, 108, 127–128
Department of Health, Education, and Welfare, 69
Department of Health and Human Services (HHS), 17–18, 60–61, 88, 98, 105–106
Department of Homeland Security, 4, 5, 66, 136, 137, 138, 180
Department of Housing and Urban Development, 17
Department of Justice (DOJ), 31–32, 70, 74, 151–153
Department of Labor, 98
Department of Transportation (DOT), 4–5, 8, 52, 57, 99
Deregulation, 72
Devolution, 120